Twists and Turns and Tangles in Math and Physics

Instructional Material for Developing Scientific and Logical Thinking

Samuel Katzoff

Volume 1

Published by The Johns Hopkins
University Center for Talented Youth
Publications and Resources Service
in collaboration with the National Aeronautics
and Space Administration
Copyright© 1992 by Samuel Katzoff

ISBN-1-881622-00-2 (Volume 1)
ISBN-1-881622-02-9 (2 Volume set)

ABOUT THE AUTHOR

The author was raised in Baltimore and received his formal education at the Baltimore Polytechnic Institute and at The Johns Hopkins University, where he received his Ph.D. in 1934. His subsequent career was with the National Advisory Committee for Aeronautics (NACA) and its successor, the National Aeronautics and Space Administration (NASA). He has published over forty scientific papers, many of which were of fundamental importance in their fields; he edited (both technically and grammatically) two extensive symposiums, Thermal Radiation of Solids (1965) and Remote Measurement of Pollution (1971); and he wrote a widely known pamphlet, Clarity in Technical Reporting. At the time he retired, he was Chief Scientist at the NASA Langley Research Center.

When he retired he was recruited to teach small classes of gifted sixth-grade students–and he thus unwittingly stepped into a small second career. Typically such an activity involves either (1) teaching the sixth graders seventh- and eighth-grade mathematics and science or (2) entertaining them with spectacular experiments–which is commonly supposed to develop interest in science. However, Dr. Katzoff felt that a scientist ought to give his students more of himself than middle-school arithmetic or showmanship. Accordingly, he emphasized mental dexterity together with the critical attitude and analytical approach on which progress is based.

For several years, Dr. Katzoff has been developing and refining instructional materials for a course entitled *"Scientific and Logical Thinking"* which he teaches in the Young Students Program of The Johns Hopkins University's Center for Talented Youth (CTY). In preparing this two volume set, Dr. Katzoff has extended the scope of his materials so that they might be useful for talented students through the twelfth grade. These *Twists and Turns and Tangles in Math and Physics* are being made available to the public through the collaborative efforts of Dr. Katzoff, the NASA Langley Research Center, and CTY. It is Dr. Katzoff's sincere wish that these materials will inspire young minds and that the availablity of this text will encourage other scientists to become involved in the nurture of talent.

Proceeds from the sale of these instructional materials will be used to establish CTY Academic Program scholarships in Dr. Katzoff's name.

CONTENTS
Volume 1

INTRODUCTION

Enriching the education of gifted children has been encouraged for many years, for they are increasingly recognized as important resources; and even if we prefer not to view them as "resources"—which seems to have a cold and materialistic flavor—and view them as people, we should nevertheless provide them means for developing themselves in accordance with their talents. Accordingly, special courses for classes of gifted students are now often provided in many subject areas—art, music, mathematics, the sciences, writing, and so on. Actually, many of these courses are similar to those taught to older students, although they may be adjusted to make them more appropriate to the particular groups of students involved. Such an approach certainly has practical advantages over using specially prepared courses, for they use available, proven textbooks and instructors that are experienced in teaching from them.

I became involved in these matters about the time that I retired from the National Aeronautics and Space Administration (NASA) and agreed to be a volunteer teacher of gifted sixth-grade children, selected from two elementary schools in Hampton, Virginia. The subject matter was to be mainly mathematics and the physical sciences, but the specific course content was left to me. I could have tried to follow the usual approach as described in the preceding paragraph. I felt, however, that simply anticipating the students' intermediate- and high-school courses offered a relatively restricted opportunity to contribute to their growth. Instead, I taught a variety of subjects, all chosen to develop the intellect along one line or another—the ability to visualize and to reason, to correlate groups of facts and ideas and then reach conclusions, and to examine ideas and experiments critically, all while learning a variety of approaches to problem solving.

Other retired scientists expressed enthusiasm for my work (perhaps merely reflecting my own enthusiasm) and expressed some interest in doing it too, although they feared that they would not know how or what to teach. This book was prepared in response to this implied need for a guide to course content. As I wrote, my own critical attitude led me to expand the material and raise its level, so that the final result can be used even with gifted high-school students, and can be used for self-study by motivated students. Thus, it is not a typical textbook that is written for a particular grade level and teaches one of the standard subjects. Furthermore, the book contains far more than can be covered reasonably well in, say, a semester, so the instructor must select what is appropriate to his class and to the available time.

As already explained, the book is not a text on a standard scholastic subject, nor are the different chapters "short courses" on their nominal subjects. The subjects of the chapters have been chosen because they provide frameworks for discussions, analyses, and exercises involving ways of looking at various types of problems and thereby learning the different types of reasoning that can be applied to them. In addition, some of the material serves mainly as mental calisthenics. Consider, for example, some of the material under Arithmetic: In adding two multidigit numbers from left to right, students learn to look ahead; in mentally multiplying together two 2-digit or 3-digit numbers, they develop their short-term memory and their concentration; in solving cryptarithmetic problems, they not only develop their arithmetic but also exercise various reasoning processes; in learning the fundamental theorem of arithmetic and in learning the casting-out-nines method of checking arithmetic they are exposed, possibly for the first time, to mathematical proofs. As to the material under Geometry, teaching a bit of Euclid is the least of its purposes, for they will study Euclid later, in geometry. More important is the development of two- and three-dimensional visualization capabilities, along with the development of geometrical reasoning. Similarly the items of scientific knowledge presented in subsequent chapters are not intended to preempt any of the students' future scientific studies, but to exemplify analyses of physical phenomena and to show the application of mathematics in such analyses. Furthermore, of course, they provide an opportunity, through experiments, to add a bit of reality and spice to the course. In particular, I might mention the chapter on surface tension. The subject may seem a rather narrow specialty in comparison with the subjects of the other chapters; yet it not only has a wealth of everyday applications but it offers a mine of opportunity for analyzing simple and interesting phenomena.

The chapter on mechanics is vulnerable to criticism in that it is not very different from a high-school course in mechanics. I trust the user will appreciate my dilemma here, for I needed to provide some background in mechanics for use in later chapters, while at the same time including items that would serve my basic goal of mental development.

Although I have thus attempted to explain and justify my choice of material, I must admit that another author approaching the same task might with equal plausibility justify a choice of different material. A book of this type reflects the author—his scientific training and career, his methods of approaching scientific problems, his incidental scientific interests, and his experience in working with gifted children, in addition to more subtle aspects of his personality. With regard to the present book, I can but hope that whatever part of my reflection is absorbed by students will be of value to them.

In a course that emphasizes reasoning, thoroughness of understanding is essential, so the instructor must not try to cover more material than can be covered well. Just how the material should be taught will have to depend on the age group of the students and the teacher's techniques. I offer only one suggestion—as soon as is reasonable, require the students to present proofs, solutions to problems, and discussions to the class. Having to present material to a bright, critical audience of their peers should make the students learn and organize their material thoroughly; in addition they will learn, with the instructor's help, to stand before a group with pointer and slide, or with chalk and blackboard, and make clear and thoughtful presentations.

The book contains many problems, although far fewer than are generally found in textbooks. Answers are usually given near the problems themselves. It is assumed that the students will have sufficient self-motivation to study each problem carefully and do their best to solve it before referring to the answer.

As a final note, I should encourage scientists who teach this material to add spice to the course by including one or two experiments that are close to their own interests. The emphasis, of course, should remain on clear analysis and discussion of the experiments; the purpose of the lesson should not be merely entertainment, with which students are already inundated.

I wish to express my admiration for and gratitude to the dedicated members of the Technical Editing Branch.

Samuel Katzoff

National Aeronautics and Space Administration
Langley Research Center
1992

Additional Guide to Contents

There is no index. However, the Contents lists all headings and sub-headings; and as further aid in finding material the following pages list other discussed items together with their page locations.

Chapter 6

Chapter 7

Chapter 10

ARITHMETIC

Addition and Subtraction

As noted in the Introduction, the following sections are intended to help develop mental acuity and mental discipline; that they promote agility in arithmetical operations and also teach a few methods of mental arithmetic are incidental benefits.

Left-to-right addition. In ordinary right-to-left addition of two integers, one never has to carry more than 1. In this example, one must carry 1 from the 4 + 8 and from the 3 + 9. The other pairs add to less than 10, so they do not give a 1 to carry. Now, instead of proceeding as usual, from right to left, see if you can perform the addition starting at the left end and proceeding to the right. As you add each pair, glance at the next pair in order to see if a 1 is to be carried from it. Thus, 4 + 5 = 9, but a glance at the next pair, 3 + 9, tells that a 1 is carried, so you write 10 instead of 9. For this next pair, 3 + 9 = 12, and since a glance at the next pair, 8 + 0, tells that a 1 is not carried, you write 2; and so on.

If, when you glance at the next pair, you see that they add up to 9, you have to glance at the pair beyond that one; if that pair also adds up to 9, you have to glance at the pair beyond that one; and so on. In this sum, every pair adds up to 9 except the last one, which adds up to 10. You should need only a few moments to see that and to write down the answer.

Do these additions, going from left to right:

> *"I couldn't afford to learn it" said the Mock Turtle with a sigh. "I only took the regular course." "What was that?" inquired Alice. "Reeling and Writhing, of course, to begin with," the Mock Turtle replied; "and then the different branches of Arithmetic—Ambition, Distraction, Uglification, and Derision."*
> —From Alice's Adventures in Wonderland, by Lewis Carroll (Charles L. Dodgson)

```
  1  1
 43864
 59028
102892
```

```
 35827
 64173
100000
```

```
  72710        88932        98712        70994
+23107       +42241       +51826       +35318
```

```
  96191        92237        57306        69298
+54509       +76060       +49199       +54224
```

```
  86385        81345        58336      123456789
+82834       +18655       +29338     + 98765432
```

Left-to-right subtraction. In the preceding examples the lower numbers are all smaller than the upper numbers. As an additional exercise of a similar kind, subtract the lower numbers from the upper numbers, again proceeding from left to right. Now you must glance from each pair to the next pair to see if a 1 has to be *borrowed*; and if the two digits of the next pair are equal you must glance at the next pair; and so on.

Left-to-right additions and subtractions are required in a number of the methods used by people who are very skilled in fast arithmetic. Many other people also use it, possibly because they enjoy the challenge and the alertness that it demands.

Among the types of problems that the more skillful can do are

(1) Adding three numbers from left to right
(2) Adding the lower two numbers and subtracting the sum from the upper number, all from left to right.

You might try both of these types of exercises with the following sets of three numbers:

86385	98165	67158	12361	16685
2467	789	7353	6482	1642
7682	4453	419	4773	5793

As a check, verify that the sum of the two results is twice the top number in every case.

Adding a column of digits. In adding a column of digits look ahead for

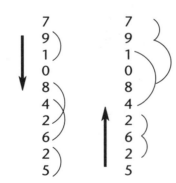

(1) Groups like 7 and 3, or 6, 2, and 2 that add up to 10.
(2) Groups like 8, 8, and 4 that add up to 20.
(3) Groups that, when added to what you already have, give a number that ends in zero. For example, if you have reached 32 and you see a 7 and a 1, add them on as a group to give 40.
(4) Any other groups that you can sum at a glance. For example, in adding this column from top to bottom, you might proceed as follows: 7, 17, 27, 37, 44, where, on the final step, the 2 and 5 were combined. In adding the column from bottom to top you might proceed as follows: 5, 15, 20, 44, where, in the last step, $8 + 9 + 7$ was recognized as $3 \times 8 = 24$ and added in one step.

All that is needed for this kind of exercise is a thorough familiarity with basic arithmetic and the ability to look ahead and recognize opportunities.

Do the following sums, first by going down the columns and then by going up the columns:

75	83	48	37	538	945
14	58	73	45	892	593
35	66	49	36	294	125
36	93	15	22	84	824
69	8	64	53	934	556
31	68	73	57	750	927
60	69	56	6	866	158
52	90	1	43	689	349
93	39	83	76	688	886
67	59	36	19	657	820

Many who are skilled in fast arithmetic add columns of digits two at a time. Taking the column farthest to the right as an example, one would have, adding two at a time, 8, 17, 30, 47, 53.

The six sums are, from left to right, 532, 633, 498, 394, 6392, 6183.

Adding a column of 2-digit or 3-digit numbers. In adding a column of 2-digit numbers, it is not very difficult to add each number as a single quantity, instead of adding the units column and then the tens column. For example, the addition on the right would proceed as follows: 72, 88, 180, 250, 332, 429, 487. Such addition is sometimes done more easily by adding some of the numbers in two steps: In order to add 82, add 80 and then add 2; in order to add 97, add 100 and then subtract 3. This addition might thus proceed as follows: 72, 88, 178, 180, 250, 330, 332, 432, 429, 489, 487.

$$72$$
$$16$$
$$92$$
$$70$$
$$82$$
$$97$$
$$\underline{58}$$

Adding a column of 3-digit numbers by taking the numbers as single quantities is, of course, some-what more difficult than a similar addition of 2-digit numbers. Adding in two steps, again, is often helpful; for example, to add 689, add 700 and then subtract 11.

As an exercise, do the preceding six additions by treating each number as a single quantity.

An everyday application of such mental addition is determining the total cost of the groceries in a supermarket basket. As an exercise, determine the total costs of the groceries in these baskets and include a 4% sales tax for each.

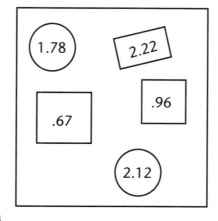

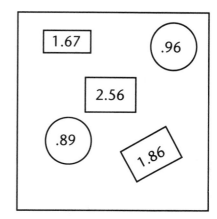

Multiplication and Division

Multiplying or dividing by 5 or 25. In order to multiply a number by 5, multiply it by 10 and divide by 2. For example, to calculate 28947×5, take $\frac{1}{2} \times 289470 = 144735$, which is easily done mentally.

In order to divide a number by 5, multiply it by 2 and divide by 10. Thus, to calculate $\frac{28947}{5}$ we take $\frac{1}{10} \times (28947 \times 2) = 5789.4$.

In order to multiply by 25, multiply by 100 and divide by 4. Thus, $28947 \times 25 = \frac{2894700}{4} = 723675$.

In order to divide by 25, multiply by 4 and divide by 100. Thus, $\frac{28947}{25} = \frac{1}{100} \times (28947 \times 4) = 1157.88$.

Exercises:
Mentally multiply and divide these numbers by 5 and 25 using

the preceding methods:

55322	78017	44768	25100	83612
41347	16834			

(Actually, direct multiplication or division by 25 is not difficult to do mentally (try it), but the methods given here are faster.)

Problem:
How would you mentally multiply by 125? Do these multiplications mentally:

$$888 \times 125 \qquad 789 \times 125 \qquad 2345 \times 125$$

Multiplying by 11. Consider this example of a multiplication by 11. The answer can easily be written down directly: The first digit of the product is the same as the first digit of the multiplicand; the next digit of the product is the sum of the first two digits; the next digit is the sum of the next two digits; and the last digit of the product is the last digit of the multiplicand.

Although this example is easily done mentally, the method becomes a bit more challenging if the digits are larger, because when some of the sums are 10 or more, there is a 1 to carry. The procedure is straightforward if we write down the answer from right to left; but if we wish to write it down from left to right we have to look ahead to see if a 1 is carried.

Do these examples mentally, first writing down the answers from right to left and then writing them down from left to right:

$$\times\,11$$

215	354	271813	4832493	89898

87074	70694	97121	94317	49160	19

Multiplying by 111. In this example of multiplication by 111, the first digit of the product is the first digit of the multiplicand; then, in order, are the sum of the first two digits, the sum of the first set of three digits, the sum of the next set of three digits, the sum of the last two digits, and the last digit. This problem is hence easy to do mentally:

$$3243 \times 111 = 359973$$

Here again, however, our example used small digits, so the sums never exceeded 9. If the digits are larger we may have a 1 or a 2 to carry, as in this example. Nevertheless, the problem is easy to do mentally if we proceed from right to left:

$$34678 \times 111 = 3849258$$

For the mental exercise, however, also do it by proceeding from left to right, always looking ahead to see whether a 1 or 2 is carried.

Do these examples mentally, first writing down the answers from right to left, and then writing them down from left to right:

Left margin column:

```
  527
 ×11
  527
 527
 5797—Last digit
       ╲ Sum of next
          two digits
        ╲ Sum of first two
          digits
        First digit
```

```
  658
 ×11
  658
 658
 7238
```

Answers:
2365; 3894; 2989943;
53157423; 988878; 957814;
777634; 1068331; 1037487;
540760; 209

```
  3243
 ×111
  3243
 3243
3243
359973
```

```
  34678
 ×111
  34678
 34678
34678
3849258
```

× 111

135035	23423	435618	35769	
78989	248376	47992	22342	19

Answers:
14988885; 2599953;
48353598; 3970359;
8767779; 27569736;
5327112; 2479962; 2109

Two-digit numbers. For mentally multiplying one 2-digit number by another, you might simply visualize the multiplication as it is usually done on paper. Keeping this picture in your mind as you perform the operations may be rather difficult, however. Mental multiplication proceeds much more easily by the following method, which involves a series of simple steps:

```
  73
×86
```

1. Multiply the tens: $7 \times 8 = 56$.
2. Cross-multiply the tens and units; combine the two cross-products: $7 \times 6 + 8 \times 3 = 42 + 24 = 66$.
3. Shift the result of step 2 one place to the right and add to the result of step 1. Add left-to-right as we did in an earlier section.
4. Multiply the units: $3 \times 6 = 18$.
5. Shift this result one place to the right and add to the result of step 3.

```
  73
  86
 438
 584
6278
```

```
  56
  66
 626
  18
6278
```

The basis of this method may be seen by writing the procedure as follows:

$$
\begin{array}{r}
73 \\
\times\,86
\end{array}
=
\begin{array}{r}
70 + 3 \\
\times\,80 + 6
\end{array}
$$

$$
\begin{array}{r}
80 \times 70 = 5600 \\
6 \times 70 + 80 \times 3 =\ \ 660 \\
6 \times 3 =\ \ \ \ 18 \\
\hline
6278
\end{array}
$$

Two suggestions for easing the mental strain are:

1. Add each cross-product separately. That is, instead of calculating $7 \times 6 + 8 \times 3 = 66$ and then adding the 66, do it in separate steps:

   $7 \times 6 = 42$; add the 42
   $8 \times 3 = 24$; add the 24

Thus:

$$
\begin{array}{ll}
\begin{array}{r} 73 \\ \times 86 \end{array} &
\begin{array}{r}
7 \times 8 = 56 \\
7 \times 6 =\ \ 42 \\
\hline
602 \\
8 \times 3 =\ \ 24 \\
\hline
626 \\
6 \times 3 =\ \ 18 \\
\hline
6278
\end{array}
\end{array}
$$

2. A sum will be easier to remember if you say it aloud instead of trying silently to visualize it. That is, as you do the first addition,

say six-0-two; as you do the next addition, say six-two-six; and as you do the final addition, say six-two-seven-eight.

Exercises: (See the following notes.)

$$
\begin{array}{cccccc}
36 & 83 & 57 & 63 & 49 & 28 \\
\times 43 & \times 38 & \times 97 & \times 67 & \times 81 & \times 87
\end{array}
$$

$$
\begin{array}{cccc}
226 & 104 & 328 & 124 \\
\times 83 & \times 33 & \times 72 & \times 337
\end{array}
$$

Answers to exercises:
1548; 3154; 5529; 4221;
3969; 2436; 18758; 3432;
23616; 41788

Notes:
1. In the third exercise (57×97), the two units digits are the same, 7. Then we can simplify the cross multiplication by taking it as $7(5 + 9) = 7 \times 14 = 98$.
2. In the fourth exercise (63×67), the two tens digits are the same and the two units digits add up to 10. The cross multiplication is then simply $6 \times 10 = 60$.
3. In the second row of these exercises are some 3-digit numbers. The same method may be applied by considering the first *pair* of digits as the tens digit. For example,

$$
\begin{array}{r}
264 \\
\times 116 \\
\hline
\end{array}
$$

$$
\begin{array}{rr}
11 \times 26 = & 286 \\
6 \times 26 + 11 \times 4 = & 200 \\
\hline
& 3060 \\
6 \times 4 = & 24 \\
\hline
& 30624
\end{array}
$$

or

$$
\begin{array}{rr}
11 \times 26 = & 286 \\
6 \times 26 = & 156 \\
\hline
& 3016 \\
11 \times 4 = & 44 \\
\hline
& 3060 \\
6 \times 4 = & 24 \\
\hline
& 30624
\end{array}
$$

Three-digit numbers. A more general way of mentally multiplying 3-digit numbers is a different extension of the method for 2-digit numbers. The following example illustrates it.

$$
\begin{array}{r}
647 \\
\times 853 \\
\hline
\end{array}
$$

$$
\begin{array}{lr}
8 \times 6 & = 48 \\
(8 \times 4) + (5 \times 6) & = 62 \\
\hline
& 542 \\
(8 \times 7) + (3 \times 6) + (5 \times 4) & = 94 \\
\hline
& 5514 \\
(5 \times 7) + (3 \times 4) & = 47 \\
\hline
& 55187 \\
3 \times 7 & = 21 \\
\hline
& 551891
\end{array}
$$

or

$$
\begin{array}{rr}
8 \times 6 = & 48 \\
8 \times 4 = & 32 \\
5 \times 6 = & 30 \\
\hline
& 512 \\
& 542 \\
8 \times 7 = & 56 \\
\hline
& 5476 \\
3 \times 6 = & 18 \\
\hline
& 5494 \\
5 \times 4 = & 20 \\
\hline
& 5514 \\
5 \times 7 = & 35 \\
\hline
& 55175 \\
3 \times 4 = & 12 \\
\hline
& 55187 \\
3 \times 7 = & 21 \\
\hline
& 551891
\end{array}
$$

The step-by-step procedure on the right is probably less liable to error. We can see here the important advantage of this procedure for mental multiplication. After each addition we need remember only that result and we can mentally erase all the earlier steps. Thus, in the preceding example, after the sixth step we have to remember only the number 5514, and we may forget all the numbers obtained in the earlier steps; then, after the next step we have to remember only the number 55175; and so on.

Exercises:

612	767	796	863
×344	×691	×252	×599
556	343	917	885
×467	×834	×571	×476
712	882		
×257	×395		

Calculating squares. Our multiplication method may, of course, be used for mentally calculating squares of 2-digit and 3-digit numbers. Suppose, for example, we wish the square of 87. According to our method we proceed as follows:

$$
\begin{array}{r}
8^2 = 64 \\
2(8 \times 7) = 112 \\
\hline
752 \\
7^2 = 49 \\
\hline
7569
\end{array}
$$

For the square of a small 3-digit number, say 127, we have

$$
\begin{array}{r}
12^2 = 144 \\
2(12 \times 7) = 168 \\
\hline
1608 \\
7^2 = 49 \\
\hline
16129
\end{array}
$$

For the square of a larger 3-digit number, say 463, we have

$$
\begin{array}{r}
4^2 = 16 \\
2(4 \times 6) = 48 \\
\hline
208 \\
2(4 \times 3) = 24 \\
\hline
2104 \\
6^2 = 36 \\
\hline
2140 \\
2(6 \times 3) = 36 \\
\hline
21436 \\
3^2 = 9 \\
\hline
214369
\end{array}
$$

Squares of integers ending in 0. The square of a multiple of 10 is easily determined:

$$10^2 = 100 \qquad\qquad 1^2 = 1$$
$$20^2 = 400 \qquad\qquad 2^2 = 4$$
$$30^2 = 900 \qquad\qquad 3^2 = 9$$
$$\cdot \qquad\qquad\qquad \cdot$$
$$\cdot \qquad\qquad\qquad \cdot$$
$$\cdot \qquad\qquad\qquad \cdot$$
$$90^2 = 8100 \qquad\qquad 9^2 = 81$$
$$100^2 = 10000 \qquad\qquad 10^2 = 100$$
$$110^2 = 12100 \qquad\qquad 11^2 = 121$$
$$120^2 = 14400 \qquad\qquad 12^2 = 144$$

Squares of integers ending in 5. The method of squaring an integer ending in 5 is illustrated by the following examples:

$$5^2 = 25 \qquad\qquad 0 \times 1 = 0$$
$$15^2 = 225 \qquad\qquad 1 \times 2 = 2$$
$$25^2 = 625 \qquad\qquad 2 \times 3 = 6$$
$$35^2 = 1225 \qquad\qquad 3 \times 4 = 12$$
$$\cdot \qquad\qquad\qquad \cdot$$
$$\cdot \qquad\qquad\qquad \cdot$$
$$\cdot \qquad\qquad\qquad \cdot$$
$$95^2 = 9025 \qquad\qquad 9 \times 10 = 90$$
$$105^2 = 11025 \qquad\qquad 10 \times 11 = 110$$
$$115^2 = 13225 \qquad\qquad 11 \times 12 = 132$$
$$125^2 = 15625 \qquad\qquad 12 \times 13 = 156$$

The rule may be given as follows: Let the number in front of the 5 be a. To get the square, write the product $a(a + 1)$ and append 25. For example, if you want the square of 115, write down the product of 11 and 12, or 132, and append 25, giving 13225. The rule is easily proved by direct multiplication:

$$\begin{array}{r} 10a + 5 \\ \times 10a + 5 \\ \hline 50a + 25 \\ 100a^2 + 50a \\ \hline 100a^2 + 100a + 25 = 100(a^2 + a) + 25 = 100a(a + 1) + 25 \end{array}$$

Square of the next larger number or of the next smaller number. The difference between the squares of two consecutive integers is the sum of the two integers. For example, the difference between 3^2 and 2^2 is $3 + 2$:

$$3^2 - 2^2 = 9 - 4 = 5 = 3 + 2$$
$$4^2 - 3^2 = 16 - 9 = 7 = 4 + 3$$
$$5^2 - 4^2 = 25 - 16 = 9 = 5 + 4$$

By using this rule we can easily calculate the square of an integer if we know the square of the next larger or next smaller integer. Thus, given $12^2 = 144$,

$$13^2 = 12^2 + (12 + 13) = 144 + 25 = 169$$

$$14^2 = 13^2 + (13 + 14) = 169 + 27 = 196$$

or, since we know 15^2,

$$14^2 = 15^2 - (14 + 15) = 225 - 29 = 196$$

(A similar rule applies even when the numbers are not integers. For example, $(14\frac{1}{2})^2 = (13\frac{1}{2})^2 + (13\frac{1}{2} + 14\frac{1}{2}) = (13\frac{1}{2})^2 + 28 = 182\frac{1}{4} + 28 = 210\frac{1}{4}$.) The rule is, again, easily proved:

Let the number be a; then the next larger number is $a + 1$. For the square of $a + 1$,

$$\begin{array}{r} a+1 \\ \times\, a + 1 \\ \hline a + 1 \\ a^2 + a \quad\quad \\ \hline a^2 + a + (a + 1) = \end{array} \; a^2 + \text{the sum of } a \text{ and } a + 1.$$

Square of the number that is two units larger or smaller. We have just seen how to go from 12^2 to 14^2 in two steps. The two steps, however, can be easily combined:

$$14^2 = 13^2 + (13 + 14) = 12^2 + (12 + 13) + (13 + 14) = 12^2 + (4 \times 13)$$

Thus, the difference between the square of a number and the square of a number that is two units larger or smaller is four times the intermediate number.

By using all of our rules for squares we may calculate mentally the square of any integer up to, say, 100 without much effort. For example

$$\begin{aligned}
60^2 &= 3600 \\
61^2 &= 3600 + 60 + 61 = 3600 + 121 = 3721 \\
62^2 &= 3600 + 4 \times 61 = 3600 + 244 = 3844 \\
65^2 &= 4225 \\
64^2 &= 4225 - (64 + 65) = 4225 - 129 = 4096 \\
63^2 &= 4225 - 4 \times 64 = 4425 - 256 = 3969 \\
66^2 &= 4225 + 65 + 66 = 4225 + 131 = 4356
\end{aligned}$$

.
.
.

A slightly different approach to getting squares of integers is based on the formulas

$$(a + b)^2 = a^2 + 2ab + b^2$$
$$(a - b)^2 = a^2 - 2ab + b^2$$

$$\begin{array}{r} a + b \\ a + b \\ \hline ab + b^2 \\ a^2 + \quad ab \quad\quad \\ \hline a^2 + 2ab + b^2 \end{array}$$

Using these formulas we have

$$60^2 = 3600$$
$$61^2 = 60^2 + 2 \times 60 \times 1 + 1^2 = 3600 + 120 + 1 = 3721$$
$$62^2 = 60^2 + 2 \times 60 \times 2 + 2^2 = 3600 + 240 + 4 = 3844$$
$$63^2 = 60^2 + 2 \times 60 \times 3 + 3^2 = 3600 + 360 + 9 = 3969$$
$$64^2 = 60^2 + 2 \times 60 \times 4 + 4^2 = 3600 + 480 + 16 = 4096$$
$$65^2 = 4225$$
$$66^2 = (70-4)^2 = 70^2 - 2 \times 70 \times 4 + 4^2 = 4900 - 560 + 16 = 4356$$
$$67^2 = (70-3)^2 = 70^2 - 2 \times 70 \times 3 + 3^2 = 4900 - 420 + 9 = 4489$$
$$68^2 = (70-2)^2 = 70^2 - 2 \times 70 \times 2 + 2^2 = 4900 - 280 + 4 = 4624$$
$$69^2 = (70-1)^2 = 70^2 - 2 \times 70 \times 1 + 1^2 = 4900 - 140 + 1 = 4761$$
$$70^2 = 4900$$

Continental method of doing long division. Americans usually learn to do long division as shown here by the example on the left. In much of Europe, however, children learn to do both the multiplications and subtractions mentally, and to write down only the remainders, as shown by the example on the right.

```
        1708
   49)83718
      49
      347
      343
       418
       392
        26 remainder
```

```
         1708
    49)83718
       347
        418
         26 remainder
```

Exercises:

Do the following divisions by the continental method:

```
92)842736        52)3054574        437)545652347
```

```
119)5994202      909)28902209      357)26586437
```

Answers:
$9160\frac{4}{23}$; $58741\frac{21}{26}$; $1248632\frac{163}{437}$; $50371\frac{53}{119}$; $31795\frac{554}{909}$; $74471\frac{290}{357}$

If you desire further to pursue studies of special methods of arithmetic, both mental and written, the following two books will be helpful:

Henry Sticker: *How To Calculate Quickly.* Dover Publications, Inc., New York. Many methods are given, together with thousands of exercises, with answers.

Karl Menninger: *Calculator's Cunning.* Basic Books, Inc., New York. This book also gives many interesting methods, with exercises and answers.

The four-4's problem. Using addition, subtraction, multiplication, and division, arrange four 4's so that they give the integers from 1 to 10. For example,

$$1 = \frac{4+4}{4+4} \text{ or } \frac{4 \times 4}{4 \times 4} \text{ or } \frac{4}{4} + 4 - 4 \text{ or } \frac{44}{44}$$

$$2 = \frac{4 \times 4}{4+4} \text{ or } \frac{4}{4} + \frac{4}{4}$$

It is possible, with four 4's to make every integer up to 100; however, for integers greater than 10, additional symbols may be required, as the square-root sign $\sqrt{4} = 2$, the factorial sign $4! = 4 \times 3 \times 2 \times 1 = 24$, the repeating decimal sign $.\overline{4} = 0.4444... = \frac{4}{9}$, parentheses $4(4+4) = 32$.

Using these additional signs when necessary, use four 4's to make the integers from 11 through 20.

Answers:

$$3 = \frac{4+4+4}{4} \qquad 4 = 4 + \frac{4-4}{4} \qquad 5 = \frac{4 \times 4 + 4}{4}$$

$$6 = 4 + \frac{4+4}{4} \qquad 7 = 4 + 4 - \frac{4}{4} \qquad 8 = 4 + 4 + 4 - 4$$

$$9 = 4 + 4 + \frac{4}{4} \qquad 10 = \frac{44-4}{4} \qquad 11 = \frac{44}{\sqrt{4 \times 4}}$$

$$12 = \frac{44+4}{4} = 4 \times 4 - \sqrt{4 \times 4} \qquad 13 = 4! - \frac{44}{4} = \frac{44}{4} + \sqrt{4}$$

$$14 = 4 \times 4 - 4 + \sqrt{4} = 4 + 4 + 4 + \sqrt{4} \qquad 15 = 4 \times 4 - \frac{4}{4} = \frac{4}{.4} + 4 + \sqrt{4}$$

$$16 = 4 \times 4 + 4 - 4 \qquad 17 = 4 \times 4 + \frac{4}{4}$$

$$18 = \frac{4}{.4} + \frac{4}{.4} = 4 \times 4 + \frac{4}{\sqrt{4}} = \frac{4}{.4} \times \frac{4}{\sqrt{4}} = 4! - \sqrt{4} - \sqrt{4} - \sqrt{4} = 4! - \frac{4}{\sqrt{4}} - 4$$

$$19 = 4! - 4 - \frac{4}{4}$$

$$20 = 4 \times 4 + \sqrt{4} + \sqrt{4} = 4^{\sqrt{4}} + \sqrt{4} + \sqrt{4} = 4\left(4 + \frac{4}{4}\right) = \frac{44}{\sqrt{4}} - \sqrt{4}$$

Problems:

Combine the given numbers, using all the given symbols. For example, combine 1 4 5 11 using $+ \times \sqrt{} =$ to obtain $\sqrt{11+5} = 4 \times 1$

a. 2 3 3 7 18 $+ - \times (\ ) =$

b. 1 3 3 4 25 $+ \times \times \sqrt{} =$

c. 9 5 7 35 63 45 $\times \times \times \sqrt{} =$

Answers:

a. $7 + 2 = 18 - (3 \times 3)$

b. $\sqrt{25} + 4 = 3 \times 3 \times 1$ or

$\sqrt{25 \times 4} = 3 \times 3 + 1$

c. $\sqrt{35 \times 63 \times 45} = 9 \times 5 \times 7$

Verifying Arithmetic

"Casting out nines" and "casting out elevens" are two methods of verifying arithmetic. They first will be described and then will be explained.

Casting out nines. Here is an example of the use of the casting-out-nines method for verifying an addition:

7013588	$7 + 0 + 1 + 3 + 5 + 8 + 8 = 32$		$3 + 2 = 5$
2654516	$2 + 6 + 5 + 4 + 5 + 1 + 6 = 29$	$2 + 9 = 11$	$1 + 1 = 2$
8559616	$8 + 5 + 5 + 9 + 6 + 1 + 6 = 40$		$4 + 0 = 4$
18227720	$1 + 8 + 2 + 2 + 7 + 7 + 2 + 0 = 29$	$2 + 9 = 11$	11
		$1 + 1 = 2$	$1 + 1 = 2$

└─Check─┘

As seen in this example, the method consists of these steps:

(1) Add the digits in each of the numbers to be added; if their sum exceeds 9, add the digits in their sum; if this sum exceeds 9, again add the digits; continue until the sum is no more than 9.

(2) Add these final sums. If the result exceeds 9, again add the digits, and so on until the result is no more than 9.

(3) Do the same with the digits of your sum. The result should be the same as the result obtained in step (2).

In the example, the final result of step (2) is 2, and the final result of step (3) is also 2; hence the method indicates that our addition is correct.

This procedure may, however, be itself prone to error when we are dealing with large numbers. It can often be greatly simplified by first crossing out all 9's and all combinations of digits that add up to 9 or to a multiple of 9, as 18 or 27. Thus, in our first number, 7013588, we can cross out 8 and 1; also 7, 3, and 8. Our procedure would then be as follows:

9-combinations

7013588	→	5		7, 3, 8 and 1, 8
2654516	→	2		6, 5, 1, 6 and 5, 4
8559616	→	13 →	4	8, 5, 5 and 9
18227720	→	2	11 → 2	1, 8; 2, 7; and 7, 2

└─Check─┘

Note that by crossing out the 9's and 9-combinations in an integer, we may sometimes cross out the whole line and leave 0. The 0 may be used as such or replaced by its equivalent, 9.

Following is an example of the use of casting out nines for verifying a multiplication:

```
    2357  →              8
    8434  → 19 →       × 1
    9428                  8
    7071
    9428
   18856
  19878938   →           8
```

$$\text{Check}$$

Following is an example of the use of casting out nines for verifying a division. The method corresponds to multiplying the divisor by the quotient and then adding the remainder in order to recover the dividend.

```
        6                6033 → 3
  724596)4372203856 → 13 → 4
         4347576                    Check
         2462785
         2173788        3 × 6 + 4 = 22 → 4
          2889976
          2173788
Remainder  716188 → 13 → 4
```

Casting out elevens. Casting out elevens is similar to casting out nines, except that one alternately adds and subtracts the digits, starting at the right-hand end. It will be illustrated here for the preceding multiplication.

```
   2357        7 − 5 + 3 − 2 =      3
 × 8434        4 − 3 + 4 − 8 =    ×−3
                                  −9
                                          + 11 = 2    Check

19878938    8 − 3 + 9 − 8 + 7 − 8 + 9 − 1 = 13    3 − 1 = 2
```

Note that when a sum or product is negative, we may add 11 or a multiple of eleven in order to make it positive. We might have achieved the same final result by crossing out −3 and −8 from 4 − 3 + 4 − 8, since they add up to −11.

An alternative procedure is to pair off the digits, starting at the right-hand ends, subtract the nearest multiple of eleven from each pair, and sum the remainders. Thus,

$$\begin{pmatrix} 57 - 55 = 2 \\ 23 - 22 = 1 \end{pmatrix} \begin{pmatrix} 34 - 33 = 1 \\ 84 - 77 = 7 \end{pmatrix}$$

```
    2357        2 + 1              3
   ×8434        1 + 7             ×8
                                 24 → 2
    − − −
  19878938    5 + 1 − 1 − 3 = 2    Check
```

This method seems easier than the standard casting-out-elevens method, and is probably less prone to error.

Neither the casting-out-nines method nor the casting-out-elevens method can provide an absolute proof of correctness, because errors might, by accident, be such that they do not affect the result. For example, in the preceding multiplication, if an error resulted in a product of 19878038 instead of 19878938, the casting-out-nines method would not detect that the answer is wrong. In this case, however, the casting-out-elevens method would show that the answer is wrong. It is most unlikely that both methods would fail to detect an error.

Question:
What kind of error would escape detection by both methods?

Why do these methods work? The methods work because of the following facts:

1. In an addition of integers, if I divide the addends and the sum separately by any given integer, *the sum of the remainders equals the remainder of the sum.* For example, if we add 62806 and 43348, and use 7 as the dividing integer, we have

$$
\begin{array}{rl}
62806 & = 7 \times\ \ 8972\ \ + 2 \\
+\,43348 & = 7 \times\ \ 6192\ \ + \underline{4} \\
\hline
106154 & = 7 \times 15164\ + 6
\end{array}
$$

    in which the remainder of the sum, 6, turns out to be the sum of the two remainders, 2 and 4. If, however, the sum of the remainders in this case were to exceed 7, we should have to subtract 7 from it (or divide it by 7 and use the new remainder). For example,

$$
\begin{array}{rl}
62809 & = 7 \times\ \ 8972\ \ + 5 \\
+\,43350 & = 7 \times\ \ 6192\ \ + \underline{6} \\
\hline
106159 & = 7 \times 15165\ + 4
\end{array}
$$

    where the two remainders 5 and 6 add up to 11; we must subtract 7 from it to get 4, or else divide it by 7 to get the remainder 4.

2. In a multiplication of two integers, if I divide the two integers and their product separately by any given integer, *the product of the two remainders will be the remainder of the product.* For example, suppose that our two integers are 7505 and 6908, and the dividing integer is again 7.

$$
\begin{array}{rl}
7505 & = 7 \times 1072 \qquad +1 \\
\times\,6908 & = 7 \times\ 986 \qquad\ \ +6 \\
\hline
& \qquad\qquad\qquad 1 \times 6 = 6 \\[4pt]
\underline{51844540} & = 7 \times 7406362 + 6
\end{array}
$$

    Again, if the product of the remainders should exceed 7, it would have to be divided by 7 to get a new remainder that is less than 7.

    The general proofs for our two basic facts follow: For the addition, let $A + B = C$, let the divisor be d, and let the remainders for

A and *B* be r_1 and r_2, respectively. Then, if

$$A = da + r_1$$
$$\underline{B = db + r_2}$$
$$C = A + B = d(a + b) + r_1 + r_2$$

(That is, when we divide *A* by *d*, the quotient is *a* and the remainder is r_1.) Thus, the remainder for the sum is the sum of the remainders.

For the multiplication, let $A \times B = C$, or $(da + r_1) \times (db + r_2) = dadb + r_2da + r_1db + r_1r_2 = d(dab + ar_2 + br_1) + r_1r_2$.

Thus, when we divide the product by *d*, the quotient is $dab + ar_2 + br_1$ and the remainder is r_1r_2. That is, the remainder for the product is the product of the remainders.

3. Now there is a special advantage to using 9 as our divisor: When we divide 10 by 9 the remainder is 1, when we divide 20 by 9 the remainder is 2, when we divide 30 by 9 the remainder is 3, and so on; when we divide 100 by 9 the remainder is 1, when we divide 200 by 9 the remainder is 2, and so on; when we divide 1000 by 9 the remainder is 1, when we divide 2000 by 9, the remainder is 2, and so on; . . . Thus, if we have any multidigit integer, say

    $$82382 = 80000 + 2000 + 300 + 80 + 2,$$

    the remainder on dividing by 9 is simply the sum of the digits,

    $$8 + 2 + 3 + 8 + 2 = 23 \rightarrow 5$$

4. The number 11 is also a convenient divisor because: When we divide 10 by 11, the remainder can be taken as –1 (that is, 10 = $11 \times 1 - 1$), when we divide 20 by 11, the remainder can be taken as –2, and so on; when we divide 100 by 11, the remainder is +1, when we divide 200 by 11, the remainder is +2, and so on; when we divide 1000 by 11, the remainder is –1 (that is, 1000 = 11 $\times 91 - 1$); when we divide 2000 by 11, the remainder is –2, and so on; . . . The remainders are similar to those for 9, except that the signs alternate. Thus, if we have any multidigit integer, say,

    $$75363 = 70000 + 5000 + 300 + 60 + 3,$$

    the remainder on dividing by 11 is (from right to left) 3 – 6 + 3 – 5 + 7 = 2.

    The alternative method, in which we pair off the digits and subtract the nearest multiple of 11 is based on the fact that on dividing 100, 10000, 1000000, etc. by 11, the remainders are all +1. Then we write 75363 as 70000 + 5300 + 63 = 70000 + (5500 – 200) + (66 – 3), for which the remainder on dividing by 11 is (right to left) –3 – 2 + 7 = 2.

Problem:

In working with decimal fractions, one may add or delete zeros at the end of a number without changing its value. For example 2.3 = 2.30 = 2.300. In the casting-out-elevens method, however, the remainder for a number will be affected by adding or deleting a final zero, and accordingly the answer, even if correct, may not be verified. Thus 2.3 gives $3 - 2 = 1$, whereas 2.30 gives $0 - 3 + 2 = -1$. Propose a method of casting out elevens from decimal fractions that would be sure to prevent such errors.

Several number tricks are based on the casting-out-nines procedure. For example, write a multidigit number, as big as you please. Add the digits. Subtract this sum from your number. In the results, cross out any digit from 1 to 9, and tell me the sum of the remaining digits. I can then tell you immediately which digit you crossed out.

Problem:
Explain this trick.

Answer:
Your original number and the sum of its digits have the same casting-out-nines remainder. Therefore, when the sum is subtracted from your number, the casting-out-nines remainder of the difference should be 9, and the sum of the digits in this difference should be a multiple of 9. If you now cross out one of the digits, the sum will be less than the multiple of nine by the value of that digit.

Example:

Original number	24769342
Sum of digits	37
Difference	24769305

Cross out the 6 (leaving 2479305) and sum the rest: 30, which is less than the next higher multiple of 9 (36) by 6.

If you cross out the 9 the sum of the rest will be 27, which is less than the next higher multiple of 9 (36) by 9. However, if you cross out the 0, the sum of the rest, 36, is also less than the next higher multiple of 9 (45) by 9. In order to avoid this confusion of 9 and 0, I had to specify that you cross out any digit from 1 to 9 (not zero).

Problem:
Remainder after division by 33.

Given a number, pair off the digits from right to left, subtract multiples of 33 from each pair, add the remainders, and reduce this sum by subtracting a multiple of 33. The final result is the remainder when the given number is divided by 33. For example, given the number 76391480, we have the pairs

	76	39	14	80
Subtract	66	33	—	66
Remainders	10	6	14	14
Sum			10 + 6 + 14 + 14 = 44.	

Subtract 33, leaving 11, which is the remainder when 76391480 is divided by 33.

Explain why this procedure gives this remainder.

Could this procedure be used for verifying arithmetic by casting out thirty-threes?

Problem:
Prove that a number is divisible by 3 if the sum of its digits is divisible by 3.

A question of divisibility. The following sample illustrates a method of determining whether a number is divisible by 17. Explain why the procedure determines the divisibility. The example number is 5546029.

5546029 45	Remove the last digit on the right (9) and subtract 5 times it (45) from what remains.
554557 35	Remove the last digit on the right (7) and subtract 5 times it (35) from what remains.
55420 10	Neglect the zero. Remove the 2 at the right end and subtract $5 \times 2 = 10$ from what remains.
544 20	Remove the 4 and subtract $5 \times 4 = 20$ from what remains.
$34 = 2 \times 17$	Yes, it is divisible by 17.

Similarly explain the following procedure for determining whether a number is divisible by 19. The example number is 91660123.

91660123 6	Remove the last digit on the right (3) and add 2 times it (6) to what remains.
9166018 16	Remove the 8 and add 16 to what remains.
916617 14	Remove the 7 and add 14 to what remains.
91675 10	Remove the 5 and add 10 to what remains.
9177 14	Remove the final 7 and add 14 to what remains.
931 2	Remove the 1 and add 2 to what remains.
95 10	Remove the 5 and add 10 to what remains.
19	Yes, it is divisible by 19.

Similarly explain the following procedure for determining whether a number is divisible by 37. The example number is 845660123.

845660123 $\underline{33}$	The last digit on the right is 3. Remove it and subtract 33 from what remains.
84565979 $\underline{99}$	The last digit on the right is 9. Remove it and subtract 99 from what remains.
8456498 $\underline{88}$	Proceed similarly to the end.
845561 $\underline{11}$	
84545 $\underline{55}$	
8399 $\underline{99}$	
$74 = 2 \times 37$	Yes, it is divisible by 37.

Explanations:

Let A be the last digit on the right (the units digit). To determine divisibility by 17, subtract A and then subtract $50A$ (by subtracting $5A$ from the tens digit). Thus $51A$ is subtracted from the number. Since 51 is divisible by 17, the method thus subtracts a multiple of 17. But if a number is divisible by 17 it will remain so if a multiple of 17 is subtracted from it. The procedure is continued until the final remainder is either 0 or an obvious multiple of 17, if it is divisible, or a non-multiple of 17 if it is not divisible. (Note that the successive remainders were actually 5545570, 55442000, and 5440000; but the procedure neglects the final 0's, because if a number is divisible by 17, it will remain so when it is multiplied by 10 or when a factor of 10 is removed.)

To determine divisibility by 19, one subtracts A and then adds $20A$. Altogether, then, one adds $19A$, which does not affect divisibility by 19.

In the case of 37, note that $3 \times 37 = 111$; hence 111, 222, 333, 444, . . . are all multiples of 37. The procedure simply subtracts whichever triplet is needed to eliminate the last digit.

Problems

1. Consecutive integers: Prove the following statements:
   The sum of two consecutive integers is odd.
   The product of two consecutive integers is even.
   The product of three consecutive integers is divisible by 6.
   Given three consecutive integers of which the middle one is odd, their product is divisible by 24.
   The product of four consecutive integers is divisible by 24.

2. There are many instances of consecutive odd numbers that are prime (11 and 13, 17 and 19, 29 and 31, 41 and 43, . . .). Show

that 1, 3, 5 and 3, 5, 7 are the *only* cases of *three* consecutive odd numbers that are prime.

Show that every prime number greater than 3 is of the form $6n - 1$ or $6n + 1$, where n is an integer. (The converse is not true.)

3. A parlor trick: Make five cards, each about 5 cm square. On one card, write 1 on one side and 2 on the other; on another card, write 3 on one side and 4 on the other; on the others, similarly write 5 and 6, 7 and 8, and 9 and 10. Show them to your audience. Toss them into the air so that they fall on the table. Turn away so that you cannot see the numbers, but ask your audience to tell you how many odd numbers are up. From this information you can tell at once the sum of all the numbers that are up. How can you do that?

Answer:
The sum of the even numbers 2, 4, 6, 8, and 10 is 30, so if only even numbers are up, the sum would be 30. Each odd number is 1 less than the even number on the other side of the card, so for each card that has an odd number up, this sum is reduced by 1. For example, if three odd numbers are up, the sum of all the visible numbers is $30 - 3 = 27$.

4. "Free" magazines: You receive a telephone call informing you that you have been selected to receive free subscriptions to ten magazines (mainly junk) for five years. Your caller asks only that you pay a small mailing cost—a mere 69 cents per week. If you accept this "gift," what would it cost you? Mentally calculate the approximate cost, and do it quickly, while your caller is waiting for you to accept.

Answer:
For a quick, approximate answer, use 70 cents per week instead of 69 cents, and use 50 weeks in a year instead of 52 weeks. Then the cost per year is 50×70 cents = \$35, and the cost for five years is $5 \times \$35 = \$175$.

5. The trial of Socrates: In Athens, in 399 B.C., Socrates was tried for teaching ideas contrary to the national religion. The trial was by jury and the verdict was decided by simple majority vote. The 501-member jury found him guilty; but Socrates noted that a shift of only 30 votes from "guilty" to "not guilty" would have acquitted him. What was the actual vote? (Do it mentally.)

Answer:
For acquittal, the vote would have had to be 250 "guilty" and 251 "not guilty." Then the vote must have been $250 + 30 = 280$ "guilty" and $251 - 30 = 221$ "not guilty."

6. Take a 3-digit number in which the first and third digits differ by at least 2. Interchange the first and third digits and subtract the smaller number from the larger number. Interchange the first and third digits of the result and add the two numbers. Show why the result is always 1089.

$$
\begin{array}{r}
763 \\
-367 \\
\hline
396 \\
+693 \\
\hline
1089
\end{array}
$$

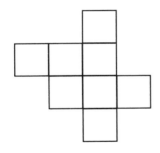

		14
8	12	16

7. I have some jacks, queens, kings, and aces. From these I select eight and arrange them as shown in the sketch, so that
   Every queen is between two kings.
   One king is between two jacks.
   No jack borders on a queen.
   There is one ace and it does not border on a king.
   At least one king borders on another king.
   Which card must be the ace?

8. Show that with a 1-gram weight, a 3-gram weight, a 9-gram weight, and a 27-gram weight, you can weigh any whole number of grams from 1 to 40.

9. In the small magic square on the left, the sums of the integers in each row, each column, and each diagonal are all the same. Fill in the five empty spaces with the missing integers.

10. There is a pile of 9 stones. Two players alternately remove 1, 3, or 4 stones. The one who removes the last stone wins. Show that the second player always wins if he plays correctly.

```
 1  2  3  4  5  6  7
 5  7  2  3  1  6  4
-4 -5  1  1  4  0  3
 4  5  1  1  4  0  3
```

11. Write down seven consecutive integers. Below them write the same integers in a different order. Subtract these from the integers above them. Delete the minus signs. Show that these seven integers cannot all be different; for example, here we have two 4's and two 1's.

Answer:
The seven integers in the differences (third line) must total zero, an even number. Deleting a minus sign is equivalent to adding an even number; for example, changing –4 to +4 is equivalent to adding 8, and changing –5 to +5 is equivalent to adding 10. Hence our final set of integers (fourth line) sums to an even number. But if our seven differences were all different, they would be 0, 1, 2, 3, 4, 5, 6, the sum of which is an odd number. Hence there is a contradiction, and we conclude that the seven differences are not all different.

Problem:
Show that this contradiction does not exist in the cases of four, five, and eight consecutive integers. In these three cases, see if you can reorder the sets of consecutive integers (second line) so that when you subtract one set from the other and delete the minus signs the differences are all different.

```
 1  2  3  4  5  6  7  8
 6  8  5  4  2  7  3  1
-5 -6 -2  0 +3 -1 +4 +7
 5  6  2  0  3  1  4  7
```

In demonstrating an approach to solving this problem, we consider the case of 8 consecutive integers. If we order them correctly, perform the subtractions, and delete the minus signs, we should get 0 1 2 3 4 5 6 7. The sum of these integers is 28. Then, before we deleted the minus signs, the positive differences must have totaled 14 and the negative differences must have totaled –14, since the sum of all the differences had to be zero. We now select some of the differences to total +14—say 7, 4, and 3—and set up our subtraction so that three of the differences will be +7, +4, and +3, one difference will be 0, and the rest will be all negative integers— –1, –2, –5, and –6. We find that, with a few trials, it is not very difficult to arrange the subtractions so that the eight differences (negative signs deleted) are all different.

Solve the case of the 8 consecutive integers by starting with another set of differences that total +14, say +6, +4, +3, and +1.

Solutions for the cases of 4 and 5 consecutive integers are

```
 1  2  3  4        1  2  3  4  5
 2  4  3  1        4  2  5  3  1
-1 -2  0  3       -3  0 -2  1  4
 1  2  0  3        3  0  2  1  4
```

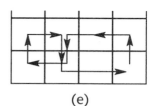

(a)

The 15-Puzzle. What Is and Is Not Possible

The 15-puzzle has been popular for over a hundred years and has even been discussed in mathematics journals. It is a frame that contains 15 movable tiles, numbered 1 to 15, and one blank space in the lower right corner (sketch (a)). If we slide the 12 down into the blank space, we get sketch (b), where the blank space has moved up to replace the 12. (It is convenient to refer to movements of the blank space, although, of course, it is the tiles that we physically move.) If we move the blank space through the closed circuit of sketch (c), the numbers along the circuit all move one space in the opposite direction (sketch (d)).

(b)

(c)

Problem:
What is the result of moving the blank space along the path shown in sketch (e)?

One's task with this puzzle is as follows: Given some arbitrary arrangement of the numbers, such as the jumble of sketch (f), with the blank space in the lower right corner, return it to the base pattern of sketch (a) by successive moves of the blank space. We shall show that this task cannot always be accomplished.

(d)

We begin by introducing the concept of inversion: In sketch (a), every number is followed by larger numbers, so there are no inversions. In any other pattern there are inversions. Specifically, wherever a number is larger than a following number we have an inversion. In sketch (f), for example, the 13 is followed by 12 smaller numbers (count them), the 12 is followed by 11 smaller numbers, the 15 is followed by 12 smaller numbers, and so on. The total number of inversions in sketch (f) is

$$(12 + 11 + 12 + 3) + (8 + 3 + 2 + 3) + (6 + 4 + 1) + 1 = 66$$

(e)

We shall want to know only whether the total is even or odd, which is easily determined by crossing out all even numbers and then crossing out pairs of odd numbers. Consider how the number of inversions is altered when we interchange two numbers in an arrangement, such as 12 and 6 in sketch (f). Let the larger number be m and the smaller number be n, and let m occur first; and of the numbers between them, let a of them be larger than m, b of them be smaller than m but

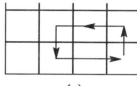

(f)

larger than *n*, and the remainder, *c*, be smaller than *n*. Then the inversions that we need consider are due to

(1) Those numbers from *m* to *n*, including *n*, that are smaller than *m* : $b + c + 1$ (when the 1 is due to *n*).
(2) Those numbers that are larger than *n* and precede it: $a + b$. The total of these two items is $a + 2b + c + 1$.

After we interchange *m* and *n*, we have

(1) Those numbers that are smaller than *n*: *c*.
(2) Those numbers that are larger than *m* and precede it: *a*. The total of these two items is $a + c$.

The difference between the two totals is $(a + 2b + c + 1) - (a + c) = 2b + 1$, an odd number. Thus, if we could interchange just two numbers, the total number of inversions would change by an odd number.

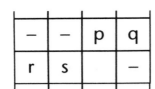

Now suppose that during the course of some rearrangement the blank space has arrived just below some number *p*. Between *p* and the blank space are three numbers: *q*, *r*, and *s*. Of these three, let *u* of them be smaller than *p*, and $3 - u$ of them be larger than *p*. The number of inversions in this group ascribed to *p* is then simply *u*. If we now slide *p* down into the blank space (which moves up to replace *p*), the number of inversions in this group ascribed to *p* changes to $3 - u$. The number of inversions has thus been changed by $(3 - u) - u = 3 - 2u$, which is an odd number. That is, a single vertical move of the blank space changes the number of inversions by an odd number.

Rearranging the numbers involves a series of vertical and horizontal moves of the blank space. Horizontal moves of the blank space do not affect the number of inversions. (You can easily see why.) Each vertical move of the blank space changes the number of inversions by an odd number, as we have just shown. Since the blank space must eventually be returned to the lower right corner, the number of vertical moves of the blank space is even; hence the number of inversions due to vertical moves of the blank space is even, because the sum of an even number of odd numbers is even. We conclude that in any change from one arrangement to another, with the blank space in the lower right corner in both arrangements, the number of inversions changes by an even number.

We saw earlier that, in interchanging a pair of numbers *m* and *n*, the number of inversions changed by an odd number. But we have just seen that the total number of inversions must be even. We conclude that it is not possible to interchange a pair of numbers unless at the same time we interchange an additional pair of numbers. An imagined arrangement made by starting with sketch (a) and interchanging pairs of numbers can actually be made only if the number of interchanges is even. For example, if someone asks you to start with sketch (a) and interchange 11 and 12 without altering the locations of any other numbers, you can state immediately that the task is impossible. For more complex tasks, if the number of interchanges is not easily determined, you can always determine the number of inversions by the method illustrated earlier for sketch (f), and thereby determine whether the task is possible.

Measuring Out Liquids With Containers of the Wrong Size

You have a milk pail containing about 15 liters of milk. You wish to measure out exactly 6 liters of milk, but you have only a 7-liter pail and a 5-liter pail.

Question:
How do you proceed?

Answer:
Find a combination of 7's and 5's that equal 6. For example, $3 \times 7 - 3 \times 5 = 6$; $4 \times 5 - 2 \times 7 = 6$. Consider the first equation. It tells us that if we fill the 7-liter pail three times but pour back three 5-liter pailfuls, 6 liters of milk will remain. Specifically, the procedure is as follows:

1. Fill the 7-liter pail.
2. Pour off 5 liters into the 5-liter pail, leaving 2 liters in the 7-liter pail. Pour back the 5 liters into the large pail, leaving the 5-liter pail empty.
3. Pour the 2 liters from the 7-liter pail into the 5-liter pail, leaving the 7-liter pail empty.
4. Fill the 7-liter pail again.
5. Pour off 3 liters into the 5-liter pail, thereby filling it and leaving 4 liters in the 7-liter pail. Again empty the 5-liter pail into the large pail.
6. Pour the 4 liters out of the 7-liter pail into the 5-liter pail, leaving the 7-liter pail empty.
7. Fill the 7-liter pail for the third time.
8. Pour off 1 liter into the 5-liter pail, filling it for the third time and leaving the desired 6 liters in the 7-liter pail. Again empty the 5-liter pail into the large pail.

Thus, you have filled the 7-liter pail three times but have returned three 5-liter pailfuls to the large pail, just as was required by the equation

$$3 \times 7 - 3 \times 5 = 6$$

Problems:
1. How do you proceed if your procedure is based on the other equation, $4 \times 5 - 2 \times 7 = 6$?
2. Using the same 7-liter and 5-liter pails, how could you measure out 1, 2, 3, 4, 6, 8, 9, 10, and 11 liters?

Question:
Could you measure out 5 liters if you had a 6-liter pail and a 4-liter pail?

Answer:
No, because any combination of 6's and 4's of the form $\pm 6a \pm 4b$ must be an even number. For example, $6a - 4b = 2(3a - 2b)$, which has 2 as a factor, regardless of the values of a and b.

Question:
Could you measure out 5 liters if you had a 9-liter pail and a 6-liter pail?

Answer:
No, because any combination of 9's and 6's of the form $\pm 9a \pm 6b$ must be a multiple of 3. Thus, $9a - 6b = 3(3a - 2b)$, which has 3 as a factor.

Then what is special about the pair 7 and 5 that permits us to combine them so as to get any integer? They have no common factor; that is, they are *relatively prime*. In fact 7 and 5 are *prime* numbers—they have no factors at all, other than themselves and 1.

$$1 \times 5 - 0 \times 7 = 5$$
$$2 \times 5 - 1 \times 7 = 3$$
$$3 \times 5 - 2 \times 7 = 1$$
$$4 \times 5 - 2 \times 7 = 6$$
$$5 \times 5 - 3 \times 7 = 4$$
$$6 \times 5 - 4 \times 7 = 2$$

We shall first show how neatly we can combine 5's and 7's to get every integer from 1 to 6, and shall then explain why 5 and 7 constitute such a convenient pair. (Of course, if we can get every integer from 1 to 6 we can then get any larger integer by adding as many 7's as are needed.)

Consider this set of combinations in which the number of 5's increases steadily, one 5 at a time, from 1×5 to 6×5, while the number of 7's increases as necessary to keep the differences less than 7. In this way, every integer from 1 to 6 has been obtained, and none are obtained twice. To show that all six integers must be different, suppose that two of them were the same, C. We have

$$5a \quad - \quad 7b \quad = \quad C$$
and also
$$\underline{5d \quad - \quad 7e} \quad = \quad \underline{C}$$
$$5(a - d) - 7(b - e) \quad = \quad 0$$

Subtract one equation from the other to get $5(a - d) - 7(b - e) = 0$. Since 5 and 7 are relatively prime, this equation requires that $(a - d) = 7$ (or a multiple of 7) while $(b - e) = 5$ (or the same multiple of 5). But since our multipliers for 5 in the preceding table varied only from 1 to 6, all possible values of $(a - d)$ must be less than 7. Hence all six combinations gave different differences, and accordingly had to include all of the six integers from 1 to 6.

Exercise:
Try to repeat the preceding proof using 6 and 9 instead of 5 and 7, in order to show where the proof goes bad. Also, repeat the proof using 3 and 8.

As this discussion showed, the essential characteristics of the pair 5 and 7 is that they are relatively prime—they have no common factor. Any other pair of relatively prime integers, such as 8 and 3, or 9 and 4, would also serve.

Problem:
You have an 11-minute hourglass and a 7-minute hourglass, and you wish to cook a 15-minute egg. How do you proceed to time it?

The answer follows directly from the preceding discussion. From the equation $2 \times 11 - 7 = 15$, we get the following procedure: Start both timers together. Put the egg into the boiling water just when the 7-minute timer has drained. Four minutes later, when the 11-minute timer has drained, turn it over and measure 11 minutes more; remove the egg at that time. It will have cooked for 15 minutes.

A shorter method is as follows: Start both timers and put in the egg all at the same time. When the 7-minute timer has drained, turn it over. Four minutes later the 11-minute timer has finished draining and 4 minutes' worth of sand has run through in the 7-minute timer. Turn over the 7-minute timer and when the 4 minutes' worth of sand has drained back remove the egg.

One question that might be raised concerning this method is the following: During the first 4-minute period, the flow-through sand was under the weight of 3 minutes' worth of sand, but during the second 4-minute period the flow-through sand did not have any extra sand above it. Might this difference in conditions affect the length of the second period? Get an egg timer and a clock that reads seconds and perform an appropriate experiment.

Problem:
You have 24 liters of milk in a large pail and you wish to divide it into three equal 8-liter portions. You have a 5-liter, an 11-liter, and a 13-liter pail. How do you proceed? (This problem is given in Ball and Coxeter.)

Answer:
Here is one solution. It is given in the form of a table, in which the four pail sizes are shown above the line and the pail contents after the successive steps are shown below the line. The first row shows the initial conditions; the next five rows show how the desired result is achieved.

	Pail size		
24	13	11	5
24	0	0	0
8	0	11	5
8	5	11	0
8	13	3	0
8	8	3	5
8	8	8	0

(Pail contents shown at left; ↑ at bottom)

Problem:
Show that during the 7-month period from May through November there is one and only one Friday the 13th.

Answer:
May 13 is a particular day of the week. Then, since May has 31 ($= 4 \times 7 + 3$) days, June 13 is 3 days later in the week. Then, since June has 30 ($= 4 \times 7 + 2$) days, July 13 is 2 more days, or a total of 5 days, later in the week. Since July has 31 ($= 4 \times 7 + 3$) days, August 13 is 3 more days, or a total of 8 days (equivalent to 1 day), later in the week. Continuing through November, we find that the six numbers are, in order, 3, 5, 1, 4, 6, 2. Thus, they include all the integers from 1 through 6. Accordingly, from May through November, the 13th day of the month occurs on seven different days of the week, of which one and only one will be Friday.

Problem:
Find all the prime numbers less than or equal to 125 by the following method: Write down, in order, all the integers from 1 to 125. Cross out all those divisible by 2—that is, cross out every second number—, but do not cross out the 2 itself. Then cross out all those divisible by 3—that is, cross out every third number—, but do not cross out the 3 itself. Continue in this way with the next three prime numbers, 5, 7, 11; but when you try to continue further with 13, 17, and 19, you will find that all numbers divisible by them have already been crossed out. The numbers that remain (not crossed out) are all the prime numbers less than or equal to 125.

(a) How many prime numbers did you find between 1 and 125?
(b) Notice that the square of 11 is the largest (prime number)^2, 121, in your list. This criterion for the largest divisor applies in general. For example, if you use the method to find all the prime numbers less than or equal to 1350, your task is completed when you cross out all the numbers divisible by 31, because $31^2 = 961$ is the largest (prime number)^2 in the list. (The next larger one is $37^2 = 1369$, which exceeds 1350.) What is the basis for this criterion?

You might note that many prime numbers occur in adjacent pairs of odd numbers; thus, 11 and 13, 17 and 19, 29 and 31, 41 and 43, 59 and 61.

Sums of Series

The arithmetic series. A series of terms in which the difference between each term and the next term is constant—for example, 2, 5, 8, 11, 14, . . .—is called an arithmetic series. To see how to sum such a series, write an arithmetic series as a sum, just below it write the sum in reverse order, and sum the pairs of terms. For example,

$$
\begin{aligned}
S &=\ \ 2 +\ \ 5 +\ \ 8 + 11 + 14 + 17 + 20 + 23 + 26 + 29 \\
\underline{S} &= \underline{29 + 26 + 23 + 20 + 17 + 14 + 11 +\ \ 8 +\ \ 5 +\ \ 2} \\
2S &= 31 + 31 + 31 + 31 + 31 + 31 + 31 + 31 + 31 + 31
\end{aligned}
$$

where the desired sum is S, the sum of the series in reverse order is, of course, also S, and the sum of both is $2S$. We see that every term in $2S$ is merely the sum of the first and last terms, and since there are 10 terms

$$
2S = 10\ (\text{first term} + \text{last term})
$$
$$
S = \frac{10 \times (\text{first term} + \text{last term})}{2} = \frac{10 \times 31}{2} = 155
$$

Problem:
Find the formula for the sum S of an arithmetic series in terms of the number of terms n, the first term a, and the constant difference d.

Answer:
The last term is $a + (n-1)d$, so our formula becomes

$$
S = \frac{n \times [a + a + (n-1)d]}{2}
$$

or,

$$S = \frac{n \times \left[2a + (n-1)d\right]}{2}$$

Problems:

1. This magic square contains all the integers from 1 to 25, arranged so that the sums of the integers in every row, every column, and each diagonal are all the same. Find (a) the sum of all 25 numbers, and (b) the sum of the numbers in each row, column, or diagonal.

17	24	1	8	15
23	5	7	14	16
4	6	13	20	22
10	12	19	21	3
11	18	25	2	9

Answer:

(a) The sum of all 25 numbers is $\frac{25 \times (1 + 25)}{2} = 325$. (b) The sum of the numbers in each row, column, or diagonal is $\frac{325}{5} = 65$.

2. The first term of an arithmetic series is 3, the last term is 31, and the sum of the series is 136. Find the series.

Answer:

$$S = 136 = \frac{n}{2}(3 + 31) = 17n$$

$$n = \frac{136}{17} = 8$$

To find d, $31 = 3 + (n-1)d = 3 + 7d$

$$d = \frac{31 - 3}{7} = 4$$

The series is 3, 7, 11, 15, 19, 23, 27, 31.

3. Prove that the sum of the arithmetic series

$$1 + 3 + 5 + 7 + \ldots + 2n - 1 = n^2$$

Answer:

$$S = \frac{n\left[1 + (2n-1)\right]}{2} = n^2$$

The geometric series. A geometric series is a series in which the ratio of each term to the preceding term is constant—for example, 2, 6, 18, 54, 162, 486,. . ., in which the constant ratio is 3. In order to sum such a series, write out the terms as a sum, S; and just above it write the same sum with all terms multiplied by the constant ratio, 3. Then subtract the lower sum from the upper sum. All the terms cancel in pairs except the last term of the upper sum and the first term of the lower sum.

$$3S = 6 + 18 + 54 + 162 + 486 + 1458 + 4374 + 13122$$
$$S = 2 + 6 + 18 + 54 + 162 + 486 + 1458 + 4374$$
$$3S - S = 2S = 13122 - 2 = 13120$$
$$S = \frac{13120}{2} = 6560$$

Note that the terms of our series of n terms are

$$2, 2 \times 3, 2 \times 3^2, 2 \times 3^3, 2 \times 3^4, 2 \times 3^5, \ldots, 2 \times 3^{n-1}; \text{ and}$$

the last term of the upper series is 2×3^n.

Problem:
Write the formula for the sum S of a geometric series in terms of the first term a, the ratio r, and the number of terms n.

Answer:

$$S = \frac{a\left(r^n - 1\right)}{r - 1}$$

Problem:
The first term of a geometric series is 3, the last term is 192, and the sum of the series is 381. Find the number of terms n and the constant ratio r.

Answer:
The sum of the series is

$$381 = \frac{192r - 3}{r - 1}, \text{ from which}$$
$$381r - 381 = 192r - 3$$
$$189r = 378$$
$$r = 2$$

Then the last term is $3 \times 2^{n-1} = 192$

$$2^{n-1} = 64 = 2^6$$

Thus $n - 1 = 6$; $n = 7$.

Infinite geometric series. Suppose that the constant ratio r is less than 1. Then the terms of the series get smaller and smaller, as in the series

$$1, \frac{1}{2}, \frac{1}{4}, \frac{1}{8}, \frac{1}{16}, \frac{1}{32}, \frac{1}{64}, \frac{1}{128}, \ldots$$

in which r is $\frac{1}{2}$. What happens to the sum of the series if we continue the series on and on—that is, if the number of terms n increases without limit? If we consider our formula for the sum

$$S = \frac{a\left(r^n - 1\right)}{r - 1}$$

we see that r^n approaches zero as n approaches infinity, so that S approaches $\dfrac{a}{1-r} = \dfrac{1}{1-\dfrac{1}{2}} = \dfrac{1}{\dfrac{1}{2}} = 2$. Thus, although the number of terms *n* increases without limit, the sum *S* approaches a finite limit, 2.

Problem:
Suppose that every flea carries five fleas of the next smaller size and is ten times as heavy as each of these next smaller fleas. How does the weight of the largest flea compare with the total weight of all the small fleas that it carries?

Great fleas have little fleas
Upon their backs to bite 'em,
And little fleas have lesser fleas
And so ad infinitum.
     Augustus DeMorgan

Answer:
Let the weight of the largest flea be 1. Then the weight of all the smaller fleas is

$$5 \times \frac{1}{10} + (5 \times 5) \times \frac{1}{10} \times \frac{1}{10} + (5 \times 5 \times 5) \times \frac{1}{10} \times \frac{1}{10} \times \frac{1}{10} + \ldots$$
$$= \frac{1}{2} + \frac{1}{4} + \frac{1}{8} + \ldots$$

which approaches 1. Thus the largest flea carries a total load of smaller fleas equal to its own weight.

A decimal fraction like 0.354354354 . . . in which a group of digits repeats ad infinitum is called a repeating decimal, recurring decimal, or circulating decimal. It can always be expressed as a common fraction. For example,

$$0.727272\ldots = 0.72 + \frac{0.72}{100} + \frac{0.72}{100^2} + \ldots = \frac{0.72}{1 - \frac{1}{100}} = \frac{0.72}{0.99} = \frac{8}{11}$$

Problems:
Convert 0.153153 . . . and 0.370370 . . . to common fractions.

Answers:

$$\frac{0.153}{0.999} = \frac{17}{111} \qquad \frac{0.370}{0.999} = \frac{10}{27}$$

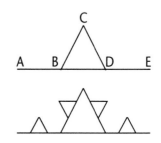

Problems:
Imagine a figure to be produced by the following procedure: Start with a segment of a straight line. Divide it into three equal parts and erect an equilateral triangle on the middle part (upper sketch). There are now four equal line segments along the upper boundary, AB, BC, CD, and DE. Divide each into three equal segments and erect an equilateral triangle on the middle one of each (lower sketch). There are now four additional triangles, and a total of 16 equal line segments along the boundary. Continue this process, adding smaller and smaller triangles, indefinitely.

1. What value does the total area of all the triangles approach in the limit? Let the area of the largest triangle be 1.
2. What value does the total length of the boundary approach in the limit? Let the length of the original line segment be 1.

Answers:

1. Each triangle has $\left(\dfrac{1}{3}\right)^2 = \dfrac{1}{9}$ the area of each of the preceding triangles, but in each step we add four of them for each triangle that we added in the preceding step. The total area thus approaches

$$1 + \frac{4}{9} + \frac{4}{9}\times\frac{4}{9} + \frac{4}{9}\times\frac{4}{9}\times\frac{4}{9} + \ldots$$

$$= 1 + \frac{4}{9} + \left(\frac{4}{9}\right)^2 + \left(\frac{4}{9}\right)^3 + \ldots = \frac{1}{1-\dfrac{4}{9}} = \frac{1}{\dfrac{5}{9}} = \frac{9}{5} = 1.8$$

2. As each triangle is added to a segment, the length of boundary along that segment is increased by the factor 4/3. Hence the addition of each new set of triangles increases the total length by 4/3. As we continue the process, the total length becomes

$$1 \times \frac{4}{3} \times \frac{4}{3} \times \frac{4}{3} \times \frac{4}{3} \times \ldots$$

and thus increases without limit; that is, it is infinite. Furthermore, as the triangles become infinitely small and infinitely numerous, the boundary of the figure becomes infinitely fuzzy.

The Fundamental Theorem of Arithmetic

The "fundamental theorem of arithmetic" states that every positive integer greater than 1 can be factored into a product of primes in only one way. We have examined many integers and have never found any integers that can be factored into a product of primes in two or more different ways; but that fact alone does not prove that there do not exist any integers that are *larger* than any we have tested and that *can* be factored into a product of primes in two or more different ways. We proceed then to argue as follows.

If there are any such large positive integers, let m be the smallest of them. Then m can be factored into a product of primes in the following two distinct ways:

$$m = p_1p_2p_3 \cdots p_r$$
$$m = q_1q_2q_3 \cdots q_s$$

whence

$$p_1p_2p_3 \cdots p_r = q_1q_2q_3 \cdots q_s$$

where none of the p's is the same as any of the q's, because if any p were the same as any q we could divide through by it and thereby get an integer *smaller* than m that can be factored into a product of primes in two different ways. In our two expressions for m, let none of the p's be smaller than p_1, and none of the q's be smaller than q_1; and let q_1 be greater than p_1.

Consider a new integer n, smaller than m, and defined as follows:

$$n = m - (p_1 q_2 q_3 \ldots q_s)$$

In this equation substitute each of the two expressions for m, thereby getting two different equations for n:

$$n = (p_1 p_2 \ldots p_r) - (p_1 q_2 q_3 \ldots q_s)$$

$$n = (q_1 q_2 \ldots q_s) - (p_1 q_2 q_3 \ldots q_s)$$

Now equate these two expressions for n, factoring them as follows:

$$p_1(p_2 p_3 \ldots p_r - q_2 q_3 \ldots q_s) = (q_1 - p_1)(q_2 q_3 \ldots q_s)$$

The left-hand product shows that p_1 is a factor of n. But p_1 cannot be the same as, or contained in, any of the factors of the right-hand product, because

1. p_1 is different from any of the q's
2. p_1 cannot be equal to, or a factor of $(q_1 - p_1)$, because that would require q_1 to be a multiple of p_1, which is contrary to our requirement that q_1 be prime. Thus, n, which is smaller than m, has been factored into a product of primes in two different ways—which contradicts our original assumption that m is the smallest integer that can be factored into a product of primes in two different ways. Our original assumption that there exists such a set of large numbers is thus shown to be invalid by the fact that there cannot exist a smallest member of the set.

Square Root and Cube Root of Prime Numbers

The square root of a prime number. The square root of a number w is the number that, when multiplied by itself, gives w. Thus, if $w = u \times u = u^2$, u is the square root of w. In symbols, $u = \sqrt{w}$. Examples are

$$\sqrt{1} = 1, \sqrt{4} = 2, \sqrt{9} = 3, \sqrt{16} = 4, \sqrt{25} = 5, \sqrt{\frac{4}{9}} = \frac{2}{3}.$$

From the fundamental theorem of arithmetic we now easily show that the square root of a prime number cannot be a common fraction $\frac{a}{b}$, where a and b are integers. For suppose that the square root of some prime number p were equal to some common fraction $\frac{a}{b}$, assumed to be in its lowest terms:

$$\sqrt{p} = \frac{a}{b} = \frac{r_1 r_2 r_3 \ldots r_m}{s_1 s_2 s_3 \ldots s_n},$$

where the r's and s's are the prime factors of a and b, respectively, and no r is the same as any s. Square both sides of the equation:

$$p = \frac{r_1 r_1 r_2 r_2 r_3 r_3 \ldots r_m r_m}{s_1 s_1 s_2 s_2 s_3 s_3 \ldots s_n s_n},$$

which is still a fraction in its lowest terms and cannot be an integer. Hence our original assumption that $\sqrt{p}$ could be expressed as a common fraction is invalid.

We can similarly show that it is impossible to express the cube root $\sqrt[3]{p}$, the fourth root $\sqrt[4]{p}$, or any other integral root of a prime number as a common fraction.

An approximate value for $\sqrt{2}$. We can find a common fraction that is very nearly equal to $\sqrt{2}$ in the following way: Start with a fraction, say 7/5, that is a fair approximation to $\sqrt{2}$.

$$\left(\frac{7}{5}\right)^2 = \frac{49}{25}$$

which is less than 2 by one part in 50. That is, if the 49 were 50, the fraction would equal exactly 2. Thus, $\frac{7}{5}$ is slightly too small. But then $2 \div \frac{7}{5} = \frac{10}{7}$ should be slightly too large:

$$\left(\frac{10}{7}\right)^2 = \frac{100}{49}$$

which now *exceeds* 2 by 1 part in 50.

Since $\frac{7}{5}$ is too small and $\frac{10}{7}$ is too large by about equal amounts, their average should be very close to $\sqrt{2}$. This average is

$$\frac{1}{2}\left(\frac{7}{5} + \frac{10}{7}\right) = \frac{99}{70} \qquad \left(\frac{99}{70}\right)^2 = \frac{9801}{4900}$$

which is indeed fairly close to 2—it exceeds 2 by about 1 part in 10000.

Again, since $\frac{99}{70}$ is thus slightly too large, $2 \div \frac{99}{70} = \frac{140}{99}$ should be slightly too small

$$\left(\frac{140}{99}\right)^2 = \frac{19600}{9801}$$

by about the same amount, and their average ought to be much more accurate:

$$\frac{1}{2}\left(\frac{99}{70} + \frac{140}{99}\right) = \frac{19601}{13860}$$

$$\left(\frac{19601}{13860}\right)^2 = \frac{384199201}{192099600}$$

which differs from 2 by only about 1 part in four hundred million

(4×10^8). Again, the average of $\dfrac{19601}{13860}$ and $2 \div \dfrac{19601}{13860}$ is $\dfrac{768398401}{543339720}$, the square of which differs from 2 by only 1 part in 6×10^{17}. You may be interested in comparing this last approximate value for $\sqrt{2}$, expressed as a decimal, with a value that is correct to 20 decimal places:

Our value: 1.41421356237309505000

Value correct to 20 decimal places: 1.41421356237309504880

This type of process, in which each value serves as a stepping stone to the next, more accurate value is called an iterative process, or a process of successive approximations.

Let us compare the accuracies of the preceding successive approximations. The squares differed from 2 by 1 part in 50, 1 part in 10000, 1 part in 4×10^8, and 1 part in 6×10^{17}. You may observe that each of these numbers is about 4 × the square of the preceding number:

$$10000 = 4 \times (50)^2$$

$$4 \times 10^8 = 4 \times (10000)^2$$

$$6 \times 10^{17} \approx 4 \times (4 \times 10^8)^2$$

If you know some algebra you should be able to derive this relation. A derivation is given in the following paragraph.

Suppose that we have a number that is very close to $\sqrt{2}$; we write it $\sqrt{2}\,(1 + a)$ where a is very small compared with 1. Its square is $2(1 + 2a + a^2) \approx 2(1 + 2a)$. For the next approximation we average $\sqrt{2}\,(1 + a)$ and $\dfrac{2}{\sqrt{2}(1+a)}$:

$$\frac{1}{2}\left[\sqrt{2}(1+a) + \frac{2}{\sqrt{2}(1+a)} \right] = \frac{1}{2}\left[\sqrt{2}(1+a) + \frac{\sqrt{2}}{(1+a)} \right]$$

$$= \frac{\sqrt{2}}{2}\left[(1+a) + \left(1 - a + a^2 - a^3 + \ldots \right) \right] \approx \frac{\sqrt{2}}{2}\left(2 + a^2\right) = \sqrt{2}\left(1 + \frac{a^2}{2}\right)$$

This number is the next approximation. Its square is approximately $2(1 + a^2)$. If we compare this new expression for the square with that of the preceding expression for the square, $2(1 + 2a)$, we see that the new fractional error is one-fourth as large as the square of the preceding fractional error:

$$a^2 = \frac{1}{4}\,(2a)^2$$

An approximate value for the cube root of 2, $\sqrt[3]{2}$. A first approximation to the cube root of 2 is 5/4. Its cube, 125/64, differs from 2 (= 128/64) by 3 parts in 128. For the second approximation, the procedure differs from that for the square root in two respects:

(1) Instead of dividing 2 by the first approximation, we divide 2 by the square of the first approximation. Thus

$$\frac{2}{(5/4)^2} = \frac{32}{25}$$

(2) Instead of taking the simple average, we take 2 × the first approximation plus 1 × the value just obtained in (1) and divide the sum by 3. Thus,

$$\text{Second approximation} = \frac{2 \times \dfrac{5}{4} + \dfrac{32}{25}}{3} = \frac{125 + 64}{50 \times 3} = \frac{189}{150} = \frac{63}{50}$$

Cubing this second approximation gives

$$\left(\frac{63}{50}\right)^3 = \frac{250047}{125000}$$

which differs from 2 by only about 1 part in 5300. Thus, in this second approximation, the accuracy has been increased about 125 times.

For the next approximation, first get

$$\frac{2}{(63/50)^2} = \frac{5000}{3969}$$

Then the next approximation is

$$\frac{2 \times \dfrac{63}{50} + \dfrac{5000}{3969}}{3} = \frac{375047}{297675}$$

the cube of which differs from 2 by about 1 part in 85000000. The fractional error in each cube is about one-third the square of the preceding fractional error. In this case,

$$\frac{1}{85000000} \approx \frac{1}{3} \frac{1}{(5300)^2}$$

An algebraic analysis of this procedure is as follows: Let N^3 be the number whose cube root N is desired and let $N(1 - a)$ be an approximate value of N, where a is a small fraction. For the next approximation our procedure gives

$$\frac{2N(1-a)+\dfrac{N^3}{\left[N(1-a)\right]^2}}{3}=\frac{2N(1-a)+N\left(1+a+a^2+a^3+\ldots\right)^2}{3}$$

$$=\frac{2N(1-a)+N\left(1+2a+3a^2+4a^3+\ldots\right)}{3}$$

$$\approx\frac{3N+3Na^2}{3}=N\left(1+a^2\right)$$

Thus, the fractional error of each cube root approximation is roughly the square of the fractional error of the preceding approximation. For their cubes, we have: Error of preceding cube is

$$[N(1-a)]^3 - N^3 = N^3(1-3a+3a^2-a^3) - N^3 \approx -3aN^3.$$

Error of the next cube is

$$[N(1+a^2)]^3 - N^3 = N^3(1+3a^2+3a^4+a^6) - N^3 \approx 3a^2N^3.$$

The fractional errors are thus $-3a$ and $+3a^2$, where we see that the second one is one-third the square of the first one.

Find the Missing Digits

In the following set of multiplications, some digits are missing in the multipliers and the products. The problem in each case is to identify the missing digits, which are represented by dots. (Examples 1, 3, 4, 5, and 6 are from Ball and Coxeter; however, the methods of solution here shown are not all the same as those therein suggested.)

1. $\cdot 1 \cdots \times 417 = 9 \cdots 057$

```
     a1bcd
    × 417
 (h)ijklm
    a1bcd
   nopqr
  9efg057
```

   Set up the problem as an ordinary multiplication. In order to facilitate explanation, unknown digits are represented by letters. The letter h is in parentheses because we do not yet know whether a1bcd × 7 has 5 digits or 6 digits.

   The solution is straightforward: The letter m must be 7; then d is 1. Then in order to give the 5 in the product, l must be 4; then c = 2 (because 7 × c ends in 4). At this point the multiplication looks like that shown on the right.

```
     a1b21
    × 417
 (h)ijk47
    a1b21
   nop84
  9efg057
```

   In order to give 0 in the product, k must be 4; then b = 9. Finally, in order to give the 9 in the product, a must be 2. The multiplicand is now complete, so the remainder of our work is simply ordinary multiplication.

```
    21921
   ×417
  153447
   21921
  87684
 9141057
```

2. $\cdot 5 \cdots \times 627 = 1 \cdots \cdot 996$

3. $\cdots \times 101 = 4 \cdot 18 \cdot$

```
        abcdef
       ×10001
        abcdef
   abcdef000
   6·80·8··51
```

4. $\cdot \times 1287 = \cdot 8 \cdot \cdot$

5. Find $6 \cdot 80 \cdot 8 \cdot \cdot 51$ knowing that it is exactly divisible by 73 and 137.

Both 73 and 137 are prime numbers, so our problem number is divisible by their product, 10001. The problem can then be set up as shown.

6. $792 \times \cdot \cdot \cdot \cdot = 70 \cdot \cdot 34 \cdot$

This problem is given in Ball and Coxeter, which also gives the following interesting method of solution: A glance at the multiplier 792 shows that it is divisible by 9 (since the sum of the digits is a multiple of 9). Dividing 792 by 9 gives 88, the product of 8 and 11. Thus we see that $792 = 8 \times 9 \times 11$. It follows that the product $70 \cdot \cdot 34 \cdot$ is divisible by 8, 9, and 11. Then

(1) Since 8 is a factor of 1000, it is a factor of any number ending in 000; hence, if it is to be a factor of our product it has only to be a factor of the number $34 \cdot$ formed by the last three digits of the product. Hence the last three digits are 344. The product is then $70 \cdot \cdot 344$.

(2) Since 9 is a factor, the sum of the digits in the product must be a multiple of 9. If we write our product as 70ef344, we have $7 + e + f + 3 + 4 + 4 = 18 + e + f = $ a multiple of 9. Then $e + f = 0, 9,$ or 18.

(3) Since 11 is a factor, $4 - 4 + 3 - f + e - 0 + 7 = 10 + e - f$ must be a multiple of 11. Then $e - f = 1$.

Comparing this condition with the preceding condition, we see that only $e = 5, f = 4$ will satisfy both conditions. Thus, the product must be 7054344. Dividing by 792 will give the multiplicand, 8907.

7. Solve the division shown at the left.

```
           x7xxx
     xxx )xxxxxxxx
   a      xxxx
   b       xxx
   c       xxx
   d       xxxx
   e       xxx
   f       xxxx
   g       xxxx
              0
```

There are four x's in the quotient. The third x is obviously 0, since after bringing down the seventh x in the dividend (line f) we have to bring down the eighth x also before it can be divided by the divisor.

Now, from line c, 7 times the divisor is a 3-digit number, but the first and last x's of the quotient, when multiplied into the divisor, give 4-digit numbers (lines a and g); hence the first and last x's of the quotient are greater than 7. The second x of the quotient must also be greater than 7, for the following reason: When 7 times the divisor (= line c) is subtracted from line b, which is a 3-digit number, the result is a 3-digit number (the first three x's of line d), but when line e is subtracted from a 4-digit number (line d), it leaves only a 2-digit number (the first two x's of line f). Thus since d is surely larger than b, while d – e is smaller than b – c, e must be greater than c. Therefore the second x in the quotient is greater than 7. It must be 8, while the first and last digits of the quotient must be 9. The quotient is thus 97809.

In order to determine the divisor, we argue as follows: It is less than 125, because 8×125 is a 4-digit number (1000) whereas line e is a 3-digit number. Then, since it is less than 125, 9 times it is less than $9 \times 125 = 1125$. Therefore the first two x's of lines f and g must not be greater than 11. Now if the divisor were 123, line 3 would be $8 \times 123 = 984$. Subtracting 984 from a 4-digit number (line d), would leave a difference of at least 16 ($1000 - 984 = 16$), which is larger than 11. Accordingly the divisor must be greater than 123. But since 125 is too large, the divisor must be 124.

```
            97809
       ┌─────────
  124 )12128316
        1116
         968
         868
        1003
         992
        1116
        1116
           0
```

8. Solve this division:

```
            xx8xx
       ┌──────────
  xxx )xxxxxxxx
        xxxx
         xxxx
          xxx
          xxxx
          xxxx
             0
```

Cryptarithmetic

Cryptarithmetic is arithmetic in code: letters are used to represent the digits 0, 1, 2, . . . 9. Our problem is to decipher the code; that is, to determine by pure reasoning which digits are represented by which letters. Here is a very simple example

$$LA \times LA = SOL$$

```
      LA
   ×  LA
   ─────
     SOL
```

We see that A multiplied by itself gives L, or else it gives a 2-digit number that ends in L. The possibilities are here listed.

A	L = A^2 or the second digit of A^2
1	1
2	4
3	9
4	6
5	5
6	6
7	9
8	4
9	1

We see that L can be 0, 1, 4, 5, 6, or 9; and it cannot be 2, 3, 7, or 8. We can immediately eliminate A = 0, 1, 5, and 6 because for these cases A and L would represent the same digit, which is not permitted. Now L cannot be as large as 4, because $40 \times 40 = 1600$, a 4-digit number, whereas our product SOL is only a 3-digit number. Then L is less than 4; but since it cannot be 2 or 3, it must be 1. Finally, since A cannot also be 1, A must be 9. Accordingly, LA = 19, and our multiplication is decoded as on the right.

```
    19
  ×19
  ───
  361
```

```
 SEND
+ MORE
-----
MONEY
```

1. The problem on the left is well known; it can be found in most collections of cryptarithmetic problems.

M=1 — The letter M must be 1, since S + M + a possible carry 1 cannot exceed 18. Then with M = 1, S + M + a possible carry 1 can be only 10 or 11. But if MO in MONEY were 11, M and O would both represent the same digit, which is not permitted.

```
 89
 10
----
MON
```

O=0 — Hence, O = 0 (zero). Then S must be 8 or 9. If S were 8, E would have to be 9, so that, with a carry 1, the result would have three digits; but the 3-digit number is 100, where O and N both represent 0—which is not permitted.

S=9 — Accordingly, S = 9.

```
 EN
 R
----
NE
```

Now consider the middle part of our sum (where O is omitted, since it is zero). Since N and E cannot represent the same digit, N = E + 1. Adding R (plus a possible carry 1) to EN gives a number in which E and N are reversed. Such reversal occurs when one adds 9, as in 12 + 9 = 21, 23 + 9 = 32, 34 + 9 = 43, and so on. However R cannot be 9, because S is 9.

R=8 — Hence R = 8, and there is a carry 1 from $\begin{smallmatrix}D\\E\\Y\end{smallmatrix}$. At this point we have identified the two smallest digits and the two largest digits 0, 1, 8, and 9, so D, E, and Y must be greater than 1 and less than 8, and D + E = a number from 12 to 17. The only possibilities are 5 + 7 and 6 + 7. Only the first of these is consistent with the rest of the problem. The final solution is

$$\begin{array}{r} 9567 \\ 1085 \\ \hline 10652 \end{array}$$

2. Solve the product shown at the left.

A = 0 — I + A = I, from which A = 0.
O × T gives a number that ends in A(= zero),
D × T gives a number that ends in T, and
G × T gives a number that ends in T. We conclude that

T = 5 — T = 5, O is an even number, and D and G are odd numbers.

```
  CAT   a
× DOG   b
------
 SPIT   c
 SOSA   d
TSST    e
------
TDGRIT  f
```

With A = 0, the multiplicand is C05; and when it is multiplied by D the result is 5SS5 (line e); that is, D × 5

D × C
S = 4
D = 9
C = 6

= S5 and D × C = 5S. By trying some values for S, we can quickly conclude that the only permissible value is S = 4, with D = 9, and C = 6.

From line d we see that $O \times T = SA$; that is, $O \times 5 = 40$.
Hence, O is 8.

$O = 8$

$$\begin{array}{r} 605 \\ \times\, 987 \\ \hline 4235 \\ 4840 \\ 5445 \\ \hline 597135 \end{array}$$

$G = 7$
$I = 3$

In line c we have $605 \times G = SPIT$, where $S = 4$ and G is odd. The only possible value for G is 7 if $G \times C$ begins with 4. Finally, $G \times T = 7 \times 5 = 35$, so $I = 3$.

3. Solve the division shown at the right.

$N = 0$
$L = 9$

From lines b, c, and d, we see that N is 0. Then, from lines f, g, and h, L must be 9.

$$\begin{array}{r} \phantom{\text{ELI)}}\text{TAU} \\ \text{ELI)}\overline{\text{VIRTUE}} \\ \underline{\text{VUAT}} \\ \text{ETNU} \\ \underline{\text{ERIS}} \\ \text{VEAE} \\ \underline{\text{VVAA}} \\ \text{LU} \end{array} \begin{array}{l} \text{a} \\ \text{b} \\ \text{c} \\ \text{d} \\ \text{e} \\ \text{f} \\ \text{g} \\ \text{h} \end{array}$$

$T = 5$

In line c, $T \times I$ gives a number that ends in T. Then either T is 5 and I is odd, or T is even and I is 6. For the present let us choose the first possibility; and if we do not find a solution we shall return to the second possibility.

The odd number I is not 9, 5, or 1, so it is 3 or 7. In line e, $E9I \times A = ERIS$. Since both $E9I$ and $ERIS$ begin with the same digit, E, we have to conclude that E is a small number, as 1, 2, or 3, and A is a larger number, as 8, 7, or 6. (Verify this statement.) Thus, our divisor ELI is one of the following five numbers:

$$193 \quad 197$$
$$293 \quad 297$$
$$397$$

while A is 8, 7, or 6.

$I = 7$
$A = 8$

By trial, we quickly find that in order for I in $ERIS$ to be the same as I in ELI, I is 7 and A is 8. The divisor is thus 197, 297, or 397.

$U = 4$
$E = 2$

We now go to line g. In order for $U \times E97$ to end in AA (that is, 88), U must be 4. Finally, in order for line g to begin with a pair, VV, E must be 2:

$V = 1$

$$297 \times 4 = 1188$$

$$\begin{array}{r} 584 \\ 297)\overline{173542} \\ \underline{1485} \\ 2504 \\ \underline{2376} \\ 1282 \\ \underline{1188} \\ 94 \end{array}$$

The two remaining letters are now easily evaluated:

$R = 3$
$S = 6$

$$R = 3 \text{ and } S = 6$$

4. Solve this division

$$\begin{array}{r} \phantom{\text{BCA)}}\text{ABAB} \\ \text{BCA)}\overline{\text{DCDEBA}} \\ \underline{\text{DFA}} \\ \text{FFE} \\ \underline{\text{BCA}} \\ \text{DAB} \\ \underline{\text{DFA}} \\ \text{FGA} \\ \underline{\text{BCA}} \\ \text{BFE} \end{array}$$

```
  AAA
  BBB
  CCC
 ─────
 DEFG
```

5. In the problem on the left, all three addends are multiples of 111; but in the sum, which is hence also a multiple of 111, all four digits are different.

   Since F is different from G, A + B + C must give a 1 or 2 to carry. The fact that E is different from F shows that A + B + C gives a 1 to carry but that a 2 is carried from the middle column to the left-hand column. It follows that A + B + C must be 19. The sum must then be 19 × 111 = 2109, in which all four digits are different, as required. The digits A, B, C must add up to 19, but none may be 2, 1, or 9. Two possibilities exist: 4 + 7 + 8 and 5 + 6 + 8

$$
\begin{array}{cc}
\begin{array}{r}
444 \\
777 \\
\underline{888} \\
2109
\end{array}
&
\begin{array}{r}
555 \\
666 \\
\underline{888} \\
2109
\end{array}
\end{array}
$$

```
 1ABCDE
 ×    3
 ──────
 ABCDE1
```

6. Find a 6-digit number beginning with 1 such that when it is multiplied by 3 the result is the same number except that the 1 is at the end.

   The solution of this problem is straightforward and involves little more than simple arithmetic. Thus, 3 × E gives a number that ends in 1; therefore E = 7, and 2 is carried. Then 3 × D must give a number that ends in 5, so that adding the carried 2 gives 7. Hence D is 5 and 1 is carried. Continuing in this way through three more steps completes the solution. The required number is 142857.

```
 1ABCD7
 ×    3
 ──────
 ABCD71
```

```
 1ABC57
 ×    3
 ──────
 ABC571
```

```
 142857
 ×    3
 ──────
 428571
```

   The problem may also be solved by means of some simple algebra: Let the 5-digit number ABCDE be our unknown, x. Putting a 1 in front of it is equivalent to adding 100000; that is $100000 + x =$ 1ABCDE. Putting a 1 after it is the same as multiplying x by 10 and adding 1; that is, $10x + 1 =$ ABCDE1. The problem states that $3(100000 + x) = 10x + 1$, from which

$$
\begin{aligned}
300000 + 3x &= 10x + 1 \\
299999 &= 7x \\
x &= 42857
\end{aligned}
$$

   so the desired number is 142857.

7. Find the number that begins with 7 and becomes one-third as large when the 7 is moved to the end.

(a) Set up the problem as a division, with only the first digit of the dividend known. Three into 7 gives 2 with a remainder of 1. Put the 2 after the 7 and continue. Three into 12 gives 4. Put the 4 after the 2 in the dividend and continue. Continue the process until a 7 is obtained in the quotient and there is no remainder. The answer is the 28-digit number

$$7,241,379,310,344,827,586,206,896,551$$

```
    2 ...
 3)7 ...
```

```
    2 ...
 3)7 2...
```

```
   24 ...
 3)724 ...
```

(b) Set up the problem as a multiplication with only the last digit of the multiplicand known. Three times 7 gives 21. Write the 1 in the product and carry the 2. Put the 1 into the multiplicand; then $3 \times 1 + 2 = 5$. Put the 5 into both the product and the multiplicand. Continue in this way until, in the last step, 7 is obtained with nothing to carry (that is, the last step gives 7, not 17 or 27).

$$\begin{array}{r} \ldots 7 \\ \times 3 \\ \hline 1 \end{array}$$

$$\begin{array}{r} \ldots 517 \\ \times 3 \\ \hline 51 \end{array}$$

Question:
What is the basic difference between this problem and problem 6?

Answer:
The basic difference is not that problem 6 is given as a multiplication whereas this problem is given as a division, because both problems can be stated in either way. This problem, for example, can be given as: "Find the number that ends in 7 such that, when it is multiplied by 3, the result is the same number except that the 7 is moved to the beginning." (The problem stated in this way, of course, is the problem that we just solved in answer (b).) Comparing this statement of the problem with the statement of problem 6 shows the basic difference. In problem 6, multiplying by 3 moves the 1 from the *front* to the *rear*; in problem 7, multiplying by 3 moves the 7 from the *rear* to the *front*.

Instead of asking that the number begin with 7, we could ask that the number begin with any other digit except 0. The answer is always the same set of 28 digits in the same order but starting at the desired digit.

Question:
How would you proceed if the number had to begin with 1 or 2?

Answer:
There are two approaches:

(a) For $3\overline{)1\ldots}$, start with "3 into 1 is 0, carry 1," giving $\begin{array}{r} 034\ldots \\ 3\overline{)1034\ldots} \end{array}$

Proceed similarly with $3\overline{)2\ldots}$, giving $\begin{array}{r} 068\ldots \\ 3\overline{)2068\ldots} \end{array}$

(b) Put the 1 or 2 at the *end* of the number and set up the problem as a multiplication.

$$\begin{array}{r} \ldots 7931 \\ \times 3 \\ \hline \ldots 3793 \end{array}$$

8. Find the integer such that when the digit on the extreme left is moved to the extreme right, the new integer is 3/2 the original integer.

    This problem is probably solved most easily by algebra: Let the integer with its first digit removed be x, let n be the number of digits in x, and let a be the first digit of the desired number. Then the desired number is $a \times 10^n + x$; and when the a is moved to the end, the number becomes $10x + a$. The problem states that

$$10x + a = \frac{3}{2}(a \times 10^n + x)$$

$$20x + 2a = 3a \times 10^n + 3x$$

$$17x = 3a \times 10^n - 2a = a(3 \times 10^n - 2)$$

$$x = \frac{a(3 \times 10^n - 2)}{17} = \frac{a(29999...98)}{17}$$

Now a is 9 or less, and since 17 is a prime number it cannot have any factors that divide a. Therefore 17 must divide 2999...98. Our procedure then is to set up this division and continue carrying down 9's until the remainder after some step is 6. Then bring down the final 8, since 68 is divisible by 17. This division is shown on the left. The quotient has 15 digits.

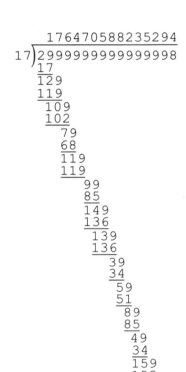

According to the last equation, x is the product of this quotient and an integer a (a = 1 to 9); and the final solution is then found by putting the integer a at the left end of this product. For example, if we choose $a = 2$, we multiply the 15-digit quotient by 2 to get the 15-digit quotient $x = 352,941,176,470,588$ and then put a 2 at the left end of x, giving the 16-digit number 2,352,941,176,470,588 as a solution.

Following are listed the solutions for a = 1 to 5:

a	Solution
1	1,176,470,588,235,294
2	2,352,941,176,470,588
3	3,529,411,764,705,882
4	4,705,882,352,941,176
5	5,882,352,941,176,470

If we choose $a = 6$, the product of our quotient and 6 is $x = 1,058,823,529,411,764$, a *16-digit* number. If now we put a 6 at the left end, it must be added to the 1, giving 7,058,823,529,411,764. This number does not fully satisfy the requirements of our problem, for if we multiply it by 3/2 we get 10,588,235,294,117,646 which corresponds to removing 6, not 7, at the left end and putting it at the right end. Using a = 7, 8, or 9 similarly yields results that do not actually satisfy the conditions of the problem. The results for a = 6 to 9 are here listed:

a	Solution
6	7,058,823,529,411,764
7	8,235,294,117,647,058
8	9,411,764,705,882,352
9	10,588,235,294,117,646

Note that the digits of all the solutions (except the "solution" for $a = 9$) form the same ordered set except that each solution starts at a different digit.

Problems without solutions.

1. Prove that the problem on the right has no solution:

$$\begin{array}{r} \text{SPEND} \\ -\text{LESS} \\ \hline \text{MONEY} \end{array}$$

From $\dfrac{\begin{array}{c}E\\E\end{array}}{N}$ we see that N is 0 or 9, depending on whether a 1 had to

be borrowed for $\dfrac{\begin{array}{c}\overset{N}{S}\end{array}}{E}$. Now if N is 9, then S is less than 9, so it is not

necessary to borrow 1 for $\dfrac{\begin{array}{c}\overset{N}{S}\end{array}}{E}$. In that case $\dfrac{\begin{array}{c}E\\E\end{array}}{N}$ would imply that

N = 0, contrary to our supposition that N = 9. If, then, we suppose that N = 0, then S is greater than 0, and it is necessary to

borrow 1 for $\dfrac{\begin{array}{c}\overset{N}{S}\end{array}}{E}$. In that case, $\dfrac{\begin{array}{c}E\\E\end{array}}{N}$ would imply that N = 9, contrary

to our supposition that N = 0. There is thus a basic inconsistency: N cannot be either 0 or 9, so the problem does not have a solution.

2. Prove that the problem on the right has no solution:

$$\begin{array}{r} \text{EIGHT} \\ -\text{THREE} \\ \hline \text{FIVE} \end{array}$$

At the left end we see that E = T + 1. At the right end we see that 2E = T + 10. The solution to this pair of equations is E = 9, T = 8. Now consider the right-hand group:

$$\begin{array}{r} \text{HT} \\ -\text{EE} \\ \hline \text{VE} \end{array} \qquad \begin{array}{r} \text{H8} \\ -99 \\ \hline = \text{V9} \end{array}$$

Subtracting 99 from H8 (borrowing 1, of course) would have to leave H9; it cannot leave V9, where V is different from H. Thus, here again is a basic inconsistency, showing that the problem has no solution.

Problems in cryptarithmetic are very popular. Since they can be found in many books of mathematical puzzles and mathematical recreations, no more will be given here. Some sources are:

Maxey Brooke: *150 Puzzles in Crypt-Arithmetic* (Dover). The book contains the reasoning used to solve the first 46 puzzles.

C. R. Wylie, Jr.: *101 Puzzles in Thought and Logic* (Dover).

W. W. Rouse Ball and H. S. Coxeter: *Mathematical Recreations and Essays* (University of Toronto Press).

Geoffrey Mott-Smith: *Mathematical Puzzles for Beginners and Enthusiasts* (Dover).

Various issues of crossword-puzzle magazines and other puzzle magazines published by Dell Publishing Co., Inc. and by Penny Press.

IF I CAN TAKE THE FIRST STEP I CAN TAKE THE NEXT STEP, AND THE NEXT, AND THE NEXT,. . .

The Tower of Hanoi

Problem and solution. The Tower of Hanoi is a fairly simple puzzle that has had some popularity for about a hundred years. It consists of a small board into which three rods have been inserted, and a set of about 8 discs of different diameters, all with center holes so that they can fit over the rods. Initially the discs are all on the same rod, with the largest disc at the bottom, and with the diameters of the successive discs decreasing toward the top. The problem is to move the tower to one of the other rods by transferring the discs, one at a time, from rod to rod in such a way that no disc is ever above a smaller disc on the same rod.

The solution is quite simple, at least in concept, and it affords a clear example of the statement in the above chapter title. Suppose, to take the simplest case, that the tower consists of only one disc. To transfer the tower from rod A to rod B, simply move the disc from rod A to rod B. This transfer of a one-disc tower is actually "the first step;" however, it seems so trivial that generalization is not obvious. Suppose, then, that the tower consists of two discs, and that it must be transferred from rod A to rod B. Consider it as a one-disc tower on top of disc 2. Proceed as follows: Transfer the one-disc tower from A to C. Then move disc 2 to rod B. Finally, transfer the one-disc tower from C to B, completing the transfer of the two-disc tower. The transfer required three moves.

Continuing, suppose that the tower consists of three discs, and that it must be transferred from rod A to rod C. Consider it as a two-disc tower on top of disc 3. Proceed as follows: Transfer the two-disc tower from A to B by the method just described, which requires three moves. Then move disc 3 to rod C, which takes one move. Then transfer the two-disc tower from B to C, building it on top of disc 3, completing the transfer of the three-disc tower. This last transfer again required three moves, so the total number of moves is 3 + 1 + 3 = 7.

The procedure should now be clear, but one more case will be given. Suppose that the tower consists of four discs, and that it must be transferred from rod A to rod B. Consider it as a three-disc tower on top of disc 4. Transfer the three-disc tower to rod C as just described, using 7 moves. Move disc 4 to rod B, which takes one move. Finally, transfer the three-disc tower from C to B, again using 7 moves. The total number of moves to transfer the four-disc tower is thus $7 + 1 + 7 = 15$.

From the preceding discussion it is clear that if we can transfer an $(n - 1)$-disc tower, then we can transfer an n-disc tower; also that the number of moves required to transfer an n-disc tower is one more than twice the number of moves required to transfer an $(n - 1)$-disc tower. The following table summarizes these results:

Number of discs in the tower, n	1	2	3	4	5	6	7	8	9	10
Number of moves to transfer the tower	1	3	7	15	31	63	127	255	511	1023
2^n	2	4	8	16	32	64	128	256	512	1024

In the third row are shown the values of 2^n, from which it appears that the general formula for the number of moves is $2^n - 1$. A formal proof of this formula for any n would be as follows:

Suppose we know that for a certain number n of discs in the tower (n may even be 1), the number of moves required to transfer the tower to another rod is $2^n - 1$. To transfer an $(n + 1)$-disc tower requires one more than twice this number; that is, $2(2^n - 1) + 1 = 2^{n+1} - 2 + 1 = 2^{n+1} - 1$, which is the same formula, with n replaced by $n+1$. In the same way if follows that the formula holds for the next larger number of discs, and then for the next larger number of discs, and so on, and hence for any number of discs. So the formula is proved for all n. This type of proof is known as proof by mathematical induction.

Practical rules for the transfer. Although the theory of the puzzle is thus simple, using this theory as the basis for the actual transfer requires an exhaustive amount of concentration and memory work if the number of discs exceeds four or five. Observation of the actual moves, however, shows that the transfer process can be guided by a few simple rules:

1. In order to transfer an n-disc tower from rod A to, say, rod B, start by moving disc 1 to rod B if n is odd, or to rod C if n is even.
2. Disc 1 is moved on alternate moves (that is, on every other move).
3. Disc 1 is always moved in the same direction. If its first move is A → B, its subsequent moves are B → C → A → B → C → A . . .; but if its first move is A → C, its subsequent moves are C → B → A → C → B → A . . ..
4. Between the alternate moves of disc 1, move one of the larger discs. No difficult decision is required for this move, however. Because of the requirement that no disc may be placed above a smaller one on the same rod, there will always be only one permissible move. Make this move and then return to disc 1.

With these four rules, one can make the moves about as fast as one can move his hand.

There are other interesting characteristics of the procedure, but it is not necessary to know them in order to effect the transfer. For example,

1. All the odd-numbered discs move in the same direction as disc 1; that is, if the moves of disc 1 are A → B → C → A → B . . ., then

the moves of discs 3, 5, 7, . . . are also A → B → C → A → B . . .; but if the moves of disc 1 are A → C → B → A → C . . ., the moves of discs 3, 5, 7, . . . are also A → C → B → A → C . . ..

2. All the even-numbered discs move opposite to the odd-numbered discs. That is, if the moves of the odd-numbered discs are A → B → C → A . . ., the moves of the even-numbered discs are A → C → B → A . . .; and vice versa.

3. Disc 1 moves on every second move (as previously noted), disc 2 moves on every fourth move, disc 3 moves on every eighth move, disc 4 moves on every sixteenth move, and so on. Thus, if there are n discs to transfer, disc 1 moves 2^{n-1} times, disc 2 moves 2^{n-2} times, . . . disc $(n-1)$ moves $2^{n-(n-1)} = 2$ times, and disc n moves $2^0 = 1$ time, for a total of $2^n - 1$ moves.

Problem:
Try to determine the reasons for the four rules and the three additional characteristics.

If the Tower is not available in any nearby shops, an adequate substitute is a set of colored plastic rings such as is sold in all toy stores as an instructional amusement for small children. An example is "Ring·A·Rounds," which consists of a base, a rod, and a set of ten brightly colored rings, all forming a step-wise-tapered tower. Additional rods are not actually necessary, because each ring fits firmly into a circular groove at the top of the next larger ring.

On Cutting Up

Cutting up a line. Consider the question of dividing a straight line into segments by putting points along it. Putting one point on a line divides it into two segments. A second point will be located on one segment or the other, dividing that segment into two parts, so that there will be three segments in all. Each additional point, no matter where it is put along the line, will produce one additional segment. In general, then, n points distributed in any manner along a line will cut it up into $n + 1$ segments.

Cutting up an area. Next consider the problem of cutting up a plane area with straight lines or, as it is often presented, "Into how many pieces can you divide a pie (or a pancake, or a pizza) with n straight cuts?"

Assume that the outer boundary of the area is everywhere convex, like a circle or an ellipse. The first line cuts the area into two parts. If the second line crosses the first line, the intersection point divides the second line into two segments (see the preceding section). Each segment cuts one of the two areas into two parts, so that there will now be four parts. If the third line crosses the first two, there will be two intersection points on it, hence three segments, each of which splits one of these parts, creating three additional parts, for a total of seven. In order to generalize, we reason as follows: If the nth line is so located that it crosses all of the preceding $n - 1$ lines, there will be $n - 1$ intersection points along it. As explained in the preceding section, these $n - 1$ points cut up this nth line into n line segments.

Each of these segments splits one of the areas, as exemplified in the little sketches; accordingly, the *n*th line will produce *n* additional areas. Thus, you start with one area. The *first* line across it produces *one* more area, so that you now have *two* areas. The *second* line produces *two* more areas, so that you now have four areas. The *third* line produces *three* more areas, so that you now have four plus three = *seven* areas, and so on. Note that in order for this rule to hold, the *n*th line must not pass through the intersection of two previous lines (as in the bottom circle on the preceding page).

The following table summarizes these results:

Number of lines, n	0	1	2	3	4	5	6	7 ...
Number of areas, m	1	2	4	7	11	16	22	29 ...

Each m is n more than the preceding m, for example, at $n = 7$, $m = 22 + 7 = 29$. It follows that each m is one more than the sum of all the integers up to and including n. This sum was found in our first chapter to be $\frac{n(n+1)}{2}$; hence $m = 1 + \frac{n(n+1)}{2}$. For example, for $n = 7$,

$$m = 1 + \frac{7 \times 8}{2} = 29.$$

In this procedure, the requirement that each line cut all the others will cause the lines to be dense in some relatively small region within the area if n exceeds 3. Making the area large will not alter this fact, although drawing the lines would be easier with the larger areas. Thus, you may be able to cut a large pizza into 16 pieces with only 5 straight cuts, but if you want the 16 pieces to be equal, you will need a different scheme for cutting it up.

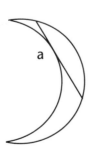

One more point will be discussed with regard to cutting up an area. We stated at the beginning that the outer boundary of the area had to be everywhere convex. If it is not, the equation derived from m will not represent the largest number of pieces obtainable with n cuts. Suppose, for example, that the area is in the shape of a crescent, which has a concave section of the boundary. If the first line is tangent to the concave arc, the point of tangency a divides the line into two parts, producing two new areas, for a total of three. A second tangent will be cut by its own point of tangency b and by the first line; thus it is divided into three parts and accordingly produces three new areas. A third tangent, if it cuts the preceding two tangents, will produce four new areas. In general, if the nth tangent cuts all of the preceding ones, it produces $(n + 1)$ new areas. The table for this case would then be:

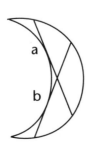

Number of lines, n	0	1	2	3	4	5	6	7
Number of areas, m	1	3	6	10	15	21	28	36

For a total of n tangent lines, the value of m is given by the sum of the arithmetic series:

$$m = 1 + (1 + 1) + (1 + 2) + (1 + 3) + \ldots + (1 + n)$$

$$= 1 + 2 + 3 + 4 + \ldots + (n + 1) = \frac{(n+1)(n+2)}{2}$$

For example, for $n = 7$, $m = \frac{8 \times 9}{2} = 36$.

Cutting up a volume. Finally, consider the problem of cutting up a convex volume, as a sphere (or a melon or a head of cheese), with n straight cuts (planes). We proceed as before. The first plane splits the volume into two parts. Assume that the second plane is so located that it intersects the first. The intersection of the two planes is a straight line, which cuts the second plane into two parts, each of which splits one of the two existing volumes, so that there are now four volumes. A suitably located third plane is cut by the first two planes along two lines and hence into four parts (see the preceding section). Each part splits an existing volume, producing four new volumes, for a total of eight. In this way, you can continue to add planes, one at a time, determining each increase in the number of volumes by using the results of the preceding section for an area.

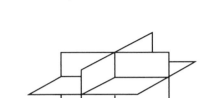

The following table summarizes the results so far obtained:

Number of lines, n points

Number of areas, n intersecting lines

Number of volumes, n intersecting planes

n	0	1	2	3	4	5	6	7	... n
Number of line segments	1	2	3	4	5	6	7	8	... $n+1$
Number of areas		1	2	4=7	11	16	22	29	... $1 + \frac{n(n+1)}{2}$
Number of volumes		1	2	4	8	15	26=42	64	... $1 + \frac{n^3+5n}{6}$

Note that each number in the table is the sum of the number immediately to its left and the number just above that one. Two examples of such summing are indicated in the table (3 + 4 = 7, 16 + 26 = 42). By following this simple rule you can extend the table, step by step, as far as you please.

This rule is equivalent to the following: In each row the value for n is 1 + the sum of the first n terms of the row above it. Thus, n intersecting planes cut up a volume into the following number of pieces:

$$1 + \left(1 + \frac{0 \times 1}{2}\right) + \left(1 + \frac{1 \times 2}{2}\right) + \left(1 + \frac{2 \times 3}{2}\right) + \ldots + \left[1 + \frac{(n-1)n}{2}\right]$$

$$= 1 + n \times 1 + \frac{1}{2}\left[1(1+1) + 2(2+1) + 3(3+1) + \ldots + (n-1)(n-1+1)\right]$$

$$= 1 + n + \frac{1}{2}\left[1 + 2 + 3 + \ldots + (n-1)\right] + \frac{1}{2}\left[1^2 + 2^2 + 3^2 + \ldots + (n-1)^2\right]$$

The first bracket is simply the sum of an arithmetic series, which has been previously discussed. The sum of consecutive squares, in the second bracket, will be derived in chapter VI. The total is given by the expression at the end of the bottom row of the table.

Again, requiring all the planes to intersect each other causes a dense concentration of the planes somewhere within the volume; so the procedure described is not really suitable for cutting up a watermelon at a party, although that is how the problem is sometimes presented.

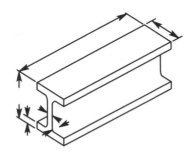

Cutting up a hyperspace. We exist in a three-dimensional space, and we cannot visualize more than three dimensions. Nevertheless, many problems involve simultaneous dependence of something on four, five, six, or more different measurable things. For example, the stiffness of a steel beam is determined by at least the six dimensions indicated in the sketch, in addition to the modulus of elasticity of the steel; and determining the stiffness might accordingly be considered as a seven-dimensional problem. In any case, the preceding table may be easily extended to more dimensions. That is, just as you determined the number of three-dimensional volumes that can be produced by passing n two-dimensional planes through a given volume, you can determine the number of pieces of a portion of six-dimensional space that can be produced by passing n five-dimensional spaces through it. The following table repeats the preceding one and extends it:

Number of Parts Into Which a Space Can Be Split
by n Dividing Elements

Number of dividing elements, n	0	1	2	3	4	5	6	7	8
One-dimensional space	1	2	3	4	5	6	7	8	9
Two-dimensional space	1	2	4	7	11	16	22	29	37
Three-dimensional space	1	2	4	8	15	26	42	64	93
Four-dimensional space	1	2	4	8	16	31	57 +	99	163
Five-dimensional space	1	2	4	8	16	32	63=120	219	
Six-dimensional space	1	2	4	8	16	32	64	127	247

The Odd Handshakers

At a party, the host greets his first guest and they shake hands. Soon another guest arrives and is greeted by the host with a handshake. Then the two guests meet and shake hands. Guests continue to arrive and shake hands with the host and with some of the earlier guests.

Problem:
Prove that at any gathering of people, the number of people who have shaken hands an odd number of times is even.

For brevity, people who have shaken hands an odd number of times will be referred to as "odd" people, the others will be referred to as "even" people. We first prove that if it is ever true it will remain true with further handshaking. There are only three cases to consider:

(a) When two even people shake hands, they both become odd; so the number of odd people increases by 2.
(b) When two odd people shake hands, they both become even; so the number of odd people decreases by 2.
(c) When an even and an odd person shake hands, the even one becomes odd and the odd one becomes even; so the number of odd people remains unchanged.

Since increasing or decreasing an even number by 2 results in an even number, we thus see that if our proposition is ever true it must remain true thereafter.

Well, then, is it ever true? Certainly—for after the host has greeted his first guest, they constitute an even number of odd people; hence the number of odd people will remain even thereafter.

Two Theorems on the Fibonacci Series

In the Fibonacci series, 1, 1, 2, 3, 5, 8, 13, 21, 34, . . ., each number is the sum of the two preceding numbers; that is, of any set of three consecutive numbers, a, b, c,

$$a + b = c$$

1. Prove that two consecutive numbers of the series do not have a common factor.

Proof:
Suppose that there is a set of three consecutive numbers of the series, a, b, and c, such that b and c have a common factor f. That is, $a + b = c$, where $b = mf$ and $c = nf$. Then, since $a = c - b$, $a = nf - mf = (n - m)f$, so a also has the factor f. But now, since a and b both have the factor f, the same reasoning shows that the number preceding a also contains the same factor f. Continuing down the series, step by step, we can similarly prove that every member of the series contains f as a factor. But the first term of the series is simply 1, which has no factor other than itself. Hence the original premise that b and c have a common factor was wrong.

2. Fibonacci's immortal-rabbits problem: You have a pair of baby rabbits, male and female. They will grow up and, after two months, produce a pair of baby rabbits, male and female; and they will continue to produce such a pair every month thereafter. Furthermore, every new pair of baby rabbits will also produce a similar pair after two months and every month thereafter. Assume that the rabbits never die. Show that the total number of pairs increases from month to month like the numbers of the Fibonacci series.

Proof:
Let the numbers of pairs in three successive months be a, b, and c, respectively. The number of pairs that were born at the second of

these three months must have been $(b - a)$. These $(b - a)$ pairs will be too young to produce baby rabbits at the next (third) month; however, all those that existed at the first month, a, will reproduce at the third month, producing a more. The total at the third month is thus $a + a + (b - a) = a + b$. That is, $c = a + b$, as in the Fibonacci series. Furthermore, we can easily see that for the first three months, the numbers of pairs are, respectively, 1, 1, 2. Then, as we have just shown, the numbers of pairs in the following months will be 3, 5, 8, 13, . . .; that is, the numbers of pairs in successive months form the Fibonacci series.

*What Color Is My Hat**

The what-color-is-my-hat problems (or games) are reasoning problems of medium complexity. The tester (teacher) has a box containing hats of two different colors, say white and red, and while standing behind the players (students) places one of the hats on each player's head. Each player must determine, from subsequently presented information, the color of his hat. "Hats" may be made of 70-cm strips of a flexible colored cardboard, formed into bands and held together near the ends by means of paper clips.

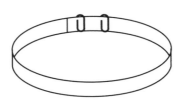

Players in a circle. In this first set of problems, each player sees all the others. We proceed from the trivial to the difficult.

(a) The first problem involves only two players. The tester puts a red hat on one player and a white hat on the other, and tells the players that whoever sees a red hat must raise his hand for a moment. He then asks them if they know the colors of their hats. Each player should have easily deduced the color of his hat. If the other player raised his hand, he knows that his own hat is red; otherwise, he knows that his own hat is white.

(b) The second problem involves three players. The tester puts red hats on two of the players and a white hat on the third player, and tells them that whoever sees at least one red hat must raise his hand for a moment. All three raise their hands. Then, on being asked if they know their colors, the two players with red hats (call them A and B) announce almost immediately that they know their hat color; the player with the white hat (C) probably remains puzzled.

Player A reasons as follows: "B can see that C's hat is white, so when B raised his hand it could only have been because my own hat is red." B's reasoning is similar. The reasoning here is perfectly straightforward and leads unambiguously to A's and B's conclusions.

Player C requires a somewhat higher level of reasoning, based on the ease with which A and B reached their conclusions. He must reason as follows: "Since A and B so quickly deduced their hat colors, my own hat must be white; for if my hat were also red

*Problems of this kind were discussed in Scientific American, May 1977, pp. 128 et seq.; June 1977, pp. 134 et seq.; July 1977, pp. 136 et seq.

each of them would see two red hats, as I do, and they would be as puzzled as I am." This type of reasoning is possibly new to you. It is important that you understand it before proceeding to the next problem.

(c) The next problem also involves three players, but now the tester puts red hats on all three. All three will be puzzled for a while, but soon the brightest will reason as follows: "If my hat were white, this problem would be the same as (b), and the other two players would quickly deduce that their hats are red. Since they remain puzzled, mine must be red."

(d) In the next problem there are four players, three with red hats and one with a white hat. The brightest of the three with red hats will reason as follows: "I see one white hat and two red hats. If my hat were also white, each of the two with red hats would quickly realize that his hat is red, just as in problem (b). Since they remain puzzled, mine must be red." An alternative way of reasoning is as follows: "Since we all raised our hands only because we saw red hats, I can disregard the white hat and consider only myself and the two players with red hats. We three are therefore in either problem (b) or problem (c). Since they seem to be puzzled, it must be problem (c); that is, my hat is red."

(e) The next problem involves four players, all with red hats. The brightest one eventually reasons as follows: "If my hat were white the problem would be reduced to problem (d). Since, however, the other three seem to be taking an *especially* long time to think it through, my hat must be red."

This series of problems may be extended, one player at a time, to as many players as we wish. However, increasing the number of players makes the reasoning increasingly unrealistic, since it requires the "brightest" player to make increasingly accurate (in fact, impossibly accurate) estimates of the length of time that the next-brightest player should remain puzzled. Even with only four players the discussion becomes questionable.

Problem (c) (three players, all with red hats) is found in many anthologies. When I first encountered it, it was presented as a competitive intelligence test used by an eastern potentate to help him choose his grand vizier from among the three brightest members of his staff. For such a purpose, however, he would surely give the same test to all three; hence, every one of them, on seeing that the others had red hats, would immediately conclude that his own was red. Furthermore, this same comment would apply even if there were twenty contestants.

These problems, beginning with *a* and continuing through *d* or *e,* when presented as games, can constitute an interesting class session. The teacher must caution the students not to give away the answers by their actions or facial expressions. For example, in problem (b), if the two red-hatted players first look blankly at the white hat but then quickly raise their hands when they see each other's red hats and then continue to stare at them, even forgetting to lower their hands, all three will know their hat colors immediately, without benefit of intricate reasoning.

Problem:
The teacher shows three students, A, B, C, that he has three red hats and two white hats. He blindfolds C and then puts a hat on each student. He then asks each student whether he knows his own hat color. A replies that he cannot tell; then B replies that he also cannot tell. Then C replies that he does know his hat color. What is it and how did he know?

Players in file. In this second set of problem-games the players are in a row, one behind the other, so that each can see only the players in front of him. They know that one of the players has a red hat and all the others have white hats. Starting from the rearmost player (no. 1), the players state in turn whether they know their hat colors. They say only Yes or No, but do not mention the color itself if they say Yes. As input for his reasoning, each player can use only what he sees in front of him and what he has heard (the Yes's and No's) behind him. It is obvious that

1. If a player sees the one red hat on some player in front of him, he knows that his own hat is white, and hence says Yes.
2. The rearmost player (no. 1) always says Yes because (a) if he sees only white hats in front of him he knows that he has the red hat, but (b) if he sees the red hat in front of him, he knows that his own hat is white. Thus, no. 1's response is always Yes; and since it is always the same and thus known in advance, it contributes no information.

(a) We begin, as before, with the trivial problem of only two players. Regardless of which player has the red hat, no. 1 will say Yes, which gives no. 2 no information, as just explained. No. 2, without any information from either in front of him or behind him, will always say No.

(b) Now consider the problem of three players. The red hat may be on no. 1, no. 2, or no. 3, but only when it is on no. 3 will no. 2 say Yes, for he will then know that his own hat is white. Furthermore, when no. 3 hears no. 2 say Yes, he will know that his own hat must be the red one. In the other two cases, no. 2 says No, from which no. 3 learns that his own hat is white. Thus, no. 3 says Yes in all three cases.

(c) Now consider the problem of four players. Only if the red hat is on no. 3 or no. 4 will no. 2 say Yes. If no. 3 sees the red hat on no. 4, he will then know that his own hat is white. If no. 3 does not see the red hat on no. 4, he will know that he himself has the red hat. As before, if no. 2 does not see the red hat in front of him, he says No, which informs nos. 3 and 4 that their hats are white. Thus, again, no. 3 says Yes in all cases.

The following table summarizes these results and extends them to the problem of six players. In the table, Y stands for Yes, N for No, w for white, and r for red.

Do I Know the Color of My Hat?
Table of Responses

Number of players: 2

Player no.	1	2
Hat colors	r	w
Responses	Y	N
Hat colors	w	r
Responses	Y	N

Number of players: 3

Player no.	1	2	3
Hat colors	r	w	w
Responses	Y	N	Y
Hat colors	w	r	w
Responses	Y	N	Y
Hat colors	w	w	r
Responses	Y	Y	Y

Number of players: 4

Player no.	1	2	3	4
Hat colors	r	w	w	w
Responses	Y	N	Y	Y
Hat colors	w	r	w	w
Responses	Y	N	Y	Y
Hat colors	w	w	r	w
Responses	Y	Y	Y	N
Hat colors	w	w	w	r
Responses	Y	Y	Y	N

Number of players: 5

Player no.	1	2	3	4	5
Hat colors	r	w	w	w	w
Responses	Y	N	Y	Y	Y
Hat colors	w	r	w	w	w
Responses	Y	N	Y	Y	Y
Hat colors	w	w	r	w	w
Responses	Y	Y	Y	N	Y
Hat colors	w	w	w	r	w
Responses	Y	Y	Y	N	Y
Hat colors	w	w	w	w	r
Responses	Y	Y	Y	Y	Y

Number of players: 6

Player no.	1	2	3	4	5	6
Hat colors	r	w	w	w	w	w
Responses	Y	N	Y	Y	Y	Y
Hat colors	w	r	w	w	w	w
Responses	Y	N	Y	Y	Y	Y
Hat colors	w	w	r	w	w	w
Responses	Y	Y	Y	N	Y	Y
Hat colors	w	w	w	r	w	w
Responses	Y	Y	Y	N	Y	Y
Hat colors	w	w	w	w	r	w
Responses	Y	Y	Y	Y	Y	N
Hat colors	w	w	w	w	w	r
Responses	Y	Y	Y	Y	Y	N

(Hat colors are r or w; Player responses are Y or N.)

Note the following characteristics of this table:

1. In any game, no more than one player will say No.
2. Odd-numbered players always say Yes; only an even-numbered player ever says No.
3. The player who must say No either has the red hat or is directly in front of the player with the red hat.

The following rules, based on these characteristics, may be used by the players to determine their responses:

1. An even-numbered player says No if everyone behind him has said Yes and he does not see the red hat in front of him. Otherwise he knows that his hat is white and says Yes.
2. An odd-numbered player always says Yes. If everyone behind him has said Yes and he does not see the red hat in front of him, he knows that he is wearing it, otherwise he knows that his hat is white.

Note how, for those cases in which player no. 2 says Yes, the problem is reduced from that for an *n*-player game to that for an (*n* – 2)-player game. Thus, in the 6-player table, the part to the right of the dashed line is the same as the 4-player table; in the 5-player table, the part to the right of the dashed line is the same as the 3-player table.

Question:
In the table, why are the first and second rows of responses identical, also the third and fourth rows of responses and the fifth and sixth rows of responses? (For example, in the 6-player table, the third and fourth rows of responses are both Y Y Y N Y Y.)

This problem, although presented as a game, is probably better for study and class discussion than for use as a game.

The last set of game-problems is a modification of the preceding set. As before, there are n players arranged in a row, one behind the other; but the teacher now has at his disposal n white hats and $n - 1$ red hats. There are $2^n - 1$ possible arrangements, since every player may have either a white hat or a red one, except that the one case in which all n players have red hats must be excluded because there are only $n - 1$ red hats.

In general, no. 1 can say Yes only when he sees all $n - 1$ red hats on the $n - 1$ players in front of him. Furthermore, in this case, all the other players also say Yes, because no. 1's response has informed them that they all have red hats. In every other case, no. 1 says No.

Player no.	1	2
Hat colors and responses	w N	w Y
	r N	w Y
	w Y	r Y

Consider first the 2-player game, for which the teacher has two white hats and one red hat. The three possible arrangements of hats and the corresponding sets of responses are shown in the table. When no. 1 says No, no. 2 knows that his own hat is white; when no. 1 says Yes, no. 2 knows that it is red. In all three cases, then, no. 2 says Yes.

Next consider the 3-player game, for which the teacher has at his disposal three white hats and two red hats. The seven possible arrangements and the corresponding responses are shown in the table on the left. As before, when no. 1 sees two red hats in front of him (case 1), he knows that his own hat is white, so he says Yes; and nos. 2 and 3, knowing that this is the only case for which no. 1 says Yes, also say Yes. When no. 1 does not see two red hats in front of him, he says No. Then if no. 2 sees that no. 3 is wearing red (cases 2 and 4), he knows that his own hat is white, so he says Yes. No. 3 then realizes from these two responses that his own hat is red, so he says Yes. In the remaining four cases (cases 3, 5, 6, 7), no. 2 sees a white hat in front of him and cannot tell whether his own hat is red or white, so he must say No. This response informs no. 3 that his own hat is white, and accordingly he says Yes. Thus, in all seven cases, no. 3 says Yes.

Case no.	Player no.	1	2	3
1		w Y	r Y	r Y
2		r N	w Y	r Y
3	Hat colors and responses	r N	r Y	w Y
4		w N	w Y	r Y
5		w N	r N	w Y
6		r N	w N	w Y
7		w N	w N	w Y

Next consider the 4-player game, of which there are $2^4 - 1 = 15$ cases. Again, if no. 1 sees all three red hats in front of him he knows that his own hat is white and says Yes; and when nos. 2, 3, and 4 hear this response they know that their own hats are red, so they also say Yes. However, if no. 1 does not see three red hats in front of him he says No. The game for players 2, 3, and 4 then becomes the 3-player game just discussed, in which no more than two red hats may be distributed among them.

Similarly, for the 5-player game, when no. 1 says No, the game is reduced to the 4-player game for the remaining four players. In general, then, in an n-player game,

1. When no. 1 says Yes, all the other players say Yes.
2. When no. 1 says No, the game for the remaining players is reduced to an $(n - 1)$-player game.

Thus, the whole series of games, for all values of *n*, can be referred back, step by step, to the simplest case—the 2-player game. As seen from the preceding two tables, the *n*th player always says Yes, the last two responses are either YY or NY, the last three responses are either YYY, NYY, or NNY; and so on.

Problem:
There are three red hats and two white hats. The tester puts a hat on each of three players, A, B, and C, who can see each other's hats; and he asks them, one at a time, whether they know the colors of their own hats. First he asks A, who replies that he cannot tell. Then he asks B, who responds similarly. What color is C's hat?

Answer:
If A sees two white hats, he will know that his own hat is red; we conclude then that A sees at least one red hat. If C's hat were white, B would know that his own hat is the red hat that A sees. But since B could not tell the color of his own hat, C's hat must be red.

The Misdirected Letters

You have written letters to various friends and relatives inviting them to your graduation, and you have also addressed the envelopes for them. Then, when you are called away to the telephone, you ask little brother to put the letters into the envelopes, seal the envelopes, and stamp them. Now, little brother loves to lick stamps and envelope flaps, but unfortunately does not yet read very well. The results of his help, therefore, is that Uncle Mortimer receives the letter that you wrote to Dear Sally, Aunt Hattie receives the letter that you wrote to Dear Uncle Mortimer, and so on.

Problem:
With *n* letters and *n* addressed envelopes, in how many ways can all the letters be put into the wrong envelopes? The following discussion is essentially that of Ball and Coxeter.

For *n* = 1 (that is, one letter and one envelope) there is no way to put the letter into the wrong envelope. For *n* = 2, there is only one way: put letter no. 1 into envelope no. 2, and letter no. 2 into envelope no. 1. For *n* = 3 the problem is more interesting. If we put letter no. 2 into envelope no. 1, there remain letters no. 1 and 3 and envelopes no. 2 and 3, for which there is only one way to misdirect both letters. We can also start by putting letter no. 3 into envelope no. 1, leaving letters no. 1 and 2 and envelopes no. 2 and 3, for which there is again only one way to misdirect both letters. Thus, of the six ways of putting three letters into three envelopes (see the table on the right), there are only two (indicated by the arrows) in which all three letters are misdirected.

Envelope no.	1 2 3
Letter no.	1 2 3
	1 3 2
	2 1 3
	2 3 1 ←
	3 1 2 ←
	3 2 1

Now consider the case *n* = 4. Suppose that, as before, we start by putting letter no. 2 into envelope no. 1, leaving

Envelopes no.   2, 3, 4
Letters no.   1, 3, 4

Envelope no.	2	3	4
Letter no.	3	4	1
	4	1	3

Envelope no.	1	2	3	4
Letter no.	2	4	1	3
	2	3	4	1
	2	1	4	3

Envelope no.	1	2	3	4
Letter no.	2	3	4	1
	2	4	1	3
	2	1	4	3
	3	1	4	2
	3	4	2	1
	3	4	1	2
	4	1	2	3
	4	3	2	1
	4	3	1	2

If letter no. 1 were letter no. 2, so that we had

> Envelopes no. 2, 3, 4
> Letters no.   2, 3, 4

the preceding paragraph tells us that there would be two ways to mismatch them all. These two ways are not affected by replacing letter no. 2 with letter no. 1, as shown by the top table. However, since letter no. 1 is not letter no. 2, we may put it into envelope no. 2, leaving letters no. 3 and 4 and envelopes no. 3 and 4, an $n = 2$ case, for which there is one way to mismatch both. At this point we have found three ways to mismatch all, as shown in the middle table. The first two rows are the two ways that correspond to $n = 3$, and the last row is the way that corresponds to $n = 2$; in order to emphasize this difference, a dashed line has been drawn between the two groups of mismatches.

Thus far, with letter no. 2 in envelope no. 1, we have found $2 + 1 = 3$ ways to mismatch the remaining letters and envelopes. With letter no. 3 in envelope no. 1 there would be three more ways, and with letter no. 4 in envelope no. 1 there would be an additional three ways. Thus, there are, in all, nine ways to mismatch all the letters and envelopes for $n = 4$. The nine ways are shown in the bottom table.

If you will review the preceding reasoning, you will see that it gives, for the total number of mismatches,

> (one less than 4, the number of letters) × (the number of mismatches for $n = 3$, plus the number of mismatches for $n = 2$), or $3(2 + 1) = 9$.

For $n = 3$, one could easily have determined, simply by inspection, the two ways of completely mismatching the letters and envelopes; and for $n = 4$, only a little more effort would have been needed to identify the nine ways. Accordingly, you might wonder about the need for our somewhat involved approach, and for the curious artifice of supposing "If letter no. 1 were letter no. 2, ..." The reason is that we are trying to develop a formula by which we relate the number of complete mismatches for any value of n, no matter how large, to the numbers of complete mismatches for $n - 1$ and $n - 2$.

As a final brief review of the method and reasoning, they will be summarized for the case $n = 5$: Put letter no. 2 into envelope no. 1 and then consider the remaining four letters and four envelopes. If letter no. 1 were letter no. 2, there would be 9 different mismatches, as just shown. But letter no. 1 is not letter no. 2, so we may put it into envelope no. 2. The remaining letters and envelopes then constitute the case $n = 3$, for which there are two different ways. Thus far, then, with letter no. 2 in envelope no. 1, we have found $9 + 2 = 11$ ways. Finally, instead of letter no. 2, we could have put letter no. 3, 4, or 5 into envelope no. 1, and found 11 ways for each. The total number of ways is then $4(9 + 2) = 44$, just as, in the preceding paragraph, the total number of ways for $n = 4$ was found to be $3(2 + 1) = 9$.

For a general formula, let D_n be the number of ways of mismatching n letters and n envelopes. Then the preceding reasoning gives

$$D_n = (n-1)(D_{n-1} + D_{n-2}) \qquad n > 2$$

Results for the first eight values of n are given in the table below, together with some other interesting relationships that will be discussed subsequently.

n		D_n	$= nD_{n-1} \pm 1$	$\dfrac{D_n}{n!}$
1		0		
2		1	$2 \times 0 + 1$	0.5
3	$2(1+0) =$	2	$3 \times 1 - 1$	.33333
4	$3(2+1) =$	9	$4 \times 2 + 1$	.37500
5	$4(9+2) =$	44	$5 \times 9 - 1$	.36666
6	$5(44+9) =$	265	$6 \times 44 + 1$	.36805
7	$6(265+44) =$	1854	$7 \times 265 - 1$	.36786
8	$7(1854+265) =$	14833	$8 \times 1854 + 1$	.36788

The third column shows a simple relationship between D_n and D_{n-1}, but it is not the same for even n as for odd n because the sign in front of the 1 alternates between + and −. However, it is easy to write the relationship in a form that holds for both even and odd n:

$$D_n = nD_{n-1} + (-1)^n \qquad n > 1$$

Problem:
Given that $D_n = (n-1)(D_{n-1} + D_{n-2})$ and that for a particular value of n we observe that

$$D_{n-1} = (n-1)D_{n-2} \pm 1 \qquad\qquad (+1 \text{ or } -1)$$

prove that $D_n = nD_{n-1} \mp 1$.

Proof:
From $D_{n-1} = (n-1)D_{n-2} \pm 1$, solve for D_{n-2}:

$$D_{n-2} = \frac{D_{n-1} \mp 1}{n-1}$$

Substitute this value of D_{n-2} into $D_n = (n-1)(D_{n-1} + D_{n-2})$:

$$D_n = (n-1)\left(D_{n-1} + \frac{D_{n-1} \mp 1}{n-1} \right)$$

$$= (n-1)D_{n-1} + D_{n-1} \mp 1 = nD_{n-1} \mp 1$$

Thus, if the formula holds for the relation between D_{n-2} and D_{n-1}, it holds for the relation between D_{n-1} and D_n; and thence, by the same reasoning, we show that it also holds for the relation between D_n and D_{n+1}. Continuing in this way, we show that it also holds for all larger pairs of adjacent values of D. Finally, since the formula holds for D_2 and D_1, it holds for all pairs of adjacent D's.

The fourth column gives the probability that little brother mismatches the complete set of n letters and n envelopes. In order to derive these values, we must first determine the number of different ways that n letters can be put into n envelopes with a different letter in each. The reasoning is as follows.

There are n different letters that can be put into envelope no. 1. For each of these n choices for the first letter, there are $n - 1$ remaining letters from which to select a letter for envelope no. 2. Thus, there are $n(n - 1)$ different ways of putting letters into the first two envelopes. There remain $n - 2$ letters from which to select a letter for envelope no. 3. Thus, there are $n(n - 1)(n - 2)$ different ways of selecting three letters for the first three envelopes. Continuing this process, we find that there are $n(n - 1)(n - 2) \ldots \times 3 \times 2 \times 1 = n!$ ways of putting n different letters into n different envelopes, all equally likely if little brother cannot read.

The probability that little brother will manage to misdirect all n letters is the fraction

$$\frac{\text{The number of ways of completely mismatching the } n \text{ letters and } n \text{ envelopes}}{\text{The total number of equally likely ways of putting } n \text{ letters into } n \text{ envelopes}} = \frac{D_n}{n!}$$

The table on the previous page shows that for $n > 3$ the probability remains at about 0.37. The more advanced student may recognize that with increasing n the probability seems to approach $1/e$, where $e = 2.7182818279 \ldots$ is an important mathematical constant, and $\frac{1}{e} = 0.36787944124 \ldots$. A proof that it approaches $1/e$ is given at the end of the chapter.

The probability that at least one letter is in the right envelope (that is, the probability that exactly one letter is in its correct envelope + the probability that exactly two letters are in their correct envelopes + . . . + the probability that all the letters are in their correct envelopes) is 1 minus the probability that none is in its correct envelope, that is, $1 - \frac{D_n}{n!}$. For n equal to 8 or more, the probability is then $1 - 0.36788 = 0.63212$.

It may seem odd that the probabilities do not change appreciably with n, but it is actually not unreasonable: as n increases from 8 to, say, 80, the chance of getting a *particular* letter into its correct envelope decreases by a factor of 10; on the other hand there are 10 times as many letters. The net result is that there is negligible change in the probability that at least one will get into its correct envelope.

Similar problems. One can easily invent problems similar to the misdirected-letters problem. For example, suppose that there are two decks of cards, A and B, of which at least one deck has been thoroughly shuffled. Compare the first card of deck A with the first card of deck B, the second card of deck A with the second card of deck B, and so on. What is the probability of comparing all fifty-two pairs of cards without getting a single match?

Here is another example: At the cry of "Fire!" all the restaurant patrons rush out, each grabbing a coat from the coat rack as he passes, expecting to exchange coats outside. What is the probability that no one grabs his own coat?

The answer in both of these cases is 0.36788, the same as for the mismatched letters.

The limiting value of $\dfrac{D_n}{n!}$ as $n \to \infty$. Use the relation $D_n = nD_{n-1} \pm 1$. Starting with $D_2 = 1$, write down the values for the subsequent D_n's as far as, say, D_6 in the following way:

$$D_3 = 3D_2 - 1 = (3 \times 1) - 1$$

$$D_4 = 4D_3 + 1 = 4[(3 \times 1) - 1] + 1$$

$$D_5 = 5D_4 - 1 = 5\{4[(3 \times 1) - 1] + 1\} - 1$$

$$D_6 = 6D_5 + 1 = 6\{\{5\{4[(3 \times 1) - 1] + 1\} - 1\}\} + 1$$

Expanding the last expression gives

$$D_6 = 6 \times 5 \times 4 \times 3 - 6 \times 5 \times 4 + 6 \times 5 - 6 + 1$$

To find the probability that all are mismatched, divide by 6! and get

$$\frac{6 \times 5 \times 4 \times 3 - 6 \times 5 \times 4 + 6 \times 5 - 6 + 1}{6 \times 5 \times 4 \times 3 \times 2 \times 1} = \frac{1}{2!} - \frac{1}{3!} + \frac{1}{4!} - \frac{1}{5!} + \frac{1}{6!}$$

As n increases beyond 6, further terms of the series, $-\dfrac{1}{7!} + \dfrac{1}{8!} - \dfrac{1}{9!} + \ldots$, are added. As n increases without limit, the number of terms in this series of reciprocal factorials also increases without limit. If we now consider the series for e^x: $e^x = 1 + x + \dfrac{x^2}{2!} + \dfrac{x^3}{3!} + \ldots$ and put x equal to -1, we get $e^{-1} = 1 - 1 + \dfrac{1}{2!} - \dfrac{1}{3!} + \dfrac{1}{4!} - \ldots$, which is the same as the limit series for our probability.

NUMBER SYSTEMS

In this chapter we shall discuss number systems other than our every-day decimal system, which is based on ten. In particular, we shall discuss the binary system, based on two, and the octal system, based on eight, because of their importance in digital computers.

The Decimal System

In order to provide the background, let us first review the decimal system. Each of the first ten cardinal numbers is represented by its individual symbol; thus, 0, 1, 2, 3, 4, 5, 6, 7, 8, 9. The next number is ten, the base of the system, which is represented as a combination of two symbols, 10, which means $1 \times$ ten + zero. The next number, eleven, is written 11, which means $1 \times$ ten + one; and so on up to nineteen, written 19, which means $1 \times$ ten + nine. The next number is written 20, which means $2 \times$ ten + zero. The two-digit numbers continue in this way up to ninety-nine (99). The next number is written 100, which means $(1 \times 10^2) + (0 \times 10) + 0$; and so on. A number written 4562, for example, means $(4 \times 10^3) + (5 \times 10^2) + (6 \times 10) + 2$.

What property makes the number 10 so special that our number system is based on it? None, although we may guess that man first learned to count with the aid of his ten fingers, and as a result eventually adopted ten as a convenient number-system base. Perhaps if we all had six fingers on each hand our number system would be based on twelve. Twelve has, in fact, been used by some cultures, and others have used other bases, as sixteen or twenty. Thus, the use of ten is not required by any mathematical law, and if some other number would be a more convenient base for certain purposes there is nothing to prevent its use.

It turns out that the electronic digital computer cannot use the decimal system in making its computations. It uses the *binary* system, based on the number two, because of the practical simplicity of electrical circuits in which switches are in either of two states—open or closed—and electric current correspondingly either flows or does not flow. As a convenient intermediate between the binary system of the computations and the decimal system of the operator, the computer also uses the octal system, based on eight, and the hexadecimal system, based on sixteen. (The hexadecimal system has now largely superseded the octal system.) As we shall see, both of these are closely related to the binary system. The following section discusses the octal system and its relation to the decimal system.

The Octal System

The following table compares decimal-system numbers with the equivalent octal-system numbers:

Decimal system	Octal system	Decimal system	Octal system
0	0	17	21
1	1	18	22
2	2	19	23
3	3	20	24
4	4	21	25
5	5	22	26
6	6	23	27
7	7	24	30
8	10 ($1 \times$ eight + 0)	25	31
9	11 ($1 \times$ eight + 1)	:	:
10	12	63	77 ($7 \times$ eight + 7)
11	13	64	100 ($1 \times$ eight^2)
12	14	65	101 ($1 \times$ eight^2 + 1)
13	15	:	:
14	16	511	777 ($7 \times$ eight^2 + $7 \times$ eight + 7)
15	17 ($1 \times$ eight + 7)	512	1000 ($1 \times$ eight^3)
16	20 ($2 \times$ eight + 0)	513	1001 ($1 \times$ eight^3 + 1)

We shall show how to convert a decimal number—for example, 4275, to its equivalent in the octal system. In order to show the principle of the method, however, we shall first go through the following trivial analysis in the ordinary decimal system.

	Remainder	Interpretation
10)4275		
10)427	5	$4275 = 427 \times 10 + 5$
10)42	7	$427 = 42 \times 10 + 7$
4	2	$42 = 4 \times 10 + 2$

$$4275 = [(\underbrace{4 \times 10 + 2}_{42}) \times 10 + 7] \times 10 + 5$$

$$= 4 \times 10^3 + 2 \times 10^2 + 7 \times 10 + 5$$

Now we shall do this same procedure using 8 as the divisors instead of 10.

	Remainder	Interpretation
8)4275		
8)534	3	$4275 = 534 \times 8 + 3$
8)66	6	$534 = 66 \times 8 + 6$
8)8	2	$66 = 8 \times 8 + 2$
1	0	$8 = 1 \times 8 + 0$

$$4275 = \{[(\underbrace{1 \times 8 + 0}_{8}) \times 8 + 2] \times 8 + 6\} \times 8 + 3$$

$$4275 = (1 \times 8^4) + (0 \times 8^3) + (2 \times 8^2) + (6 \times 8) + 3$$

Hence $4275_{10} = 10263_8$

where the subscripts 10 and 8 indicate the bases of the number systems.

Can we now convert this octal system back to the original decimal number by using the same technique? There should be no difficulty—except that we are used to doing our arithmetic in the decimal system, and we may find it very confusing to do our arithmetic in the unfamiliar octal system. (It would be a challenging mental exercise, however, and you should try it.) In order to help with the conversion, we first prepare the octal-system multiplication table shown here.

Octal-System Multiplication Table

	1	2	3	4	5	6	7	10	11	12	13
1	1	2	3	4	5	6	7	10	11	12	13
2	2	4	6	10	12	14	16	20	22	24	26
3	3	6	11	14	17	22	25	30	33	36	41
4	4	10	14	20	24	30	34	40	44	50	54
5	5	12	17	24	31	36	43	50	55	62	67
6	6	14	22	30	36	44	52	60	66	74	102
7	7	16	25	34	43	52	61	70	77	106	115
10	10	20	30	40	50	60	70	100	110	120	130
11	11	22	33	44	55	66	77	110	121	132	143
12	12	24	36	50	62	74	106	120	132	144	156
13	13	26	41	54	67	102	115	130	143	156	171

By using this table we shall find the successive divisions to be fairly easy and straightforward. The subscripts 8 will help to remind us that the divisions are in the octal system. The conversion method is basically the same as the method that we used for converting from a decimal number to an octal number: For the conversion from decimal to octal, we repeatedly divided the decimal number by 8_{10}; for the conversion from octal to decimal, we shall repeatedly divide the octal number by 12_8 (= 10_{10}).

$$12_8\overline{)10263_8}$$
$$12_8\overline{)653_8} \qquad \text{Remainder}$$
$$12_8\overline{)52_8} \qquad\qquad 5$$
$$4 \qquad\qquad\quad 7$$
$$\qquad\qquad\qquad 2$$

Thus, $10263_8 = 4275_{10}$. Here is an additional example:

$$12_8\overline{)14721_8}$$
$$12_8\overline{)1224_8} \qquad \text{Remainder}$$
$$12_8\overline{)102_8} \qquad\qquad 11_8 = 9_{10}$$
$$6 \qquad\qquad\quad 0$$
$$\qquad\qquad\qquad 6$$

Thus, $14721_8 = 6609_{10}$. Note that a remainder may equal or exceed 10_8, in which case it has to be converted to the equivalent decimal number.

The conversion method just shown was presented partly to show the general applicability of this method of converting from one number system to another. Other useful methods are:

1. Convert simply by using the basic meaning of a multidigit number. Thus, to take the preceding example,

$$14721_8 = 1 \times 8^4 + 4 \times 8^3 + 7 \times 8^2 + 2 \times 8 + 1$$

$$1 \times 8^4 = 4096$$
$$4 \times 8^3 = 2048$$
$$7 \times 8^2 = 448$$
$$2 \times 8 = 16$$
$$1 = \underline{1}$$
$$6609_{10}$$

2. Starting at the left end of a multidigit number, multiply the first digit by 8 and add the second digit; multiply the result by 8 and add the third digit; and so on. Thus, to take the same example, 14721_8,

$$1 \times 8 = 8$$
$$\underline{+\ 4}$$
$$12 \times 8 = 96$$
$$\underline{+\ 7}$$
$$103 \times 8 = 824$$
$$\underline{+\ 2}$$
$$826 \times 8 = 6608$$
$$\underline{+\ 1}$$
$$6609_{10}$$

This calculation can be done mentally if the number is no bigger than this one.

Both of these methods can also be used for the conversion from decimal to octal. Thus, by the first method,

(1) $6609_{10} = 6 \times 12_8^3 + 6 \times 12_8^2 + 0 \times 12_8 + 11_8$

$6 \times 12_8^3 = 6 \times 1750_8 = 13560_8$

$6 \times 12_8^2 = 6 \times 144_8 \quad = \quad 1130_8$

$$\frac{11_8}{14721_8}$$

$$12_8$$
$$\underline{\times 12_8}$$
$$144_8$$
$$\underline{\times 12_8}$$
$$1750_8$$

(2) 6609_{10}:

$6 \times 12_8 = 74_8$

$$\underline{+ 6}$$

$102_8 \times 12_8 = 1224_8$

$$\underline{+ 0}$$

$1224_8 \times 12_8 = 14710_8$

$$\underline{+ 11}$$
$$14721_8$$

Exercises:

Convert the following numbers from the decimal system to the octal system and then convert back to the decimal system, using all three methods.

   15638, 93730, 1934759, 21816, 610642, 6444270

Question:

In the octal-system multiplication table, many of the products look the same as decimal products—for example $6 \times 11 = 66$, $12 \times 13 = 156$, $13 \times 10 = 130$, ... Other products look different—for example, $6 \times 5 = 36$, $13 \times 13 = 171$, $7 \times 6 = 52$, ... When do the products look the same and when do they look different?

Answer:

If none of the steps in the process of multiplying produces a number that exceeds 7, the products will look the same—for example,

$$
\begin{array}{r}
12 \\
\times 13 \\
\hline
36 \\
12 \\
\hline
156
\end{array}
$$

just as in the decimal system; but if any step produces a number that exceeds 7, the products must look different—for example,

$$
\begin{array}{r}
13 \\
\times 13 \\
\hline
41 \\
13 \\
\hline
171
\end{array}
\qquad
\begin{array}{r}
22 \\
\times 13 \\
\hline
66 \\
22 \\
\hline
306
\end{array}
$$

In the first example, 3×3 gives a number, 9_{10}, that exceeds 7 and must be taken as 11_8; in the second example, the sum $6 + 2$ exceeds 7 and must be taken as 10_8.

Problems:
Identify these two sequences, given that all the numbers are in the base-7 system.

1. 2, 4, 6, 11, 13, 15, 20, 22
2. 2, 4, 11, 22, 44, 121, 242, 514

The first is an arithmetic series; the second is a geometric series.

3. In what number system is 41 an exact multiple of 14?

The Binary System

The relation between the decimal system and the binary system is illustrated in the following comparisons:

Decimal system	Binary system
0	0
1	1
2	10 (1×2)
3	11 $(1 \times 2 + 1)$
4	100 $(2^2 + 0 \times 2 + 0)$
5	101 $(2^2 + 0 \times 2 + 1)$
6	110 $(2^2 + 2 + 0)$
7	111 $(2^2 + 2 + 1)$
8	1000 $(2^3 + 0 \times 2^2 + 0 \times 2 + 0)$
9	1001 $(2^3 + 0 \times 2^2 + 0 \times 2 + 1)$
10	1010 $(2^3 + 0 \times 2^2 + 1 \times 2 + 0)$
11	1011
12	1100
13	1101
14	1110
15	1111
16	10000
17	10001
18	10010

A binary number has about three times as many digits as the equivalent decimal number.

Following are shown an addition, a subtraction, a multiplication, and a division in the binary system.

$$\left(\begin{array}{c} 93_{10} \\ +11_{10} \\ \hline 104_{10} \end{array} \right) \qquad \begin{array}{r} 1011101 \\ +1011 \\ \hline 1101000 \end{array} \qquad \left(\begin{array}{c} 104_{10} \\ -11_{10} \\ \hline 93_{10} \end{array} \right) \qquad \begin{array}{r} 1101000 \\ -1011 \\ \hline 1011101 \end{array}$$

$$\left(\begin{array}{r}93_{10}\\ \times 11_{10}\\ \hline 1023_{10}\end{array}\right)$$

$$\begin{array}{r}1011101\\ \times 1011\\ \hline 1011101\\ 1011101\\ 10111010\\ \hline 1111111111\end{array}$$

$$\begin{array}{r}93_{10}\\ 11_{10}\,\overline{)1023_{10}}\end{array}$$

$$\begin{array}{r}1011101\\ 1011\,\overline{)1111111111}\\ 1011\\ \hline 10011\\ 1011\\ \hline 10001\\ 1011\\ \hline 1101\\ 1011\\ \hline 1011\\ 1011\\ \hline 0\end{array}$$

The methods of doing these four elementary operations are similar to those used with decimal-system numbers and do not require discussion. In the subtraction, however, the repeated borrowing tends to be confusing, and the following suggestion should be useful: After a 1 (that is, 10) is borrowed from the adjoining digit, repay it into the subtrahend. The steps in the subtraction would then be as follows:

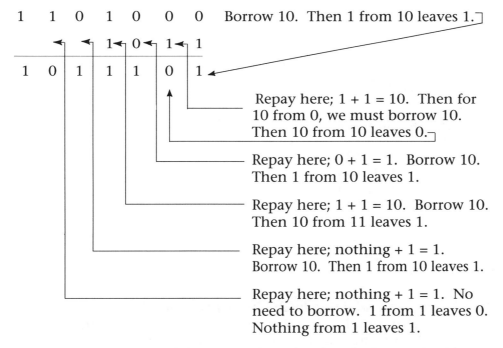

A simpler method is as follows: In the subtrahend, change the 0's to 1's and the 1's to 0's. Add this number to the minuend. Thus,

$$\begin{array}{r}1101000\\ -1011\\ \hline \end{array}\quad\rightarrow\quad\begin{array}{r}1101000\\ +1110100\\ \hline 11011100\end{array}$$

Add 1 to this result and delete the 1 at the left-hand end to get the final result, 1011101. Computers must use this method because their basic operation is addition—they are unable to subtract.

Question:
Why is this procedure equivalent to the desired subtraction?

Answer:
Changing the 1's to 0's and the 0's to 1's is equivalent to subtracting from 1111111. Thus,

$$\begin{array}{r} 1111111 \\ -1011 \\ \hline 1110100 \end{array}$$

which we add to the minuend. After we add the 1 at the right-hand end, we will have added a total of $1111111 + 1 = 10000000$. Deleting the 1 at the left-hand end removes this extraneous number. Then all that remains is the desired subtraction.

Exercises:
1. In the decimal system, do the subtractions by both of the preceding methods:

$$\begin{array}{r} 9909000 \\ -9099 \end{array} \qquad \begin{array}{r} 489763 \\ -54389 \end{array}$$

2. Perform the following subtractions:

$$\begin{array}{r} 101010101 \\ -111 \end{array} \quad \begin{array}{r} 111000 \\ -101001 \end{array} \quad \begin{array}{r} 101000 \\ -10011 \end{array} \quad \begin{array}{r} 100001 \\ -10111 \end{array}$$

3. Verify this addition:

$$\begin{array}{r} 1001101 \\ 1110100 \\ 1000110 \\ 1011101 \\ 110010 \\ 101000 \\ 1001011 \\ \hline 1000001001 \end{array}$$

Multiplying by 2; dividing by 2; binary fractions. In order to multiply by 2 ($=10_2$), simply add a 0 at the end of the number. In order to divide by 2, shift the "binary point" (corresponding to the decimal point in the decimal system), one space to the left.

In the binary system, 0.11 represents one half + one fourth, or three fourths, while in the decimal system 0.11 represents one tenth + one one-hundredth, or about one ninth. Thus, the digits on the right side of the point represent a larger number in the binary system than in the decimal system; the reverse is true for digits on the left side of the point.

Conversions between octal and binary numbers. Conversion from a binary number to the equivalent octal number, and the reverse conversion from octal to binary, are so simple that they can be performed on sight. The procedure is as follows: Given a binary number, say 11011001010, break it into groups of three digits, starting from the right, giving 11 011 001 010. Interpret each group as a separate number. In this case, the numbers are 3, 3, 1, and 2; then the equivalent octal number is 3312_8.

The reason why the conversion works out in this way is as follows: The given binary number, $\underline{11}\ \underline{011}\ \underline{001}\ \underline{010}$, expressed as the sum of powers of 2, is

$$\underbrace{2^{10} + 2^9} + \underbrace{2^7 + 2^6} \underbrace{+\ 2^3} \underbrace{+\ 2} =$$

$$2^9(2 + 1) + 2^6(2 + 1) + 2^3 + 2 =$$

$$8^3(2 + 1) + 8^2(2 + 1) + 8 + 2 =$$

$$3 \times 8^3 + 3 \times 8^2 + 1 \times 8 + 2 = 3312_8$$

Conversion from octal to binary goes in the opposite direction over the same steps. For example, to convert 2176_8 to binary, simply convert the four digits to binary and write the four binary numbers in sequence: $\underset{2}{\underline{10}}\ \underset{1}{\underline{001}}\ \underset{7}{\underline{111}}\ \underset{6}{\underline{110}}$. Thus, $2176_8 = 10001111110_2$.

Problem:
Prove that the same procedure can convert between octal and binary fractions; for example, $0.100110001001_2 = 0.4611_8$.

Conversions between octal and decimal fractions. A decimal fraction is interpreted as a sum of tenths, hundredths, thousands, and so on. For example,

$$0.596_{10} = \frac{5}{10_{10}} + \frac{9}{100_{10}} + \frac{6}{1000_{10}}$$

An octal fraction is interpreted similarly, except that the tenths, hundredths, thousandths, ... are to base 8. For example,

$$0.374_8 = \frac{3}{10_8} + \frac{7}{100_8} + \frac{4}{1000_8} = \frac{3}{8_{10}} + \frac{7}{64_{10}} + \frac{4}{512_{10}} = 0.4921875_{10}$$

In order to convert from 0.596_{10} to an octal fraction, determine, first, how many eighths are contained in 0.596_{10}:

$$0.596 \times \frac{8}{8} = \frac{4.768}{8}$$

Thus, there are 4 whole eighths and 0.768_{10} eighths:

$$0.596_{10} = \frac{4}{8} + \frac{0.768}{8}$$

Then the first digit to the right of the octal point is 4. Now determine how many sixty-fourths are contained in 0.768 eighths:

$$\frac{0.768}{8} \times \frac{8}{8} = \frac{6.144}{64}$$

Thus, there are 6 whole sixth-fourths and 0.144 sixty-fourths in 0.768 eighths. Then the second digit to the right of the octal point is 6. Continuing,

$0.144 \times 8 = 1.152$, so the third digit is 1

$0.152 \times 8 = 1.216$, so the fourth digit is 1

$0.216 \times 8 = 1.728$, so the fifth digit is 1

$0.728 \times 8 = 5.824$ Stop the process here and let the sixth digit be 6.

The answer is then $0.596_{10} = 0.461116_8$.

In order to convert back, proceed as follows, using the octal multiplication table:

$$0.461116_8 \times \frac{10_{10}}{10_{10}} = 0.461116_8 \times \frac{12_8}{12_8} = \frac{5.753414_8}{12_8}$$

Then the first digit to the right of the decimal point is 5. Continuing,

$$0.753414_8 \times 12_8 = 11.463170_8$$

so the second digit is $11_8 = 9_{10}$

$$0.463170_8 \times 12_8 = 6.00026$$

so the third digit is 6. Stop at this point since the next three digits will be 0. The reverse conversion has thus given

$$0.461116_8 = 0.596000_{10}$$

(With the aid of a small calculator, one can easily perform this conversion by interpreting 0.461116_8 as $\frac{4}{8} + \frac{6}{8^2} + \frac{1}{8^3} + \frac{1}{8^4} + \frac{1}{8^5} + \frac{6}{8^6}$.)

Problems:
Convert from decimal to octal and check your answers by converting them back to decimal.

0.6064_{10}, 0.935_{10}, 0.1071_{10}, 0.0871_{10}, 0.995_{10}

Conversions between decimal and binary fractions. The procedures for converting from decimal to binary and from binary to decimal are similar to the procedures just described, and the reasoning will not be repeated. With the same decimal number, 0.596, the procedure is as follows:

```
 0.596        0.144        0.216        0.824
   ×2           ×2           ×2           ×2
 1.192        0.288        0.432        1.648
   ×2           ×2           ×2           ×2
 0.384        0.576        0.864        1.296
   ×2           ×2           ×2           ×2
 0.768        1.152        1.728        0.592
   ×2           ×2           ×2
 1.536        0.304        1.456
   ×2           ×2           ×2
 1.072        0.608        0.912
   ×2           ×2           ×2
 0.144        1.216        1.824
```

The result thus far is $0.596_{10} = 0.10011000100100110111 0_2$. To convert back to a decimal fraction multiply repeatedly by $10_{10} = 1010_2$:

$$0.100110001001001101110_2 \times 1010_2 =$$

$101.1111010111000010011 0 \times 1010 =$	$101_2 = 5_{10}$
$1001.1001100110010111 11 \times 1010 =$	$1001_2 = 9_{10}$
$101.111111111101101 1 \times 1010 =$	$101_2 = 5_{10}$
$1001.1111111101000 111 \times 1010 =$	$1001_2 = 9_{10}$
$1001.111110001100 011 \times 1010 =$	$1001_2 = 9_{10}$
$1001.101101111011 110 \times 1010 =$	$1001_2 = 9_{10}$
$111.0010110101011 =$	$111_2 = 7_{10}$

The reverse conversion thus gives 0.5959997.

These conversions between decimal and binary fractions were given mainly as an exercise, for, in a practical sense, they were superfluous: Since the octal equivalent of the decimal fraction 0.596_{10} had already been obtained, it had only to be converted to a binary fraction by the simple method already described. Or, conversely, if the conversion to the binary equivalent had been done first, it could have been converted to the octal equivalent without having to use the octal multiplication table.

Uses of the binary system in problems and puzzles.

1. Think-of-a-number game I: Think of a number from 0 to 31, inclusive. I can determine it by means of five questions, to each of which you must answer yes or no. Suppose, for example, that your number is 26. The questions and answers are as follows:

Questions	Answers	Conclusion
1. Is it at least 16?	Yes	
2. Is it at least 24?	Yes	
3. Is it at least 28?	No	
4. Is it at least 26?	Yes	
5. Is it 27?	No	Then it is 26.

Thus the questioner begins with 16 and in the next three questions he adds or subtracts 8, 4, and 2, respectively. After the fourth question has been answered, only two possibilities remain, and the answer to the fifth question identifies the correct one. The basis for this method of determining the number is as follows: In the binary system, the range 0 to 31 is 00000 to 11111, and the five questions are equivalent to Is the first digit (on the left) 1? Is the second digit 1? and so on. How many questions would you have to ask in order to identify a number from 0 to 255?

2. Think-of-a-number game II. There are six cards with different sets of numbers, as shown. Think of a number from 1 to 63 and tell me on which of the cards the number appears. I can tell you what the number is. Examine the six sets of numbers and explain my method.

4	5	6	7	12	13	14	15
20	21	22	23	28	29	30	31
36	37	38	39	44	45	46	47
52	53	54	55	60	61	62	63

1	3	5	7	9	11	13	15
17	19	21	23	25	27	29	31
33	35	37	39	41	43	45	47
49	51	53	55	57	59	61	63

2	3	6	7	10	11	14	15
18	19	22	23	26	27	30	31
34	35	38	39	42	43	46	47
50	51	54	55	58	59	62	63

8	9	10	11	12	13	14	15
24	25	26	27	28	29	30	31
40	41	42	43	44	45	46	47
56	57	58	59	60	61	62	63

32	33	34	35	36	37	38	39
40	41	42	43	44	45	46	47
48	49	50	51	52	53	54	55
56	57	58	59	60	61	62	63

16	17	18	19	20	21	22	23
24	25	26	27	28	29	30	31
48	49	50	51	52	53	54	55
56	57	58	59	60	61	62	63

1	1
2	10
3	11
4	100
5	101
6	110
7	111
8	1000
9	1001
10	1010
11	1011
12	1100
13	1101
14	1110
15	1111

Explanation:

Shown here on the left are the first fifteen integers expressed in binary. Note that:

1. Every odd number (1, 3, 5, ...) has a 1 in the first position, at the right end. All of these numbers are on the card that begins with 1.
2. The numbers 2, 3, 6, 7, 10, 11, ... all have a 1 in the second position from the end. All of these numbers are on the card that begins with 2.
3. The numbers 4, 5, 6, 7, 12, 13, ... all have a 1 in the third position from the end. All of these numbers are on the card that begins with 8.
4. The numbers 8, 9, 10, ... all have a 1 in the fourth position from the end. All of these numbers are on the card that begins with 8.

Similarly, the other two cards, beginning with 16 and with 32, contain all the numbers that have 1 in the fifth and sixth positions, respectively, from the end.

Hence, when you identify the cards that contain your number, I have only to add the numbers in the upper left corners in order to determine it. For example, if your number is on the cards that begin with 1, 4, 8, and 32, its binary form is 101101 and its value is $32 + 8 + 4 + 1 = 45$.

3. The game of Nim: In this ancient game there are several groups of counters (stones, beans, . . .) and there are two players who play alternately. Each player, when his turn comes, removes as many counters as he likes from any one group, even removing the entire group if he wishes. The winner is the one who takes the last counter. If there is only one group, the first player wins by re-moving the entire group. Otherwise the knowledgeable player uses the following strategy:

Determine the numbers of counters in the separate groups and write them down in the binary system, one below the other. For example, suppose there are five groups of counters, containing, respectively, 8, 15, 6, 21, and 32 counters. Then write

Decimal	Binary
8	1000
15	1111
6	110
21	10101
32	100000
	112322

At the bottom of each column write the number of 1's in that column, as shown. Three of these numbers are odd, namely 1, 1, and 3. The strategy consists of making all the numbers even by removing an appropriate number of counters from one of the groups. In the present case change the set of six numbers from 112322 to 022422 by changing 100000 to 010100; that is, by removing 12 counters from the 32-group, thereby changing it to a 20-group. The other player now removes some counters from one of the groups, and when he does so, he must, of course, alter its binary designation: at least one 1 is changed to 0 and one or more 0's may be changed to 1's. Thus, no matter what he does he must change one of the sums at the bottom from an even number to an odd number. Then the first player again removes what is necessary to make all the sums even. The game continues in this way until the first player takes the final counter, or group, and wins, because his opponent must always leave at least one odd sum and hence must leave *something*.

If all the sums are even at the beginning, the first player must lose unless his opponent blunders or is unaware of the correct strategy.

3a. Reverse Nim: Suppose that the object of the game is changed by making the player who takes the last counter be the loser. The knowledgeable player uses the same strategy as before, making all the sums even, until near the end. When he sees that this strategy would, in the next move, leave only an even number of "groups" containing only a single counter, he changes the strategy so as to leave an odd number of such 1-counter groups. His opponent will

Decimal	Binary
8	1000
15	1111
6	110
21	10101
20	10100
	22422

1	1
1	1
1	1
11	→ 1
14	4

thereby be forced to take the last counter. For example, if there remain four groups containing 1, 1, 1, and 3 counters, his Nim strategy would require him to remove 2 counters from the 3-group, as shown in the additions on the right; but at this point he must change his strategy and remove the entire 3-group, leaving three 1-groups.

Problems:

(1) There remain a group of 2 counters and a group of 3 counters, and it is your move. Show how you proceed to win if the object is to take the last counter. Show how you proceed to win if the object is to make your opponent take the last counter.

(2) For reverse Nim, could you assure a win by reversing the strategy for normal Nim—that is, by always leaving all *odd* sums? Presumably, by leaving only odd sums, you ensure that on your opponent's next move he must change at least one of the odd sums to an even sum, which you can then change to odd, thus always leaving him only odd sums.

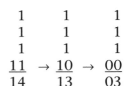

The fallacy is that the even sum that he leaves you may be 0, and if it is the sum that is farthest to the left you cannot change it to 1 by removing some counters. At this point, then, it will be you who are faced with all odd sums. Consider again the preceding example. If you change the 3-group to a 2-group, as shown, you leave only odd sums; but if your opponent then removes this 2-group, there will not remain an even sum that you can then make odd.

4. Given that a and b are positive integers, and $b > 2$, show that $2^a + 1$ is never divisible by $2^b - 1$. That is, no number of the set 9, 17, 33, 65, 129, 257, 513, ... is divisible by a number of the set 7, 15, 31, 63, 127, 255, 511, ...

   In binary form, $2^a + 1$ is of the form 1000...001

   $2^a - 1$ is of the form 111...111

   The division proceeds as follows:

$$111 \ldots 111 \overline{)1000 \ldots 00000 \ldots \ .. 001}$$
$$\underline{111 \ldots 111}$$
$$1000 \ldots \quad 0$$
$$\underline{111 \ldots 111}$$
$$1000 \ldots \text{ and so on}$$

```
1000 ... 001
 111 ... 111
          10
```

At best, the end of the division is like this, with a remainder of 2.

Why was it necessary to specify that $b > 2$?

5. A card-riffling trick: In riffling a deck of cards, one splits the deck into two packs of 26 cards each, grasps a pack with each hand, raising a bottom corner of the pack with the thumb, brings the two corners together, and lets the cards drop, one by one, in such a way that the cards of each pack become interleaved with the

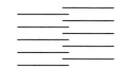

cards of the other pack. The two packs are then pushed together to form a complete deck. The lower half of the deck is again separated from the upper half and the two packs are again riffled together. For a card game, several riffles and some ordinary shuffling are combined, in order to achieve a random distribution of the cards.

In a perfect riffle every card of each pack is separated from its neighbor by a card of the other pack. An expert magician, capable of performing perfect riffles repeatedly, can do the following trick: He shows you the top card of the deck and offers to shuffle the cards in such a way that the card will be moved to any location in the deck that you wish. The trick is done as follows: Suppose that you ask him to make it the 15th card in the deck. He first subtracts 1 from 15 and expresses the result in binary: $14_{10} = 1110_2$. He then riffles the cards four times, once for each binary digit. For the digit 1, he riffles so that the top card of the deck becomes the second card of the deck. For the digit 0, he riffles so that the top card remains on top. For this

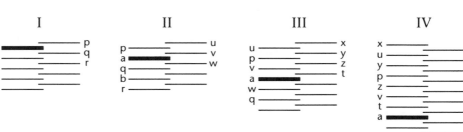

example, then, he performs three successive riffles of the first type and a final riffle of the second type. The card that was originally on top will then be found to be the fifteenth card of the deck. The four perfect riffles are diagrammed in these sketches, in which the original top card is indicated by the heavy line. Only the top few cards of the deck are shown.

In the first riffle, the top card becomes the second card of the deck. In the second riffle, this second card becomes the fourth card of the deck. In the third riffle, this fourth card becomes the eighth card of the deck. In the fourth riffle, this eighth card becomes the fifteenth card of the deck. Note that in the first type of riffle the location number of the card is doubled ($1 \to 2 \to 4 \to 8$); in the second type of riffle, the location number becomes one less than twice the preceding number ($8 \to 16 - 1 = 15$).

Problem:
Why does the procedure work?

Consider the first two riffles and the corresponding first two digits of our binary number. The first digit is always 1, and accordingly the top card goes to position 2, 1 more than 1. If the second digit is also 1 (the binary number is then 11, which is 3), the card goes to the position $2 \times 2 = 4$, 1 more than 3. If the second digit is 0 (the binary number is then 10, which is 2), the card goes to position $2 \times 2 - 1 = 3$, 1 more than 2. To generalize, let the binary number at some point in the process be n, with the card at position $n + 1$. If the next binary digit is 0, the binary number becomes $2n$ and the card goes to position $2(n + 1) - 1 = 2n + 1$; or if the next binary digit is 1, the binary number becomes $2n + 1$ and the card goes to position $2(n + 1) =$ $2n + 2$. In both cases, the card position is one more than the value of the binary number, in conformity with the rule.

Exercise:
Determine the successive locations of the card if it is to go to location 20, to location 22, to location 29.

Gates. The circuitry within a computer is often discussed with the aid of schematic representations of certain basic circuit elements called "gates." The sketches show representations of three of the most important gates.

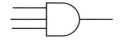

AND gate. The output on the right is 1 only if all the inputs on the left are 1; otherwise the output is 0.

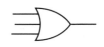

OR gate. The output is 1 if one or more of the inputs is 1; otherwise the output is 0.

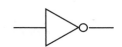

NOT gate, or INVERTER. The output is 1 if the input is 0, and 0 if the input is 1.

Some circuitry elements. Various combinations of gates serve as the basic operational units that perform the computations. One important combination is the "flip-flop," shown in this sketch on the left. The name emphasizes a similarity to such instruments as the ordinary spring-loaded electric-light switch—once the switch has been flipped to either ON or OFF, it remains firmly in that position even after the force that flipped it is removed. The sketch shows a flip-flop made of two OR gates and two NOT gates. In general, the important input lines are A and D. If the A input is 1, the output at Q is 1 while the output at P is 0. If the input at A is now removed, the two outputs remain unchanged, because the input at B received from Q maintains the condition. The flip-flop is thus a storage device—Q stores the momentary input at A, and, furthermore, its value may be read as necessary without deleting it from storage. A momentary 1 input at D, however, erases the 1 at Q and puts a 1 at P; and if P is connected to other parts of the circuitry they will then be activated. Be sure to trace the circuitry to verify these characteristics of the flip-flop.

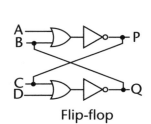

Flip-flop

This diagram on the left represents a "half-adder." Trace the schematic circuitry to show that:

(a) If both inputs are 0, the sum is 0 and there is nothing to carry.

(b) If either input is 1 and the other input is 0, the sum is 1 and nothing is carried.

(c) If both inputs are 1, the "sum" is 0 and 1 is carried.

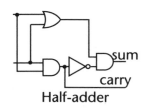

Half-adder

The arrangement is called a half-adder because it cannot accommodate a carry-1 from the preceding step.

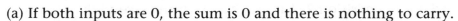

The next diagram represents a "full-adder," which accommodates three inputs, including the carry. Since each input may be 0 or 1, there are $2 \times 2 \times 2 = 8$ possible combinations of inputs. Trace the schematic circuitry for these possible combinations to show that the output is correct for every case.

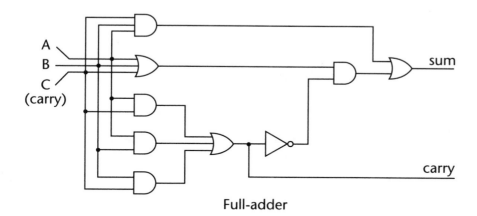

Full-adder

Inputs				Outputs	
A	B	C		Sum	Carry
0	0	0		0	0
0	1	0		1	0
0	0	1		1	0
0	1	1		0	1
1	0	0		1	0
1	1	0		0	1
1	0	1		0	1
1	1	1		1	1

When the host at a party suggests that you try some of the tuna salad or some of the cheese mixture, he would be pleased to see you try both. The OR gate with, say two input lines, interprets "or" in the same way—the output is 1 if either input is 1 or if both inputs are 1. Such an OR is sometimes referred to as an "inclusive-OR" since it includes this latter meaning. In non-computer language, "and/or" is sometimes used to cover the two possible meanings. (A judge once angrily invalidated a legal document because it contained the expression "and/or," claiming that it could not be interpreted. Perhaps "or (inclusive)" might be acceptable in its place.)

But "or" can be used to mean "either but not both." For example, if a recipe calls for 3 or 4 large apples, the cook may not use 7 large

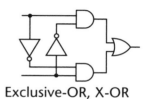

Exclusive-OR, X-OR

apples. Correspondingly, there is an exclusive-OR, or X-OR gate whose output is 1 when only one input is 1, but 0 when both inputs are 1. Trace the schematic circuitry in this sketch to verify that it represents an X-OR gate.

Trace the schematic circuitry in this sketch to verify that two half-adders and an OR gate can serve as a full-adder.

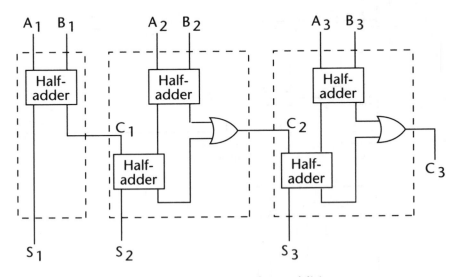

The first three steps of an addition, showing the use of two half-adders and an OR gate to make a full-adder.

A, B inputs
S   sum
C   carry

HOW MANY WAYS?

Problems that require finding the number of ways that something can be done, or the number of ways that something can happen, often occur in science and also crop up in non-technical areas. We discuss here only a few samples of such problems. Many more can be found in books on probability and statistics.

1. Three books, A, B, and C, are to be placed side by side on a book shelf. In how many ways can the three be arranged?

   The first one (the book on the left) may be A, B, or C. For each of these three possible choices, there remain only two books from which to choose the second one. Since each of the first three possible choices can thus be coupled with either of the remaining two, there are $3 \times 2 = 6$ possible arrangements of the first two books. After the second book has been chosen, there remains only one book—that is, there is only one "choice" for the third book. (Such a choice without an alternative is sometimes referred to as "Hobson's choice.") The reasoning just given may be represented by the tree diagram on the right.

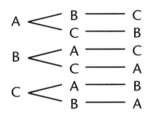

   If there are n different items to be arranged in order, the reasoning is similar: There are n choices for the first position; after that choice has been made, there remain $(n-1)$ choices for the second position; and so on. Then the total number of possible arrangements is $n \times (n-1) \times (n-2) \times ... \times 2 \times 1$. This product is called "n factorial" and written $n!$.

   The various possible orders of the same items (as the 6 possible orders of the three books) are commonly referred to as *permutations*. If the order is not significant, the group is simply a *combination*. Thus, in the problem of the three books there are 6 permutations but only 1 combination.

2. Seven students are to be seated on the seven chairs around a table.

   (a) In how many ways might the students be arranged?

   Number the chairs from 1 to 7. There are seven students from whom to select the one to sit in chair no. 1. After he has been chosen, there remain six students from whom to select the one to sit in chair no. 2. Thus far, then, there are $7 \times 6 = 42$ ways to select occupants for the first two chairs. Continuing in this way, we find that there are $7! = 5040$ ways to distribute the seven students around the table.

   (b) One of the students, Kate, does not hear very well, so her friend Michelle always sits beside her, on her right, in order to help when necessary. How does that affect the number of ways that the students may be arranged?

Kate may sit in any one of the seven chairs. Michelle must sit on her right and hence has no choice. Thus, Kate-Michelle may be in any one of the seven locations. The remaining five students may be distributed among the remaining five chairs in 5! ways. Thus, the total number of possible arrangements is

$$7 \times 5! = 840$$

(c) Not only must Kate and Michelle sit together but they must sit in the two chairs that are closest to the teacher. How does that affect the answer?

Since their locations are no longer subject to choice, the problem concerns only the distribution of the remaining five students among the remaining five chairs. The number of arrangements is 5! = 120.

(d) If Michelle may sit on either side of Kate, how does that affect the answers in (b) and (c)?

It doubles both. The answers become 1680 and 240, respectively.

(e) Suppose that the table has ten chairs around it. In how many ways can seven students now be arranged?

Student no. 1 can be placed in any one of the ten chairs. For every one of these ten choices, there remain nine chairs from which to choose a location for student no. 2. Continuing in this way, we find

$$10 \times 9 \times 8 \times 7 \times 6 \times 5 \times 4 = \frac{10!}{(10-7)!} = \frac{10!}{3!} = 604800$$

ways in which to arrange the students.

(f) Suppose that there are ten students but the table is too small for more than seven chairs. In how many ways can seven students be selected and arranged around the table?

This problem is essentially the same as the preceding problem, except for reversed wording. Thus, chair no. 1 can be occupied by any one of ten students; then chair no. 2 can be occupied by any one of the remaining nine students; . . . ; chair no. 7 can be occupied by any one of the remaining four students. As before, the answer is $\frac{10!}{3!}$.

(g) Suppose that in problem (a) we do not wish to differentiate between arrangements that are essentially the same as each other but merely shifted, as a unit, around the table. That is, we shall consider two arrangements to be the same provided that every student has the same right-hand neighbor. How many essentially different arrangements are there now?

The location of student no. 1 is irrelevant. But regardless of where he sits, there are six choices for the student who sits in the seat on his right, five choices for the student who sits in the next seat, and so on. Then the number of essentially different arrangements is one-seventh of what was found in problem (a):

$$\frac{7!}{7} = 6! = 720$$

(h) If, in addition, it does not matter whether a student is on the right side or the left side of his neighbor, as long as they are adjacent, each arrangement is essentially equivalent to its mirror image. Then the number of essentially different arrangements is only half as much as before:

$$\frac{6!}{2} = 360$$

3. A group of six girls and four boys are lined up in single file. In how many ways can they be arranged?

$$10! = 3628800$$

If each girl is to be in front of all shorter girls, and each boy is to be in front of all shorter boys, how many arrangements are possible?

In any selection of six locations in this file, there can be 6! different arrangements of the six girls; but in only one of these 6! arrangements is each girl in front of all shorter girls (similarly for the four boys). Hence the number of arrangements must be reduced from 10! to

$$\frac{10!}{6! \times 4!} = 210$$

4. In the Baseball World Series, the American-League team (A) and the National-League team (N) play until one or the other has won four games. Thus, the Series may be over after the fourth game or it may continue through as many as seven games.

(a) In how many different sequences of wins can, say, the American-League team win the series?

The question is equivalent to the following: In how many different ways can we insert A's in four of a sequence of seven spaces (for example, -AA-AA-)? The answer is not $7 \times 6 \times 5 \times 4$ because that product applies for four *different* objects, whereas our four A's are indistinguishable. Using the expression $7 \times 6 \times 5 \times 4$ would indicate that we have counted every arrangement of the four A's 4! times; hence, for our purpose, we must divide the expression by 4! The correct answer is then

$$\frac{7 \times 6 \times 5 \times 4}{4!} = \frac{7!}{3! \; 4!} = 35$$

The National-League team can similarly win the Series in 35 different sequences. Thus, there are 35 + 35 = 70 different possible sequences of wins and losses in the World Series.

(b) In how many of these sequences does A win in seven games?

In order for the series to end with the seventh game, it must be tied 3 to 3 at the end of the sixth game. The question is therefore the same as "In how many ways can we put three A's in the first six spaces?" The answer is

$$\frac{6!}{3!\ 3!} = 20 \text{ possible sequences}$$

(c) In how many of these sequences does A win in six games? Now we ask: In how many ways can A win three of the first five games?

$$\frac{5!}{2!\ 3!} = 10$$

(d) In how many sequences does A win in five games?

$$\frac{4!}{1!\ 3!} = 4$$

Another way of seeing this result is to note that in order for A to win three of the first four games, N must win one of the four games, which it can do in four ways. That is, it must win the first, second, third, or fourth game.

(e) There is only one way for A to win in four games. The total number of ways in which A can win the Series is thus 20 + 10 + 4 + 1 = 35, in agreement with the previous result.

Notes:

(1) From (d), since $\frac{4!}{1!\ 3!} = 4$, we see that 1! must be interpreted as 1.

(2) In (e), if we use the same reasoning as in (b), (c), and (d), the answer should be given by the expression $\frac{3!}{0!\ 3!}$. Since we know that the answer is 1, we see that 0! must also be interpreted as 1.

5. A certain organization has 40 members, 10 of whom are physicians. In how many ways can a committee of 6 members be selected so as to include at least one physician?

There are

$$\frac{40!}{34!\ 6!} = 3838380$$

ways to select a committee of six without regard to its composition. The number of ways to select a 6-member committee that contains *no* physicians is the number of ways to select it from the 30 members who are not physicians:

$$\frac{30!}{24! \, 6!} = 593775$$

The difference 3838380 − 593775 = 3244605 is the number of 6-member committees that contain at least one physician.

Here, again, note that the 6! in the denominators of both fractions is needed because the order in which the 6 members are selected is immaterial; if we omit the 6! we shall count every possible 6-member group 6! times.

But suppose that when the 6 members are selected, their functions on the committee are specified; for example:

> A is to be chairman.
>
> B is to be vice-chairman.
>
> C is to be treasurer, and so on.

Then, for each of the 6-member groups that have been found, there are 6! ways of organizing them. Accordingly, the total number of committees that contain at least one physician is

$$3244605 \times 6! = 2336115600$$

Another approach is to start at the beginning and proceed as follows: If we neglect the requirement for one or more physicians, there are 40 ways to select the chairman, 39 ways to select the vice-chairman, and so on, giving 40!/34! possible committees. Of these, we must subtract the number of committees that contain no physicians, 30!/24!, giving

$$\frac{40!}{34!} - \frac{30!}{24!} = 2336115600$$

6. In how many ways can a group of 3 letters be chosen from the letters a, b, c, d, e if repetitions are allowed and order is immaterial (for example, aad is not different from ada or daa)?

Two ways of solving the problem are given:

A. There are three types of groups:

(1) All three letters are alike.

(2) Only two letters are alike.

(3) All three letters are different.

(1) There are five different groups of the first type.

(2) For the second type, there are five ways of choosing the letter that is used twice, and then four ways of choosing

the other letter. Hence, the number of groups of this type is

$$5 \times 4 = 20$$

(3) For the third type, there are $\dfrac{5!}{2!\ 3!} = 10$ different groups.

The total number of ways is then $5 + 20 + 10 = 35$.

B. Consider a row of 8 spaces in which we place the 5 letters, in order, and 3x's, where an x means that the letter in front of it has been chosen. For example, abxxcdxe means bbd. There are only 7 permissible locations for the x's since an x may not be placed in the first space. (The letter a must be in the first space.) Then the number of different ways of distributing the three x's in these 7 spaces is

$$\frac{7!}{4!\ 3!} = 35$$

7. The automobile license plates in many states have 3 letters and 3 digits, as WGR-736, where a letter or a digit may be repeated. If the letters I, O, and Q are not used, how many different license plates are possible?

$$23 \times 23 \times 23 \times 10 \times 10 \times 10 = 12167000$$

8. In how many ways can we write a sum of integers that add up to 20? Consider the same set of integers written in different orders as being different ways; for example, $2 + 7 + 11$ and $7 + 11 + 2$ are two different ways.

Write a sum of twenty 1's between parentheses, as follows:

$$(1 + 1 + 1 + 1 + 1 + 1 + 1 + 1 + 1 + 1 + 1 + 1 + 1 + 1 + 1 + 1 + 1 + 1 + 1 + 1) = 20$$

Around any of the 19 + signs we can put a pair of reversed parentheses, as) + (, in order to enclose groups of 1's. For example, in

$$2 \quad + \quad 4 \quad + \quad 6 \quad + \quad 6 \quad + \ 2 \ = 20$$
$$(1 + 1) + (1 + 1 + 1 + 1) + (1 + 1 + 1 + 1 + 1 + 1) + (1 + 1 + 1 + 1 + 1 + 1) + (1 + 1) = 20$$

we have inserted four pairs of reversed parentheses in order to make the sum $2 + 4 + 6 + 6 + 2 = 20$. In order to solve our problem consider that around each of the 19 + signs we can choose either to place a pair of reversed parentheses or to omit them; that is, there are two choices for each + sign. There are thus 2^{19} ways of placing pairs of reversed parentheses. However, if we omit all the pairs of reversed parentheses we get simply $20 = 20$, which cannot really be considered as a way of expressing 20 as a sum of integers. Omitting this one case leaves $2^{19} - 1 = 524287$ ways of expressing 20 as a sum of integers.

9. Braille is a system of printing for the blind in which the characters are represented by groups of raised dots. The basic "Braille cell" is

a group of six locations—the corners and the middles of the sides of a rectangle (typically 5 mm × $2\frac{1}{2}$ mm); and the various charac- ters are represented by combinations of raised dots at these loca- tions. Examples of Braille characters are

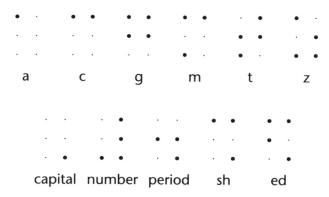

a   c   g   m   t   z

capital number period   sh   ed

(The letters a, b, c, ... j preceded by the number symbol represent the numbers 1, 2, 3, ... 0, respectively.) How many different characters can be formed by combinations of raised dots in the Braille cell?

Each of the six locations may be used or not used. However, if none are used, the result is simply a smooth surface; hence that case must be excluded. The total number of possible characters is therefore $2^6 - 1 = 63$.

10. How many 3-digit integers are there?

There are 10 choices (0 to 9, inclusive) for the digit in the units place and 10 choices for the digit in the tens place. There are only 9 choices (1 to 9, inclusive) for the digit in the hundreds place, since the integer may not begin with 0. Then the answer is $10 \times 10 \times 9 = 900$ integers—the number of integers from 100 to 999.

How many of them are even?

There are now only 5 choices for the units place (0, 2, 4, 6, 8). The answer is then $5 \times 10 \times 9 = 450$.

How many of them are divisible by 9?

11.(a) In how many ways can 52 different cards be distributed to four players, each player getting 13 cards?

$$\frac{52!}{13!\ 13!\ 13!\ 13!}$$

(b) How many different combinations may be in, say, group no. 1?

$$\frac{52!}{39!\ 13!}$$

After you have examined group no. 1, how many different combinations may be in group no. 2?

$$\frac{39!}{26! \ 13!}$$

After you have also examined group no. 2, how many different combinations may be in group no. 3?

$$\frac{26!}{13! \ 13!}$$

After you have similarly examined group no. 3, how many different combinations may be in group no. 4?

Since 39 cards have already been accounted for, the remaining 13 must be the fourth group; that is, only 1 combination is possible for the fourth group. If we use the form of the last three expressions, we get

$$\frac{13!}{0! \ 13!} = 1$$

The product of our four results is

$$\frac{52!}{39! \ 13!} \times \frac{39!}{26! \ 13!} \times \frac{26!}{13! \ 13!} \times \frac{13!}{0! \ 13!} = \frac{52!}{13! \ 13! \ 13! \ 13!}$$

Thus, as you should expect, the fact that you are examining the groups, one after the other, does not alter the total number of possible distributions to the four players.

(c) In how many ways can the 52 cards be divided into four groups of 13 each? The four groups are not assigned to four players or given any other identifications.

$$\frac{52!}{13! \ 13! \ 13! \ 13! \ 4!}$$

12. In how many numbers between 0 and 9999 does the digit 5 occur at least once?

The digit does not occur in $9 \times 9 \times 9 \times 9 = 6561$ numbers. Then it does occur in $10000 - 6561 = 3439$ numbers.

In how many of these numbers does 5 occur just once? twice? three times? four times?

13. In how many ways can a 6-digit number be formed from the digits 1, 2, 3, 4, 5, 6, 7, 8, 9 if all the digits must be different, three digits must be even, and three digits must be odd?

$$\left(\frac{4!}{3! \ 1!} \times \frac{5!}{3! \ 2!} \right) 6! = \left(4 \times 10 \right) 6! = 40 \times 720 = 28800$$

14. In this arrangement of letters, along how many different paths can we spell out the word UNDERSTAND?

```
                    U
                   U N U
                  U N D N U
                 U N D E D N U
                U N D E R E D N U
               U N D E R S R E D N U
              U N D E R S T S R E D N U
             U N D E R S T A T S R E D N U
            U N D E R S T A N A T S R E D N U
           U N D E R S T A N D N A T S R E D N U
```

Proceed backward, starting with the letter D in the middle of the bottom row. Using the left half of the arrangement, including the center column, we have two choices at each step: up or to the left. That is, from the D we can go up to N or left to N; then, from each of these two N's we can go up to A or left to A; and so on. There are 9 steps in proceeding backward from D to U; hence there are 2^9 possible paths in this left half of the arrangement. In the right half, again including the center column, there are similarly 2^9 paths. The total number of paths is then $2 \times 2^9 - 1 = 2^{10} - 1 = 1023$, where the 1 is subtracted because the path up the center column was counted twice.

15. We have n identical groups of three items, A, B, and C: (ABC), (ABC), . . . (ABC). If we select one item from every group, in how many ways can we select p A's, q B's, and r C's, where $p + q + r = n$?

There are $\dfrac{n(n-1)(n-2)\ldots(n-p+1)}{p!}$ ways of selecting the p A's;

then there remain $\dfrac{(n-p)(n-p-1)\ldots(n-p-q+1)}{q!}$ ways of selecting

the q B's; and finally there remain $\dfrac{(n-p-q)(n-p-q-1)\ldots 1}{r!}$ ways

of selecting the r C's. Since $n - p - q = r$, this last term is simply $r!/r! = 1$. Thus, since we have taken our A's from p of the groups and our B's from q of the groups, there remain only $n - p - q = r$ groups from which to take our r C's, so there is only one way to select the C's.

The total number of ways is the product of the preceding three expressions,

$$\frac{n!}{p!q!r!}$$

An application of this result is in the expansion of $(a + b + c)^n = (a + b + c)(a + b + c) \ldots (a + b + c)$. If we do the indicated multiplication we get a series of terms of the form $a^p b^q c^r$ (where $p + q + r = n$), where the p a's were obtained from p of the parentheses, the q b's were obtained from q other parentheses, and the r c's were obtained from the remaining r parentheses. From the preceding problem we know that the number of different ways of selecting p a's, q b's, and r c's is

$$\frac{n!}{p!q!r!}$$

which is hence the number of times that the term $a^p b^q c^r$ occurs in this product; that is, it is the coefficient of $a^p b^q c^r$ in the expansion. For example, in the expansion of $(a + b + c)^6$, the coefficient of $a^3 bc^2$ is

$$\frac{6!}{3!\ 1!\ 2!} = 60$$

When there are only two items in the parentheses, as in $(a + b)^n$, the coefficient of $a^p b^q$ $(p + q = n)$ is $\dfrac{n!}{p!q!}$. These coefficients are known as the binomial coefficients; they are listed, for ranges of values of n and p, in many mathematical tables.

Problem:
Show that in the expansion $(a + b + c)^4 = a^4 + 4a^3 b + . . .$, the total number of terms is 15. (See problem 6, solution method B.)

Additional problems.

1. How many even numbers of four different digits can be formed of the digits 0, 1, 2, 3, 4, 5, 6, 7 if every number must be less than 4000?

2. How many numbers, each of three different digits and formed of the digits 1, 2, 3, 4, 5, 6 are divisible by 4?

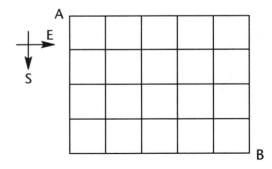

3. In going from A to B, one must go five blocks east and four blocks south. How many different such 9-block paths are there?

4. Eight people are entered in a ping-pong singles tournament. In how many ways can four pairs of contestants be selected for the first round?

5. You have a penny, a nickel, a dime, a quarter, a half-dollar, and a dollar. In how many ways can we combine two or more of these six coins?

Answers:
1. Each number must begin with 1, 2, or 3. If it begins with 1, it ends in one of the four even numbers 0, 2, 4, 6. Of the remaining 6 digits, one goes into the tens place and one goes into the hundreds place. Hence there are $4 \times 6 \times 5 = 120$ even numbers that begin with 1. Similarly there are 120 even numbers that begin with 3. If the number begins with 2, there remain only three even numbers for the units place: 0, 4, 6. Then there are $3 \times 6 \times 5 = 90$ even numbers that begin with 2. The total is $120 + 120 + 90 = 330$.

2. If the number is divisible by 4, it ends in 12, 16, 24, 32, 36, 52, 56, or 64. For each of these 8 cases we have 4 choices for the first digit. Hence there are $4 \times 8 = 32$ different numbers that satisfy our requirements.

3. The question is equivalent to "In how many different ways may we order 5 E's and 4 S's?" The answer is

$$\frac{9!}{5!\ 4!} = 126$$

4. For the first pair there are $\frac{8 \times 7}{2} = 28$ ways. From the six remaining entrants, there are $\frac{6 \times 5}{2} = 15$ ways of selecting a pair. From the four remaining entrants there are $\frac{4 \times 3}{2} = 6$ ways of selecting a pair. Only two entrants remain for the final pair. Then the total number of ways is $\frac{28 \times 15 \times 6 \times 1}{4!} = 105$, where we divide by 4! because each group of four pairs could have been chosen in 4! different ways.

5. Any one of the six coins may be used or not used. That would give 2^6 possibilities; however, we must delete the case in which none is used, and also the six cases in which only one coin is used. The answer is therefore $2^6 - 1 - 6 = 57$.

PROBABILITY

Definitions

Probability as a fraction. Suppose that a certain type of action or test yields a particular result for the fraction p of the time and some other result for the fraction q of the time, where $p + q = 1$. We then say that the probability of that particular result is p, and the probability of not getting that result is q.

Sometimes the value of a probability is obvious, as from considerations of symmetry. For example, consider the result of throwing a die—a cube whose six sides are numbered (with spots) 1, 2, 3, 4, 5, 6. From the symmetry of the die we assume that when it comes to rest after being thrown, all sides are equally likely to be on top. Then, for a large number of throws, we suppose that each side will, on the average, be up after one-sixth of the throws; that is, the probability that any particular number will be up after a throw is 1/6. Also, since three of the numbers are even and three of them are odd, the probability that it will be even is $3 \times \frac{1}{6} = \frac{1}{2}$, which is also the probability that it will be odd.

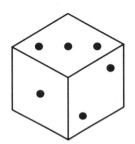

Some probabilities, however, are not obvious and must be determined by experiment. For example, consider the probability that a tack that is brushed off a table top onto the floor will come to rest with its point up $\perp$ rather than with its point down $\curlywedge$. In order to determine this probability you might empty several boxes of tacks onto the table, brush them off the table onto the floor, and count the number of tacks that lie each way. If you then find that 741 tacks lie with their points up and 1532 tacks lie with their points down, you conclude that the probability of coming to rest with the point up is

$$\frac{741}{741 + 1532} = \frac{741}{2273} = 0.326 \approx \frac{1}{3}$$

and the probability of coming to rest with the point down is

$$\frac{1532}{2273} = 0.674 \approx \frac{2}{3}$$

If you repeat the experiment with the same tacks, you will, very likely, get slightly different values. Averaging the corresponding results from the two experiments would give values that are more trustworthy than those from either experiment. In general, the greater the number of experiments the more trustworthy are the results.

---

*I have seen this quotation ascribed to F. P. Adams, to Damon Runyan, and to Jimmy the Greek.

In the case of our symmetrical die, the probability 1/6 assigned to each number is more accurate than any experimental values obtainable even in a thousand throws. Similarly, in flipping a coin, we may assume that the probability of getting a head equals the probability of getting a tail, so that both probabilities are 1/2. Yet, if we flip a coin a large number of times, we should not expect to get exactly as many heads as tails—we should expect only that the ratio (number of heads)/(number of tails) will be close to 1 and will tend to get closer to 1 as the number of flips increases. (The difference from 1 tends to vary inversely with the square root of the number of flips.) Nevertheless the number of flips would have to be enormous if high accuracy is to be obtained. For example, if a coin is flipped 10000 times, a result like 5050 heads and 4950 tails would not be at all unlikely. In one experiment 5087 heads and 4913 tails were obtained. True, such deviation from equality is a bit large, but not surprisingly so: the chance that the deviation would have been this large or larger (about 1/14) is comparable to the chance of getting four heads when a coin is flipped four times (1/16)—a bit unusual but not especially rare or remarkable

Problem:
Following is an excerpt from an article on testing people for drug use. Derive the probability values given in the last two sentences.

"A peculiar feature of all tests (whatever the kind) is that they are least reliable when the condition being tested for is least common. Let's assume you have a drug test that produces false positives 0.5% of the time and false negatives 0.5% of the time. As tests go, that's pretty good. But if the population you are screening has only one drug user per 1000, a positive result has only a 16% chance of being accurate. Even if 1% of the population are using the drug, a third of the positive results will still be in error."

Answer:
(1) Assume a population of, say, 1000 people, among which is only one drug user. The drug user is almost certain (99.5% probability) to test positive. In addition, on the average, 5 non-users (0.5% of 999) will test positive. Of these 6 people who test positive, only one is really a drug user (although you do not know which one). Accordingly, the probability that a person who tested positive is actually a drug user is 1/6, or 17%.
(2) Again assume a population of 1000 people, among which are 10 drug users. These 10 are almost certain to test positive. Of the remainder, on the average, 5 (= 0.5% of 990) will also test positive. Of the 15 who test positive, then, 5 are not drug users; that is, a third of the positive results are in error.

Odds. Suppose that the probability of a certain result is p and the probability of the alternative result is q, where $p + q = 1$. Then we say that the "odds in favor of" the first result are p to q; or the odds in favor of the alternative result are q to p. We may also say that the "odds against" the first result are q to p; or the odds against the alternative result are p to q. Also,

1. If possible, odds are given in terms of integers. For example, where, in the case of the tacks, we found

   probability of point up is 1/3
   probability of point down is 2/3,

   we do not say that the odds in favor of point down are 2/3 to 1/3; we say that the odds are 2 to 1.
2. Many people like to give the larger integer first and also prefer to give "odds in favor of" rather than "odds against." Thus, for the tacks, "odds in favor of point down are 2 to 1" is usually the preferred form, although "odds against point up are 2 to 1," "odds in favor of point up are 1 to 2," and "odds against point down are 1 to 2" may also be used.

If someone wishes to bet with you against a tack's coming to rest point up he should offer you odds of 2 to 1. Then, if you accept his offer, if it comes to rest point down, you give him say, 1 dollar, but if it comes to rest point up, he gives you 2 dollars. Alternatively, you put 1 dollar into "the pot" and he puts 2 dollars into the pot, and whoever wins takes the pot.

Multiple Events

Equally likely results. I shall flip a coin three times. What is the probability that the three results will be head, head, tail (H, H, T) in that order? The first flip will give H or T with equal likelihood. Independently of the first result, the second flip will also give H or T with equal likelihood. Similarly for the third flip. To the right is a tree diagram for this 3-flip experiment and also a list of the possible results.

The tree diagram shows how, with two possible results for each flip, there is a total of $2 \times 2 \times 2 = 8$ possible results. All eight are equally likely, so the probability of H H T (or of any one of the other seven) is 1/8.

(1) (2) (3)

```
        H < H
    H <     T
        T < H
            T

        H < H
    T <     T
        T < H
            T
```

```
H  H  H
H  H  T
H  T  H
H  T  T
T  H  H
T  H  T
T  T  H
T  T  T
```

Probability as a product. The probability of H for the first flip is 1/2; the probability of H for the second flip is 1/2; the probability of T for the third flip is 1/2. Since each flip is an independent experiment, the result of which is not biased by the results of the preceding flips, we may multiply the three possibilities and find that the probability of H H T is

$$\frac{1}{2} \times \frac{1}{2} \times \frac{1}{2} = \frac{1}{8}$$

The justification for multiplying together the three component probabilities is easily seen: The $2 \times 2 \times 2$ in the denominator of this product is the same $2 \times 2 \times 2$ that gave the number of possible (and equally likely) arrangements in the preceding paragraph.

Independent events. Consider further the multiplication of separate probabilities to get the probability of the combined result. In the preceding paragraph we indicated that such multiplication is permissible if the result of each experiment is not biased by the results of the other experiments. For further clarification, compare the following two problems:

1. A bag contains three white balls and two black balls. You reach in and draw out two of the balls. What is the probability that one is white and the other is black?

   Image that you draw them out one at a time. Since there are three white balls in the total of five, the probability of drawing a white ball on the first draw is $\frac{3}{5}$. Suppose that a white ball is actually drawn. Then only four balls now remain, of which two are white and two are black, so the probability of getting a black ball on the second draw is $\frac{2}{4}$. Then the probability of drawing first a white ball and then a black ball is $\frac{3}{5} \times \frac{2}{4} = \frac{3}{10}$. Now consider the probability of drawing first a black ball and then a white ball: The probability of first drawing a black ball is $\frac{2}{5}$, since only two of the five balls are black; and, then, if a black ball is actually drawn, the probability of drawing a white ball is $\frac{3}{4}$, since three of the remaining four balls are white. Thus, the probability of drawing a white ball is $\frac{2}{5} \times \frac{3}{4} = \frac{3}{10}$. (Compare with the preceding product and note how the two numerators are interchanged while the two denominators remain the same.) The total probability of drawing two balls of different colors is the sum $\frac{3}{10} + \frac{3}{10} = \frac{3}{5}$.

   In this problem, if we forget to imagine one drawing to occur *after* the other, we might argue that the probability of drawing a white ball is $\frac{3}{5}$ and the probability of drawing a black ball is $\frac{2}{5}$, so the probability of drawing both is $\frac{3}{5} \times \frac{2}{5} = \frac{6}{25}$, which is wrong. The source of confusion here is that as soon as the fingers start to close over one ball, the number of balls remaining for the second choice is reduced to four, so the probability for the second drawing has a 4 in the denominator. This problem, thus, may be considered as involving two separate experiments, one after the other.

   As noted in the paragraph before the last, if the first drawing is white, the next drawing is from a group of 2 white and 2 black, whereas if the first drawing is black, the next drawing is from a group of 3 white and 1 black. Thus, the result of the first experiment affects the make-up of the second experiment, and in this sense one might say that the two results are not independent. However, for our purpose, we refer to them as independent, because we consider that one experiment occurs *after* the other and is thus as separate from it as if the remaining four balls were contained in a separate bag; and since they are independent we may multiply the probabilities in order to find the probability of both results.

2. By contrast, consider the following problem: If you flip a coin three times, what is the probability that (1) the third flap gives a head while (2) you get exactly two tails? One might reason that (1) the probability that the third flip gives a head is $\frac{1}{2}$, and (2) of the eight results shown in the previous list, three (T T H, T H T, H T T) have exactly two tails; hence the probability of exactly two tails is $\frac{3}{8}$; then the probability of satisfying both conditions is the product $\frac{1}{2} \times \frac{3}{8} = \frac{3}{16}$. But this answer is wrong, because the first condition limits the number of ways that the second condition can be fulfilled. There is, in fact, only one way (T T H) to satisfy both conditions simultaneously, and the probability is hence $\frac{1}{8}$. The two events here considered are not independent.

Problem:
We earlier listed the eight possible results for three flips of a coin. Similarly list the possible results for the two drawings from the bag containing three white and the two black balls. From the list determine the probability of drawing one white ball and one black ball.

Let the three white balls be w_1, w_2, and w_3, and the two black balls be b_1 and b_2. The possible pairs are listed on the right. There are ten pairs, all equally likely, of which six include one white and one black ball. Hence the probability of one white ball and one black ball is 6/10, or 3/5, as was previously derived.

w_1	w_2
w_1	w_3
w_1	b_1
w_1	b_2
w_2	w_3
w_2	b_1
w_2	b_2
w_3	b_1
w_3	b_2
b_1	b_2

The total probability of all the possibilities. In the preceding problem of the white and black balls, we found that the probability of drawing two balls of different colors was 3/5. We can similarly show that the probability of drawing two white balls is $\frac{3}{5} \times \frac{2}{4} = \frac{3}{10}$ and the probability of drawing two black balls is $\frac{2}{5} \times \frac{1}{4} = \frac{1}{10}$. The total probability of all three possibilities is

$$P(w, b) + P(b, w) + P(w, w) + P(b, b) = \frac{3}{10} + \frac{3}{10} + \frac{3}{10} + \frac{1}{10} = 1.$$

The total probability is 1, which means merely that it is *certain* that one of these results must occur—which is obvious, for there are no other possibilities.

Problem:
When six coins are tossed (either all together or one at a time), what is the probability that exactly one will fall with the head up?

Consider six consecutive flips. Any particular arrangement, say, H T T T T T, has probability $\frac{1}{2} \times \frac{1}{2} \times \frac{1}{2} \times \frac{1}{2} \times \frac{1}{2} \times \frac{1}{2} = \frac{1}{64}$. However, the one H need not occur on the first flip—it may occur on the second flip, or the third flip, or . . ., or the sixth flip. The desired probability is the sum of all six probabilities, which is $6 \times \frac{1}{64} = \frac{3}{32}$.

Problem:
What is the probability that exactly two will fall with the head up? As in the preceding problem, any particular arrangement, as T H T T H T, has probability $\frac{1}{64}$. The number of ways of distributing two H's among six spaces is $\frac{6!}{2!\,4!} = 15$. That is, of the 64 different ways, all equally likely, of distributing T's and H's among six spaces, 15 have exactly 2H's and 4T's. Then the desired probability is $\frac{15}{64}$.

Problem:
What is the probability that *at least* one will fall with the head up? We could calculate the separate probabilities for 1, 2, 3, 4, 5, and 6 heads and add them, but a far simpler way is to calculate the probability of no heads and subtract from 1: The probability of no heads, or T T T T T T, is $\frac{1}{64}$; hence the probability of at least one head is $1 - \frac{1}{64} = \frac{63}{64}$.

Problem:
The TV weatherman predicts the weekend weather as follows: The probability of rain on Saturday is 50% and the probability of rain on Sunday is 50%; therefore the probability of rain this weekend is 100%. Discuss this conclusion.

Answer:
The weatherman can do simple arithmetic but he seems confused about simple probability theory. According to our earlier discussion, one might calculate the probability as follows: The probability of no rain on Saturday is $\frac{1}{2}$; the probability of no rain on Sunday is $\frac{1}{2}$, the probability of no rain on either day is $\frac{1}{2} \times \frac{1}{2} = \frac{1}{4}$, and the probability of rain this weekend is therefore $1 - \frac{1}{4} = \frac{3}{4}$, or 75%.

Actually, however, weather prediction has complicating aspects. Suppose, for example, that a weatherman expects that a brief rain will pass through the area during the weekend; but its approach is so irregular that he cannot predict whether it will pass through on Saturday or on Sunday. Accordingly, he assigns a probability of 50% to rain on Saturday, a probability of 50% to rain on Sunday, and a probability of 100% to rain on the weekend. In this case, the two 50% probabilities are not independent: If the rain arrives on Saturday, it will be gone by Sunday, and if the weather is clear on Saturday, the rain will surely arrive on Sunday. The matter is thus different from that in flipping pennies where, if the first flip results in head, the second flip results in head or tail quite independently of the first result.

Problems:
1. In one bag are 9 balls, numbered 1 to 9; in another bag are 6 balls numbered 1 to 6. If one ball is drawn from each bag, what is the probability that the two balls have the same number?

2. A bag contains 5 balls numbered 1 to 5. Three balls are drawn from the bag. What is the probability that the sum of their numbers is 10?

3. If 6 coins are flipped, what is the chance that none will turn up heads? What is the chance of getting exactly one head? exactly two heads? exactly three heads? exactly four heads? exactly five heads? exactly six heads? Verify that the sum of these probabilities is 1.

4. A bag contains exactly 2 white balls, 2 red balls, and 2 black balls. If you reach in and pull out two of the balls, (a) What is the probability that both will be the same color? (b) What is the probability that neither is white? (c) That one is red and one is black? (d) That one is white and one is another color? (e) That the two colors are different?

Answers:

1. The ball drawn from the second bag may have any number from 1 to 6. The probability that the ball drawn from the first bag will match it is simply $\frac{1}{9}$.

2. In order for the sum to be 10, the three numbers must be either 1, 4, 5 or 2, 3, 5. The probability of either group is $\frac{1}{5} \times \frac{1}{4} \times \frac{1}{3} \times 3! = \frac{1}{10}$, so the probability of drawing one or the other is $\frac{1}{10} + \frac{1}{10} = \frac{1}{5}$.

3.
$$P(0) = \left(\frac{1}{2}\right)^6 \qquad = \frac{1}{64}$$

$$P(1) = \left(\frac{1}{2}\right)^6 \times 6 \qquad = \frac{6}{64}$$

$$P(2) = \left(\frac{1}{2}\right)^6 \times \frac{6 \times 5}{2} \quad = \frac{15}{64}$$

$$P(3) = \left(\frac{1}{2}\right)^6 \times \frac{6!}{3! \; 3!} \quad = \frac{20}{64}$$

$$P(4) = \left(\frac{1}{2}\right)^6 \times \frac{6!}{4! \; 2!} \quad = \frac{15}{64}$$

$$P(5) = \left(\frac{1}{2}\right)^6 \times \frac{6!}{5! \; 1!} \quad = \frac{6}{64}$$

$$P(6) = \left(\frac{1}{2}\right)^6 \qquad = \frac{1}{64}$$

$$\frac{64}{64} = 1$$

4. (a) The first ball may be any one of the three colors. The probability that the second ball matches it is $\frac{1}{5}$.

(b) P (neither is white) $= \frac{4}{6} \times \frac{3}{5} = \frac{2}{5}$

(c) P (one black, one red) $= \frac{2}{6} \times \frac{2}{5} \times 2 = \frac{4}{15}$

(d) P (one white, one red or black) $= \frac{2}{6} \times \frac{4}{5} \times 2 = \frac{8}{15}$

(e) The first may be any one of the three colors. The probability that the second is another color is $\frac{4}{5}$.

The Baseball World Series. Suppose that in the Baseball World Series the two opposing teams are evenly matched. That is, the probability that the American League team (A) wins any particular game is 1/2, and the probability that the National League team (N) wins any particular game is 1/2. What is the probability that A wins the series (that is, wins 4 games) in the first 4 games? in 5 games? in 6 games? in 7 games?

Following are listed the probabilities (refer to the discussion of the Baseball World Series under "How Many Ways?"):

1. A wins in 4 games: $\left(\frac{1}{2}\right)^4 = \frac{1}{16}$

2. A wins in 5 games: $\left(\frac{1}{2}\right)^5 \times 4 = \frac{1}{8}$

   (N wins 1 of the first 4 games, which it can do in 4 ways.)

3. A wins in 6 games: $\left(\frac{1}{2}\right)^6 \times \frac{5!}{3! \, 2!} = \frac{5}{32}$

   (N wins 2 of the first 5 games.)

4. A wins in 7 games: $\left(\frac{1}{2}\right)^7 \times \frac{6!}{3! \, 3!} = \frac{5}{32}$

   (N wins 3 of the first 6 games.)

$$\text{Sum} = \frac{1}{2}$$

The total probability that A wins the Series is thus 1/2, as it should be. The probabilities for N, of course, are the same as for A.

The probability that the Series goes all the way to 7 games is $\frac{5}{32} + \frac{5}{32} = \frac{5}{16}$, or slightly less than 1/3. If the two teams are not evenly matched, the probability that the Series goes to 7 games is even less. It turns out, however, that appreciably more than 1/3 of the World Series go all the way to 7 games. The only reason that has been suggested is that when a team fears that it is losing, its members manage to put forth efforts exceeding their normal capabilities (or perhaps the members of the other team unconsciously relax slightly). A similar "back-to-the-wall effect" seems to apply in basketball games, in which the final scores of opposing teams are often remarkably close, like 128–126.

Problem:

In a series of games between two teams, A and B, the team that wins four games will be the winner. After five games have been played, team A is ahead 3 to 2. A long period of bad weather then sets in and the series is never completed.

Two people have bet each other one dollar on the outcome of the series. Since the odds were thus 1 to 1, we may suppose that the teams were essentially evenly matched. What should be done with the two dollars in the pot?

The simplest answer, perhaps, is for each person to take back his dollar. However, the person whose team is ahead feels that the pot should be his or, at least, that he should get the larger part of the pot. Propose an equitable way of dividing the pot.

Answer:

This type of problem is of historical interest, for when it was proposed to a famous mathematician in about 1650, it launched the modern study of probability theory, which has become one of the most important branches of mathematics.

The most equitable division of the pot is based on the teams' relative probabilities of winning four games. As mentioned, we suppose that the teams are evenly matched, so that each team's probability of winning or losing a game is 1/2. Team A needs to win only one more game, which it can do in two different ways:

P (A wins the sixth game) = $\dfrac{1}{2}$

P (A loses the sixth game and wins the seventh game) = $\dfrac{1}{2} \times \dfrac{1}{2} = \dfrac{1}{4}$

P (A wins the series) = $\dfrac{3}{4}$

Team B needs to win both of the next two games:

P (B wins the sixth and seventh games) = $\dfrac{1}{2} \times \dfrac{1}{2} = \dfrac{1}{4}$

Thus, A's probability of winning the series is three times as much as B's. The most reasonable way to divide the pot, then, is in the ratio of 3 to 1; that is, the person whose team was ahead gets $1.50, and the person whose team was behind gets $0.50.

The numbers game. In the numbers games (also known as the numbers racket), the player guesses a 3-digit number and puts up as much money as he wishes, say a dollar. Many hundreds of people in a community may play the game every day. At the end of the day the winning number is found from the day's statistics—for example, it might be the last three digits of the number of shares of stock traded that day on the New York Stock Exchange.

Since there are one thousand 3-digit numbers (000 to 999), all equally likely, the probability that the player guessed the winning number is

1/1000. Hence, on the average, he must play the game one thousand times for each win. Then, if the game is fair, he should be paid $1000 when he wins. Actually, the pay-off to a winner is typically between $500 and $600, and the remainder stays with the operators. The game is played mainly by the gullible or by those who do not mind the unfairness if they can, every few years, experience the thrill of winning and the pleasure of bragging about it for months afterwards. Of course there is no certainty of winning once in 1000 times (or about once in four years if one plays every day). Many players play several different numbers each day, so the thrill occurs oftener. Also, many players feel that they improve their luck by playing their house numbers, numbers seen in their dreams, and so on. But their "luck" does not seem to affect the operators' enormous profits.

Privately operated numbers games are generally illegal. However, several of our states operate numbers games, called state lotteries. The players are presumably aware of the unfairness, but they can at least feel that they are helping to provide money for running the states' governments. Playing the lottery seems to be less painful and more interesting than paying increased taxes.

Problem:
It was previously mentioned that there is no certainty of winning once in 1000 tries. Just what is the probability of one or more wins in 1000 tries?

The probability of not winning in any particular try is $\dfrac{999}{1000}$; then the probability of not winning in a thousand tries is $\left(\dfrac{999}{1000}\right)^{1000} = 0.3677$, so the probability of at least one win is $1 - 0.368 = 0.632$, or just a little more than 5/8.

Problem:
Using the value just given for 0.999^{1000}, calculate approximate values for the probabilities of winning exactly once in 1000 tries; exactly twice; . . .; exactly five times. The sum of these five probabilities should be nearly equal to the probability of getting at least one win in 1000 times, as determined in the preceding problem.

The probability of winning exactly once is

$$\left[\left(\frac{999}{1000}\right)^{999} \times \frac{1}{1000}\right] \times 1000 \qquad\qquad = 0.368$$

$$\text{twice} \qquad \left[\left(\frac{999}{1000}\right)^{998} \times \left(\frac{1}{1000}\right)^2\right] \times \frac{1000!}{998!\ 2!} \approx \frac{0.368}{2} = 0.184$$

three times $\left[\left(\dfrac{999}{1000}\right)^{997} \times \left(\dfrac{1}{1000}\right)^{3}\right] \times \dfrac{1000\,!}{997\,!\ 3!} \approx \dfrac{0.368}{6} = 0.061$

four times $\left[\left(\dfrac{999}{1000}\right)^{996} \times \left(\dfrac{1}{1000}\right)^{4}\right] \times \dfrac{1000\,!}{996\,!\ 4!} \approx \dfrac{0.367}{24} = 0.015$

five times $\left[\left(\dfrac{999}{1000}\right)^{995} \times \left(\dfrac{1}{1000}\right)^{5}\right] \times \dfrac{1000\,!}{995\,!\ 5!} \approx \dfrac{0.366}{120} = \dfrac{0.003}{0.631}$

The four favorite marbles. A bag contains thirteen differently colored marbles, among which are your four favorites.

Problems:
1. If you draw four marbles out of the bag, what is the probability that they are your four favorites?
2. If you draw six marbles out of the bag, what is the probability that your four favorites are among them?

Answers:

1. $\dfrac{4}{13} \times \dfrac{3}{12} \times \dfrac{2}{11} \times \dfrac{1}{10} = \dfrac{4!\ 9!}{13!} = \dfrac{1}{715} \approx 0.0014$

2. The answer to problem 1 must be increased in proportion to the number of ways that the favorite four can be distributed (regardless of order) among the six.

   The desired probability is then

   $\dfrac{4!\ 9!}{13!} \times \dfrac{6!}{4!\ 2!} = \dfrac{9!\ 6!}{13!\ 2!} = \dfrac{3}{143} \approx 0.0210$

Games Played With Dice

Basic probabilities. We have already seen that when a single die is cast the probability that any one of the six numbers will be on top is 1/6. For a pair of dice, the probability of any particular pair of numbers, say 2 on the first die and 3 on the other, is $\dfrac{1}{6} \times \dfrac{1}{6} = \dfrac{1}{36}$. However, if we ask for the probability of rolling a 5 (where 5 is the sum of the two numbers on the dice), we must take into account the fact that a 5 can be obtained in four ways: 2 and 3, 3 and 2, 1 and 4, 4 and 1. The probability of each of these pairs is $\dfrac{1}{36}$, so the total probability of rolling a 5 is $\dfrac{4}{36} = \dfrac{1}{9}$.

In the following table are listed the various numbers that can be rolled, from 2 to 12, with the ways that they can be obtained and their total probabilities.

Number	Ways	Total Probability
2	(1, 1)	$\dfrac{1}{36}$
3	(2, 1), (1, 2)	$\dfrac{2}{36} = \dfrac{1}{18}$
4	(3, 1), (2, 2), (1, 3)	$\dfrac{3}{36} = \dfrac{1}{12}$
5	(4, 1), (3, 2), (2, 3), (1, 4)	$\dfrac{4}{36} = \dfrac{1}{9}$
6	(5, 1), (4, 2), (3, 3), (2, 4), (1, 5)	$\dfrac{5}{36}$
7	(6, 1), (5, 2), (4, 3), (3, 4), (2, 5), (1, 6)	$\dfrac{6}{36} = \dfrac{1}{6}$
8	(6, 2), (5, 3), (4, 4), (3, 5), (2, 6)	$\dfrac{5}{36}$
9	(6, 3), (5, 4), (4, 5), (3, 6)	$\dfrac{4}{36} = \dfrac{1}{9}$
10	(6, 4), (5, 5), (4, 6)	$\dfrac{3}{36} = \dfrac{1}{12}$
11	(6, 5), (5, 6)	$\dfrac{2}{36} = \dfrac{1}{18}$
12	(6, 6)	$\dfrac{1}{36}$
	Sum	$\dfrac{36}{36} = 1$

The game of craps. The preceding table contains the information needed to discuss the game of craps. In this game, the player (or "shooter") and his opponent each put up the same amount of money and the shooter then starts to cast the pair of dice. If the first roll is 2, 3, or 12, he loses immediately (but retains the dice if he wishes) and his opponent takes the money. If the first roll is 7 or 11, he wins immediately (and retains the dice) and he takes the money. If the first roll is any of the other numbers (4, 5, 6, 8, 9, 10), he continues to cast the dice until either (a) he repeats the number of his first roll, in which case he wins, or (b) he rolls a 7, in which case he loses and passes the dice to his opponent (or to the player on his left if there are several players). For example, suppose his first roll is a 4. Then he continues to cast the dice until he rolls either a 4 or a 7. For this final deciding roll, which is either a 4 or a 7, the probability that it is a 4 rather than a 7 is

$$\frac{P(4)}{P(4) + P(7)} = \frac{\dfrac{3}{36}}{\dfrac{3}{36} + \dfrac{6}{36}} = \frac{1}{3}$$

Correspondingly, the probability that it is a 7 rather than a 4 is

$$\frac{P(7)}{P(4) + P(7)} = \frac{\frac{6}{36}}{\frac{3}{36} + \frac{6}{36}} = \frac{2}{3}$$

Thus, if his first roll is a 4, he is twice as likely to lose as to win; that is, the odds are 2 to 1 against him.

Following are listed the probabilities of the various ways of winning:

P (success)

$$P(7) = \qquad\qquad\qquad \frac{1}{6}$$

$$P(11) = \qquad\qquad\qquad \frac{1}{18}$$

$$P(4) \times P \text{ (4 rather than 7)} = \frac{1}{12} \times \frac{\frac{1}{12}}{\frac{1}{12} + \frac{1}{6}} = \qquad \frac{1}{36}$$

$$P(5) \times P \text{ (5 rather than 7)} = \frac{1}{9} \times \frac{\frac{1}{9}}{\frac{1}{9} + \frac{1}{6}} = \qquad \frac{2}{45}$$

$$P(6) \times P \text{ (6 rather than 7)} = \frac{5}{36} \times \frac{\frac{5}{36}}{\frac{5}{36} + \frac{1}{6}} = \qquad \frac{25}{396}$$

$$P(8) \times P \text{ (8 rather than 7)} = \frac{5}{36} \times \frac{\frac{5}{36}}{\frac{5}{36} + \frac{1}{6}} = \qquad \frac{25}{396}$$

$$P(9) \times P \text{ (9 rather than 7)} = \frac{1}{9} \times \frac{\frac{1}{9}}{\frac{1}{9} + \frac{1}{6}} = \qquad \frac{2}{45}$$

$$P(10) \times P \text{ (10 rather than 7)} = \frac{1}{12} \times \frac{\frac{1}{12}}{\frac{1}{12} + \frac{1}{6}} = \qquad \frac{1}{36}$$

Total probability of winning = $\qquad \dfrac{244}{495}$

Total probability of losing = $\qquad 1 - \dfrac{244}{495} = \dfrac{251}{495}$

The shooter's probability of winning is thus slightly less than his probability of losing. The difference is fairly small, however; and, in any case, the shooter will eventually have the advantage when his opponent becomes the shooter. In a gambling casino, however, the shooters play only against "the house" (that is, the casino), so the house always has the advantage. The difference between $\frac{244}{495}$ and $\frac{251}{495}$ may not seem very large; but it suffices to provide a good profit to the casino, where thousands of games are played every day.

In ordinary craps, bystanders may place side bets with each other while watching the game; in a casino, however, betting is only against the house and is always at odds that are slightly favorable to the house. For example, if the shooter's number is 6, the bystander may bet that the shooter "makes his point"—that is, that a 6 finally comes up rather than a 7. As shown in the earlier table, the probability of a 6 is only 5/6 the probability of a 7, so the true odds against the by-stander are 6 to 5. However, the odds offered him by the house are usually just "even"—that is, 1 to 1. The house makes its profit by always offering odds that are slightly unfair.

But now suppose that, before the shooter begins, a bystander wishes to bet against him. Does the house permit him to take advantage of the 251-to-244 true odds against the shooter? No, the house changes the rules in order to shift the odds in its favor. The change is in only one particular; namely, the house does not pay off to the bystander if the shooter loses by rolling a 2 on his first roll. The bystander does not lose his bet in this case; the result is considered a tie, and his bet remains on the table to be played in the next game. Since the probability of rolling a 2 is 1/36, his probability of winning is reduced to $\frac{251}{495} - \frac{1}{36} = \frac{949}{1980}$. His probability of losing (= the shooter's probability of winning) is still $\frac{244}{495} = \frac{976}{1980}$; so the odds are against him by 976 to 949. Thus, the odds are against him by about as much as 251-to-244 would have been in his favor. The two probabilities, $\frac{949}{1980}$ and $\frac{976}{1980}$ do not add up to 1; the difference, $\frac{1}{36}$, is the probability of the "tie."

Dishonest dice. There are several ways to make a dishonest die, that is, a die for which the probability that a particular number is up exceeds, or is less than, 1/6. The best known method is to add some extra weight near the opposite face, which then tends to be down. Such a die is said to be loaded. If a die is suspected of being loaded it may be tested by letting it fall through a tall cylinder full of water. If it is loaded, it will gradually turn so that the heavier side will be at the bottom by the time the die completes its fall.

Thou shalt not steal; an empty feat
When it's so lucrative to cheat.
A. H. Clough

As mentioned, however, there are other ways of making dishonest dice. Here is a simple example of cheating with crooked dice. Suppose that the dice are slightly flattened (shown exaggerated in the sketch) so that the 1- and 6-faces are slightly larger than the other faces. The probabilities of 1 and of 6 are then slightly greater than 1/6, and the probabilities of the other four numbers are all correspondingly reduced to less than 1/6.

Then, on the first throw, the shooter's probability of getting a 2, 3, or 12—that is, P(1,1) + P(1,2) + P(2,1) + P(6,6)—and thus losing immediately is much greater than it should be, while his probability of getting a 7 or 11, and thus winning immediately, is only slightly greater than it should be. Furthermore, if the shooter's first throw is a 4, 5, 6, 8, 9, or 10, the probability that he will throw it again before he throws a 7 is appreciably reduced. Accordingly, the cheater always bets against the shooter, or against the shooter's making his point.

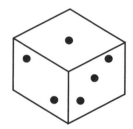

Of course, the flaws in the dice must not be so gross that they are apparent to the victims. The cheater needs only a slight change in the probabilities; for since he plays many games, this slight change suffices to provide his livelihood.

Problem:
Assume that for the dishonest dice the probabilities of 1 and 6 have been increased from 1/6 to 0.18, while the probabilities of 2, 3, 4, and 5 have been correspondingly reduced from 1/6 to 0.16. (Note that the sum of these six probabilities is 1, as it should be.) Verify the preceding statements concerning the changes in the shooter's probabilities.

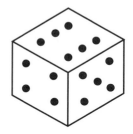

He was a stranger and they took him in.

On Gambling

Suppose that you are given ten dollars and sent to the market with a list of groceries needed for dinner. On the way you meet a friend who is on a similar errand, also with ten dollars. He offers to let you flip a coin for the money. It is a fair bet, and if you win you will get his ten dollars, but do you agree to play? No, because if you lose, what will you have for dinner, besides a scolding?

Our first rule, then, is

(1) Do not bet more than you can easily afford to lose. Decide in advance how much that is, and when you have lost it, quit. Playing further in order to recover your losses, or to avoid being called a quitter, can lead to catastrophe. Would you rather be a fool than a quitter?

Other rules are

(2) Quit, if possible, if you were lucky enough to win. In a game that depends only on chance, the fact that you were lucky in one game promises nothing about your luck in subsequent games.
(3) Do not gamble with strangers, and avoid out-of-the-way gambling joints. There are many dishonest tricks practiced by people whose livelihood depends on winning from suckers. If you do play, play only with your friends, and for small stakes. Your purpose should not be to make money but to enjoy the mental exercise, the excitement, and the banter.

Problems

1. In a group of 100 people, 70 are engineers and 30 are lawyers. Concerning one of them, you are told "He is 30 years old and

married. He is considered to be very able and highly motivated, and promises to be very successful in his field. He is friendly and well liked by his colleagues." What is the probability that the man is a lawyer?

2. In a certain town there are a large hospital and a small hospital. In the large hospital there are about 100 births per month; in the small hospital there are about 20 births per month. You examine the records of each hospital to find the months in which 60 percent or more of the babies born in the hospital were girls. Which hospital do you expect to have more such months?

3. If you flip a coin six times, how does the probability of getting H H H H H H compare with the probability of getting H T H H T T?

4. A certain club has 10 members. How does the number of possible 6-member committees compare with the number of possible 4-member committees?

5. A bag contains 30 white marbles and 50 black marbles. You withdraw the marbles one by one, putting the white marbles into one box and the black marbles into another box. What is the probability that at least once during this procedure the two boxes contain the same number of marbles?

6. I shuffle a jack, a queen, a king, and an ace, and lay the four cards face down on the table. However, I accidently brush one of the cards off the table with my sleeve, and it lies face down on the floor. If I pick one of the three remaining cards from the table, what is the probability that it is an ace?

Answers:

1. The description gives no way of distinguishing between engineer and lawyer. Hence, we remain with only the information given in the first sentence, and must conclude that the probability is 0.3.

2. The larger the number of births, the smaller is the expected deviation from 50% girls—50% boys. Hence it is at the smaller hospital where we should expect to find more frequent large percentage deviations.

3. The probabilities are equal. Similarly, in a bridge game the probability of being dealt all 13 cards of a specified suit equals the probability of being dealt any other specified set of 13 cards.

4. The two are equal: For each 6-member committee that can be chosen, there remains a 4-member group that is available for a committee.

5. Consider, as an example, that the initial drawings are, in order, WWBWBWWBBB. . ., in which the number of B's equals the number of W's at the tenth drawing. The probability of drawing this initial sequence is the same as the probability of drawing any other initial sequence of ten marbles containing 5W's and 5B's; in particular, it is equal to the probability of drawing the reverse sequence BBBWWBWBWW. . .

Now if the first marble drawn is a W, the number of B's drawn must, at some point, equal the number of W's, since the total number of B's exceeds the total number of W's. The probability that this first marble is a W is $30/(30 + 50) = 3/8$. Also, we have seen that for every initial sequence starting with a W, there is an equally probable initial sequence, starting with B, in which the B's and W's are in reverse order. Then the total probability of having as many B's as W's at least once during the drawing is $\frac{3}{8} + \frac{3}{8} = \frac{3}{4}$.

6. The probability is $\frac{1}{4}$.

Life Insurance and Life-Expectancy Tables

Here is the final portion of an old life-expectancy table, prepared about 1880. The table starts with 1000 children at age 10 and shows the average number still alive at subsequent birthdays. The portion shown here is for ages 88 to 100.

Age	88	89	90	91	92	93	94	95	96	97	98	99	100
Number alive at that birthday	28	21	15.7	11.3	8.0	5.5	3.7	2.4	1.5	0.9	0.5	0.2	0

Suppose that a person takes out life insurance on his 88th birthday, paying $100 then and expecting to pay $100 on every subsequent birthday while he is alive. The insurance company expects to receive from him a total of $100 + $100 × (probability that he is alive on his 89th birthday) + $100 × (probability that he is alive on his 90th birthday) + . . . =

$$\$100 \left(1 + \frac{21}{28} + \frac{15.7}{28} + \frac{11.3}{28} + . . . + \frac{0.2}{28}\right) = \$100 \times \frac{98.7}{28} = \$352.50$$

A mathematically fair insurance to be paid on his death is then $352.50. This calculation, however, is oversimplified. For example, the insurance company invests your money so that its value increases; also it must take a certain amount for expenses and profit.

Radioactivity

Most of the chemical elements that we encounter, as ordinary hydrogen, oxygen, sulfur, iron, . . ., are extremely stable—their atoms remain unchanged for billions of years. Some atoms, however, are radioactive—their nuclei emit characteristic radiations and change to other kinds of nuclei, usually nuclei of different elements. Two isotopes that exist as minute fractions of ordinary carbon and potassium are radioactive.

The probability of the change is often expressed in terms of half-life. For example, if we say that a certain type of radioactive atom has a half-life of one year, we mean that the probability that the atom will still exist after one year is 1/2. Or, if we have today one gram of the material (roughly 10^{22} atoms) one year from now only 1/2 gram of it will remain; the rest will have been transformed.

Consider the half-gram that remains. With so many of their partners gone, are the atoms now old and on the verge of being transformed too? No, they are as fresh as ever, with a half-life of one year. That is, half of this remainder, or $\frac{1}{2} \times \frac{1}{2} = \frac{1}{4}$ of the original gram, will remain after the second year. Half of this quantity, or $\frac{1}{2} \times \frac{1}{2} \times \frac{1}{2} = \frac{1}{8}$ gram will remain after the third year; and so on. In other words, the probability that an atom will be transformed is independent of its age; no matter when we ask the question, the probability that it will still exist after a year is 1/2.

If we ask how much will remain after a half-year, the answer is $\frac{1}{\sqrt{2}}$ = 0.71 gram; then, after the second half-year, the amount remaining will be $\frac{1}{\sqrt{2}} \times \frac{1}{\sqrt{2}} = \frac{1}{2}$ gram, as it should be. The amount remaining after a quarter-year is $\frac{1}{\sqrt[4]{2}}$ = 0.84 gram; and again, after four quarter-years, the amount remaining is

$$\frac{1}{\sqrt[4]{2}} \times \frac{1}{\sqrt[4]{2}} \times \frac{1}{\sqrt[4]{2}} \times \frac{1}{\sqrt[4]{2}} = \frac{1}{2} \text{ gram}$$

A similar type of arithmetic applies in various other scientific matters, for example, the absorption of light. Suppose that after a beam of green light of a certain wavelength has penetrated 1 cm into a cup of tea, its intensity has been reduced to 0.8 of the initial intensity. Then after it has penetrated a second cm its intensity will be $0.8 \times 0.8 =$ 0.64 of the initial intensity, and so on. If we consider the beam as a stream of light quanta, or photons, we say that the probability is 0.8 that a photon will remain unabsorbed after passing through 1 cm of the tea; and then the arithmetic becomes very analogous to that of the preceding paragraphs.

Problems:
Consider a type of atom that has a half-life of 1 year.

1. If we start with only 4 atoms, what are the probabilities that after 1 year there will remain 0, 1, 2, 3, 4 atoms of the original kind?
2. If we start with 8 atoms, what are the probabilities that after 1 year there will remain 0, 1, 2, 3, 4, 5, 6, 7, 8 atoms of the original kind?
3. If we start with 4 atoms, what are the probabilities that after 2 years there will remain 0, 1, 2, 3, 4 atoms of the original kind?
4. For problems 1, 2, and 3, plot the probabilities against the numbers of remaining atoms.

Answers:
1. The probability that n atoms will remain and $4 - n$ atoms will have disintegrated after 1 year is

$$\left(\frac{1}{2}\right)^n \left(\frac{1}{2}\right)^{4-n} \frac{4!}{n!(4-n)!}$$

where the last factor represents the number of ways of selecting the n atoms that will remain.
2. The probability is

$$\left(\frac{1}{2}\right)^n \left(\frac{1}{2}\right)^{8-n} \frac{8!}{n!(8-n)!}$$

3. The probability that an atom will remain after 2 years is P(it remains after the first year) × P(if it remains after the first year, it will still remain after the second year) = $\frac{1}{2} \times \frac{1}{2} = \frac{1}{4}$. The probability that it will not remain after 2 years is then $1 - \frac{1}{4} = \frac{3}{4}$. The probability that *n* atoms will remain after 2 years is

$$\left(\frac{1}{4}\right)^n \left(\frac{3}{4}\right)^{4-n} \frac{4!}{n!(4-n)!}$$

4. The results for problems 1, 2, and 3 are plotted in sketches (a), (b), and (c), respectively. Note that in (a) and (b) the curves between the points do not represent reality, since they show probabilities for fractional numbers of remaining atoms. They have been drawn only to help show how, with increasing numbers of atoms, the probability clusters more closely about the most probable

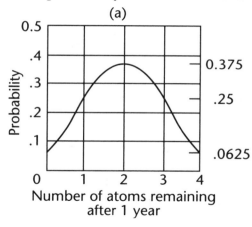

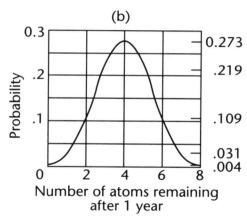

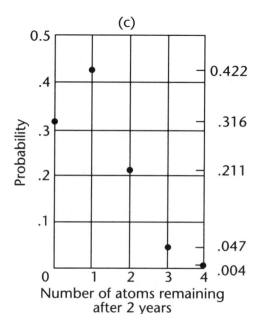

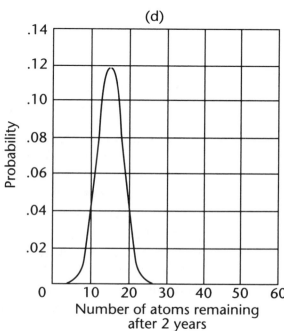

number of remaining atoms. A further example of this clustering is shown in sketch (d), which plots the probabilities after 2 years when the original number of atoms is 60. As expected, there is a sharp peak at 15, one-fourth of the original number; also the probabilities for remainders of less than 5 or greater than 25 are extremely small. But these numbers of atoms (4, 8, 60) are still unrealistically small. Even with the smallest weighable amount of material, the number of atoms is extremely large (about 10^{16}), and then essentially all of the probability is clustered so closely about the most probable remainder that the probability of a measurable deviation from this value is negligible.

Two Matching-Pennies Games

A game of chance. A has one penny and B has two pennies. They match pennies until one or the other has lost all his pennies. What is the probability that A wins both of B's pennies? We give two different ways of solving this problem:

Solution 1: Add the probabilities of all the ways that B can lose his two pennies:

B loses his first and then his second penny (B, B). Probability of B, B is $\frac{1}{2} \times \frac{1}{2} = \frac{1}{4}$.

B loses a penny, then A loses a penny, then B loses both his pennies. $P(B, A, B, B) = \frac{1}{2} \times \frac{1}{2} \times \frac{1}{2} \times \frac{1}{2} = \frac{1}{16}$.

B loses, then A loses, then B loses, then A loses, then B loses both his pennies. $P(B, A, B, A, B, B) = \frac{1}{2} \times \frac{1}{2} \times \frac{1}{2} \times \frac{1}{2} \times \frac{1}{2} \times \frac{1}{2} = \frac{1}{64}$.

Continuing in this way we have the infinite series.

$$P(\text{B loses}) = \frac{1}{4} + \frac{1}{16} + \frac{1}{64} + \ldots = \frac{1}{4}\left(1 + \frac{1}{4} + \frac{1}{16} + \ldots\right) = \frac{1}{4}\left(\frac{1}{1 - \frac{1}{4}}\right) = \frac{1}{3}.$$

Thus the probability that A wins both B's pennies is $\frac{1}{3}$ and the probability that B wins A's penny is $\frac{2}{3}$.

Solution 2: Consider that the pot consists of the three pennies (one from A, two from B). Since matching pennies is a fair game, we expect that A will, on the average, win back his penny, and that B will, on the average, win back his two pennies. Then the probability that A wins the pot is $\frac{1}{3}$ (since $\frac{1}{3} \times 3$ pennies = 1 penny) and the probability that B wins the pot is $\frac{2}{3}$ (since $\frac{2}{3} \times 3$ pennies = 2 pennies). If the numbers of pennies are large, the first method requires a long and involved calculation, while the second method is simple. For example, if A has 5 pennies and B has 7 pennies, the second method tells immediately that A's chance of winning is $\frac{5}{5+7} = \frac{5}{12}$, while B's chance of winning is $\frac{5}{5+7} = \frac{7}{12}$. Be sure that you understand this reasoning: The game is based on matching pennies so it is basically fair; then, on the average, each player wins back his stake.

Chance plus strategy. A and B play the following game: Each places a penny on the table, with the head or tail up according as he wishes (that is, the players do not flip their pennies), but he keeps his hand over it so that his opponent does not see it. Then they uncover the pennies and compare them, and one player pays the other according to the following table:

1 head and 1 tail	B pays A 2 pennies
2 heads	A pays B 3 pennies
2 tails	A pays B 1 penny

Problem:
Is the game fair?

For each player we multiply the probability of winning by the amount that he gets if he wins, and subtract the probability of losing multiplied by the amount that he pays when he loses. The result is the average amount that he wins on each play. We consider several cases, as follows:

1. Suppose that each player plays head or tail at random, just as if he flipped his penny. Then A wins, on the average,

$$P(H, T) \times 2 - P(H, H) \times 3 - P(T, T) \times 1 = \frac{1}{2} \times 2 - \frac{1}{4} \times 3 - \frac{1}{4} \times 1 = 0$$

    For B we simply reverse the signs. Obviously, B also wins 0 on the average. Thus far, then, the game seems fair.
2. If A plays head or tail purely at random, while B has studied his chances, B will always play head. Then B can expect to win, on the average,

$$P(H, H) \times 3 - P(H, T) \times 2 = \frac{1}{2} \times 3 - \frac{1}{2} \times 2 = \frac{1}{2} \text{ penny per game}$$

    (Note that P(H,H) is 1/2, not the usual 1/4, because B always plays head so that the only uncertainty concerns A's penny, for which the probability of head is 1/2. Similarly for P(H,T).)

    Presumably, A will eventually perceive that B is always playing head, and then he will always play tail. A will then win 2 pennies per game until B realizes that his strategy has been discovered.
3. If B plays head or tail purely at random, while A plays only tail, A will win, on the average,

$$P(H, T) \times 2 - P(T, T) \times 1 = \frac{1}{2} \times 2 - \frac{1}{2} \times 1 = \frac{1}{2} \text{ penny per game}$$

Presumably, B will eventually perceive that A is always playing tail, and then will also always play tail. B will then win 1 penny with every game, until A realizes that his strategy has been discovered.

Thus far, our discussion has not shown either A or B to have a very clear advantage. Nevertheless, A has a definite advantage, although not a very big one. For suppose A plays head 1/3 of the time and tail 2/3 of the time, randomly distributed so that B cannot predict which one he will play. Then if B always plays head, A wins, on the average,

$$P(H_B, T_A) \times 2 - P(H_B, H_A) \times 3 = \left(1 \times \frac{2}{3}\right) \times 2 - \left(1 \times \frac{1}{3}\right) \times 3 = \frac{1}{3} \text{ penny per game,}$$

if B always plays tail, A's average win is

$$P(H, T) \times 2 - P(T, T) \times 1 = P(H_A, T_B) \times 2 - P(T_A, T_B) \times 1$$

$$= \left(\frac{1}{3} \times 1\right) \times 2 - \left(\frac{2}{3} \times 1\right) \times 1 = 0$$

and if B plays head or tail with equal probabilities, A's average win is

$$P(H, T) \times 2 - P(H, H) \times 3 - P(T, T) \times 1$$

$$= [P(H_A, T_B) + P(T_A, H_B)] \times 2 - P(H_A, H_B) \times 3 - P(T_A, T_B) \times 1$$

$$= \left(\frac{1}{3} \times \frac{1}{2} + \frac{2}{3} \times \frac{1}{2}\right) \times 2 - \left(\frac{1}{3} \times \frac{1}{2}\right) \times 3 - \left(\frac{2}{3} \times \frac{1}{2}\right) \times 1 = \frac{1}{6}$$

which is the average of 1/3 and 0, as was to be expected.

If B is aware of A's method and always plays tail in order to keep A's average win at 0, A will recognize the strategy and play head oftener. Thus, no matter how B plays he cannot make A's average win less than 0. Of course, if, when B is playing only tail, he recognizes when A has started to play head oftener, he may play head occasionally in order to get A off balance. The game then becomes a battle of wits in which, however, A has essentially the better position.

Furthermore, if A wishes to avoid such a confused battle of wits, he can change his strategy to playing head 3/8 of the time and tail 5/8 of the time. Then if B always plays head, A's average win is

$$\frac{5}{8} \times 2 - \frac{3}{8} \times 3 = \frac{1}{8};$$

and if B always plays tail, A's average win is

$$\frac{3}{8} \times 2 - \frac{5}{8} \times 1 = \frac{1}{8}$$

In this way, whether B plays only head, only tail, or any mix of the two, A's average win is 1/8 penny per game.

Is It Prior or Posterior Probability?

Problem:
At a certain traffic circle the traffic is so congested and confused that one's chance of having an accident while driving through it is 0.01. One day a man has a collision while driving through the circle and dents a fender. The chance of having an accident there on two successive days is 0.01 × 0.01 = 0.0001. Accordingly, when he drives through the circle on the following day he feels more confident than

usual because of this small probability of having two accidents in a row. Is his increased confidence justified?

The value 0.0001 is the *prior* probability of having an accident on each of two given days. But after he has already had an accident, the probability of that accident is not 0.01, it is 1 (that is, it is a fact). The combined probability of that accident and another on the following day is then $1 \times 0.01 = 0.01$. In other words, the probability of a future accident is not affected by the past accident (unless, for example, the past accident induces the driver to be more careful).

Many additional interesting probability problems can be found in textbooks on probability or on high-school or college algebra.

Inference: What Is the Probability That That Is How It Was (or Is)?

Method. I tell you that I threw 10 with a pair of dice. What is the probability that I threw two 5's?

A 10 can be obtained in three equally likely ways: 5 and 5, 6 and 4, 4 and 6. Then, since they are equally likely, the probability of each is 1/3; in particular the probability of 5 and 5 is 1/3.

As a step toward the next problem, we shall do this problem slightly differently by considering the initial probabilities of throwing a 10:

$$P(5, 5) = P(6, 4) = P(4, 6) = \frac{1}{36}$$

Then, knowing that 10 has been thrown, we write

$$P(5, 5) = \frac{P(10 \text{ via } 5,5)}{\text{Total } P(10)} = \frac{P(10 \text{ via } 5,5)}{P(10 \text{ via } 5,5) + P(10 \text{ via } 6,4) + P(10 \text{ via } 4,6)}$$

$$P(5, 5) = \frac{\frac{1}{36}}{\frac{1}{36} + \frac{1}{36} + \frac{1}{36}} = \frac{1}{3}$$

In the next problem we consider not only the initial probabilities of certain results but also the probabilities that these results can lead to a particular subsequent event.

Problem:
There is a box containing 6 white balls and 3 black balls. From this box I draw two balls at random and put them into a second box. You now reach into this second box and draw one ball, which turns out to be white. What is the probability that both balls in this box were white?

The *initial* probability that I put two white balls into the box is $P_1(w, w) = \frac{6}{9} \times \frac{5}{8} = \frac{5}{12}$. The initial probability that I put in one white ball and one black ball is $P_1(w, b) = \frac{6}{9} \times \frac{3}{8} \times 2 = \frac{1}{2}$. The initial probability that I put in two black balls need not be considered, because we know that the box contained at least one white ball.

Let $P_2(w, w)$ be the inferred probability of two white balls *after* you drew out a white ball. Then

$$P_2(w, w) = \frac{P(w \text{ via } w,w)}{\text{Total } P(w)}$$

$$= \frac{P(w \text{ via } w,w)}{P(w \text{ via } w,w) + P(w \text{ via } w,b)}$$

$$= \frac{P_1(w,w) \times P(w \text{ from } w,w)}{P_1(w,w) \times P(w \text{ from } w,w) + P_1(w,b) \times P(w \text{ from } w,b)}$$

$$= \frac{\frac{5}{12} \times 1}{\frac{5}{12} \times 1 + \frac{1}{2} \times \frac{1}{2}} = \frac{\frac{5}{12}}{\frac{5}{12} + \frac{1}{4}} = \frac{5}{8}$$

Thus, on the basis of the evidence—that you drew a white ball from the box—the probability that the box contained two white balls has increased from $\frac{5}{12}$ to $\frac{5}{8}$.

Problem:
In the preceding experiment, after you draw the white ball you return it to the second box, shake the box, and again draw a ball, which again turns out to be white. Now that you have drawn a white ball twice, what is the probability that both balls in the box were white?

$$P_2(w, w) = \frac{P(\text{drawing } w \text{ twice via } w,w)}{\text{Total } P(\text{drawing } w \text{ twice})}$$

$$= \frac{P(\text{drawing } w \text{ twice via } w,w)}{P\left(\begin{array}{c}\text{drawing } w \\ \text{twice via } w,w\end{array}\right) + P\left(\begin{array}{c}\text{drawing } w \\ \text{twice via } w,b\end{array}\right)}$$

$$= \frac{\frac{5}{12} \times (1 \times 1)}{\frac{5}{12} \times (1 \times 1) + \frac{1}{2} \times \left(\frac{1}{2} \times \frac{1}{2}\right)} = \frac{\frac{5}{12}}{\frac{5}{12} + \frac{1}{8}} = \frac{10}{13}$$

Thus, after you have repeated the experiment and got the same result, the probability that both balls are white is increased from $\frac{5}{8} = 0.625$ to $\frac{10}{13} = 0.769$. The greater the number of times you repeat the experiment and get the same result (that is, draw a white ball), the greater is the probability that both balls are white. However, if one of the draws yields a black ball, the probability drops to zero.

Initial probability unknown. In the preceding problem we started with an initial value for the probability of w, w, and we gradually changed the value as the experimental results were received—the value was initially 5/12 but after two experiments it had increased to 10/13. In certain related types of problems an initial value for the probability is simply an estimate based vaguely on experience, or perhaps a pure guess based on nothing more than desires or prejudices. Following is an example:

While you are riding in a train or airplane, the person beside you offers to help pass the time by betting small amounts on the toss of a coin (his coin). Such betting is fair, with 1-to-1 odds, and the game involves no skill, so you agree. It is always possible, however, that the person is a cheat whose coin looks the same on both sides; however, he seems honest and aboveboard, so you guess that the probability of such knavery is small—say, 1/10. However, after the first five tosses you realize that he has bet on head all five times and that head has come up all five times. You now make a new estimate of the probability that he is tossing a two-headed coin.

For this new estimate you must first start with your earlier estimate that the probability is 1/10 (and the probability that the coin is normal is 9/10).

$$P_2(\text{2-headed coin}) = \frac{P_1(\text{5 heads via a 2-headed coin})}{\text{Total P(5 heads)}}$$

$$= \frac{P_1(\text{2-headed coin}) \times P(\text{5 heads if a 2-headed coin})}{P_1(\text{2-headed coin}) \times P\left(\begin{array}{c}\text{5 heads if a}\\\text{2-headed coin}\end{array}\right) + P_1(\text{normal coin}) \times P\left(\begin{array}{c}\text{5 heads if a}\\\text{normal coin}\end{array}\right)}$$

$$= \frac{\frac{1}{10} \times 1}{\frac{1}{10} \times 1 + \frac{9}{10} \times \left(\frac{1}{2}\right)^5} = \frac{\frac{1}{10}}{\frac{1}{10} + \frac{9}{320}} = \frac{32}{41}$$

Thus, your estimate of the probability that your fellow passenger is dishonest has increased from $\frac{1}{10}$ to $\frac{32}{41}$. But note that in order to make this calculation you had to use your original estimates, namely, $P_1(\text{he is dishonest}) = \frac{1}{10}$, and $P_1(\text{he is honest}) = \frac{9}{10}$. If you were a very trusting person, these probabilities would have been different, say $\frac{1}{100}$ and $\frac{99}{100}$, respectively; and the revised estimate after five heads would be $\frac{32}{131}$. On the other hand, if you were a more suspicious person, your initial estimates of the probabilities might have been, say $\frac{1}{3}$ and $\frac{2}{3}$, respectively; and the revised estimate of his dishonesty would then be $\frac{16}{17}$. (Derive this value and the preceding value of $\frac{32}{131}$.) Thus, your own judgment determines not only your initial estimates but also, indirectly, your revised estimates.

But note also that if you were a completely trusting person, with complete faith in everyone's honesty, your first estimate of your fellow passenger's dishonesty would be simply zero; and then, according to our formula, it would remain zero thereafter, regardless of the evidence. Like Job's faith, your trust would remain unshaken, for you are a completely trusting person.

After you have digested this result, consider the following related paradox: We are fond of saying that in our legal system a person is presumed to be innocent until proven guilty. But if everyone were presumed innocent (P_1(guilt) = 0), no amount of evidence could prove him otherwise; that is, P_2(guilt) = 0 regardless of evidence. Indeed, no one would ever be suspected or arrested in the first place. Any evidence of guilt would have to be shrugged off as merely an interesting coincidence; and keeping a "suspect" in jail or making him post bond would have to be considered as outrageous treatment of a presumably innocent person. Or, to state the matter in terms of our earlier discussion, if the law insists that the first estimate of the probability of guilt must be zero, all subsequent estimates must also be zero.

The method of analysis used in deriving this paradox is the same as that used in the earlier problem concerning the black and white balls; however, mathematical justification for applying the method is somewhat elusive when the initial value of probability is a guess (or, as in the preceding paragraph, prescribed by law). As far as it goes, it gives answers that are reasonable—the trusting person needs a great deal of evidence before he loses his trust, while the suspicious person needs very little evidence in order to feel that his suspicions are confirmed. But how these persons feel may not be relevant; what is needed is an objective method of calculating the probability that the coin is 2-headed or that the suspect is guilty. A method of evaluating probability that is based on an initial guess cannot yield a usable result, and many mathematicians refuse to have anything to do with the method.

The prisoner's paradox. The jail contains three prisoners, A, B, and C, but in order to reduce crowding the town council has decided to parole two of them. The warden knows which two have been selected but he may not tell them until the following week. Until then, each prisoner must be content with knowing that the probability of his release is 2/3.

Prisoner A, however, is impatient and begs the warden to tell him, at least, the name of one of the others who will be released. But then he is horrified when he calculates that this information will reduce his chance of being released from 2/3 to 1/2. Thus, suppose the warden tells him that B is to be released. Then along with B, either A or C will be released, with equal probabilities, so that A's probability of being released is reduced to 1/2. The result is the same if the warden tells him that C is to be released. Since the warden would say either B or C, A cannot now avoid the reduced probability. Yet A's situation would not change in any way if the warden tells him that, say, B will be released.

Problem:
Explain the paradox.

It is true that if, say, the warden says B, then the two prisoners to be released will be either A and B or C and B. But if A and B are the lucky pair, the warden *must* say B, since he may not say A; while if B and C are the lucky pair, the warden will say either B or C, with probability 1/2 for each. Accordingly, when the warden says B, it is twice as likely that A will go with him as that C will go with him:

$$P_2(\text{A will be released}) = \frac{P\left(\begin{array}{c}\text{warden says B because}\\ \text{A and B will be released}\end{array}\right)}{P(\text{warden says B})}$$

$$= \frac{P_1(\text{A and B will be released}) \times P(\text{warden says B})}{P_1\left(\begin{array}{c}\text{A and B will}\\ \text{be released}\end{array}\right) \times P(\text{warden says B}) + P_1\left(\begin{array}{c}\text{C and B will}\\ \text{be released}\end{array}\right) \times P\left(\begin{array}{c}\text{warden}\\ \text{says B}\end{array}\right)}$$

$$= \frac{\frac{1}{3} \times 1}{\frac{1}{3} \times 1 + \frac{1}{3} \times \frac{1}{2}} = \frac{2}{3}$$

Thus, if the warden says B (or if he says C), the probability that A will also be released is still 2/3.

Problem:
In response to A's request, the warden says B; the next day, having forgotten that he already answered A's request, he again mentions B. What is now the probability that A will be released?

The probability is now increased from 2/3 to 4/5 (refer to the second problem).

The paradox of the two aces. The four kings and four aces are taken from a deck of cards and shuffled; and from these eight cards someone draws two cards. What is the probability that both cards are aces?

$$P(\text{2 aces}) = \frac{4}{8} \times \frac{3}{7} = \frac{3}{14}$$

Problem:
The person is asked "Do you have an ace?" and he says "Yes." What is the probability that he has two aces?

The prior probability of two aces is 3/14, as just shown; the prior probability of one ace and one king is $\frac{4}{8} \times \frac{4}{7} \times 2 = \frac{4}{7}$; the prior probability of two kings need not be considered, because we know that he has at least one ace. Then

$$P_2(2 \text{ aces}) = \frac{P(1 \text{ ace via 2 aces})}{\text{Total P(1 ace)}} = \frac{\frac{3}{14}}{\frac{3}{14} + \frac{4}{7}} = \frac{3}{11}$$

Paradox: But suppose the person is asked to name the ace, and he says "I have the ace of spades." What is now the probability that he has two aces? One might reason as follows: The prior probability of having the ace of spades and one other ace is $\frac{1}{8} \times \frac{3}{7} \times 2 = \frac{3}{28}$. The prior probability of having the ace of spades and a king is $\frac{1}{8} \times \frac{4}{7} \times 2 = \frac{1}{7}$. Then

$$P(\text{ace of spades and another ace}) = \frac{\frac{3}{28}}{\frac{3}{28} + \frac{1}{7}} = \frac{3}{7}$$

But how can simply naming the ace change the probability of having two aces from 3/11 to 3/7? This calculation, in fact, is wrong for a reason similar to that discussed in the previous paradox: Again, we must use the fact that he *said* "I have the ace of spades." If he has only the one ace, he *must* say this; but if he has two aces, he could name either, with probability of 1/2 for each. Then

$$P_2(2 \text{ aces}) = \frac{P(\text{He says "ace of spades" if 2 aces})}{\text{Total P(He says "ace of spades")}}$$

$$= \frac{P_1(2 \text{ aces, including ace of spades}) \times P(\text{He says "ace of spades"})}{P_1\left(\begin{array}{c}2 \text{ aces, including} \\ \text{ace of spades}\end{array}\right) \times P\left(\begin{array}{c}\text{He says} \\ \text{"ace of spades"}\end{array}\right) + P_1\left(\begin{array}{c}\text{ace of spades} \\ \text{and a king}\end{array}\right) \times P\left(\begin{array}{c}\text{He says} \\ \text{"ace of spades"}\end{array}\right)}$$

$$= \frac{\frac{3}{28} \times \frac{1}{2}}{\frac{3}{28} \times \frac{1}{2} + \frac{1}{7} \times 1} = \frac{3}{11}$$

which agrees with the answer previously derived. Thus, naming the ace does not change the probability that he has two aces.

We may help to clarify this inference problem by using the list on the next page of the 28 equally likely pairs. The four aces are designated a_1, a_2, a_3, and a_4; and the four kings are similarly designated k_1, k_2, k_3, and k_4. The left-hand column lists the six possible pairs of aces and the six possible pairs of kings; the right-hand column lists the 16 possible pairs containing one king and one ace.

The prior probability of two aces is 6/28 = 3/14, of two kings is 6/28 = 3/14, of one king and one ace is 16/28 = 4/7. After we learn that the pair includes at least one ace, we may eliminate the six pairs of kings, leaving 6 + 16 = 22 pairs. The probability of two aces is now 6/22 = 3/11, as previously derived, while the probability of one ace and one king is 16/22 = 8/11.

The paradox arises as follows: If the ace is identified as, say, a_1, we examine the list and find that a_1 is in three of the pairs of aces and in four of the pairs that contain one ace and one king. Is the probability of two aces now 3/(3 + 4) = 3/7? We return to the earlier reasoning and write

a_1a_2	a_1k_1
a_1a_3	a_1k_2
a_1a_4	a_1k_3
a_2a_3	a_1k_4
a_2a_4	a_2k_1
a_3a_4	a_2k_2
	a_2k_3
k_1k_2	a_2k_4
k_1k_3	a_3k_1
k_1k_4	a_3k_2
k_2k_3	a_3k_3
k_2k_4	a_3k_4
k_3k_4	a_4k_1
	a_4k_2
	a_4k_3
	a_4k_4

P(pair of a's if he says a_1)

$$= \frac{\text{No. of } a_1a_n \text{ pairs} \times P(\text{he says } a_1)}{\text{No. of } a_1a_n \text{ pairs} \times P(\text{he says } a_1) + \text{no. of } a_1k_n \text{ pairs} \times P(\text{he says } a_1)}$$

$$= \frac{3 \times \frac{1}{2}}{3 \times \frac{1}{2} + 4 \times 1} = \frac{3}{11}$$

Problem:
(This problem appeared recently under "Ask Marilyn" in Parade magazine.) In a game show, the host shows three doors and states that the prize, a new car, is behind one of the doors, while goats are behind the others. The contestant must correctly guess which door hides the car.

The contestant guesses, say, door 1. His probability of being correct is, of course, 1/3. The host does not immediately open door 1, however; instead he opens door 3, showing a goat, and asks the contestant whether he would care to change his selection to door 2. Have the relative probabilities for doors 1 and 2 changed?

Answer:
We argue as follows: If the car is behind door 1, the host may open either door 2 or door 3, so the probability that he opens door 3 is 1/2. But if the car is behind door 2, the host *must* open door 3, so the probability that he opens door 3 is then 1.

$$P(\text{door 1}) = \frac{P(\text{host opens 3 if the car is behind 1})}{P\left(\begin{array}{c}\text{host opens 3 if} \\ \text{the car is behind 1}\end{array}\right) + P\left(\begin{array}{c}\text{host opens 3 if} \\ \text{the car is behind 2}\end{array}\right)}$$

$$= \frac{\frac{1}{2}}{\frac{1}{2} + 1} = \frac{1}{3}$$

$$P(\text{door 2}) = \frac{P(\text{host opens 3 if the car is behind 2})}{P\left(\begin{array}{c}\text{host opens 3 if}\\ \text{the car is behind 1}\end{array}\right) + P\left(\begin{array}{c}\text{host opens 3 if}\\ \text{the car is behind 2}\end{array}\right)}$$

$$= \frac{1}{\frac{1}{2}+1} = \frac{2}{3}$$

The contestant should change to door 2, which now is twice as likely to hide the car as door 1.

Laws of Heredity

Mendel's laws. Gregor Johann Mendel (1822—1884) was a monk in the Augustinian monastery of Brunn, Moravia (now Brno, Czechoslovakia), and taught science at the local technical high school until he was elected abbott of the monastery in 1868. In 1865 he reported the results of his research to the local scientific society, which published the work in its Transactions in 1866. The value of the research remained unrecognized until after similar research was done, about 1900, by three scientists who then found it while searching the previous scientific literature.

He studied heredity in the garden pea, in which he identified seven pairs of alternative hereditary traits: plant height, colors of the blossom and of the leaf axil, seed color, seed shape, position of the flower on its stem, and form of the pod. For all of these, inheritance follows the same rules. Here, to be specific, we shall discuss plant height, and shall describe the plant as either tall (about 1-1/2 meters tall) or dwarf (about 1/2 meter tall).

The experiments began with crossbreeding, or hybridizing, tall plants with short plants, both originally purebred. Crossbreeding consists, in this case, of:

1. Removing the anthers (which hold the pollen) from the flowers of, say, the dwarf plants.
2. Collecting the pollen from the anthers of the flowers of the tall plants.
3. Applying the tall-plant pollen to the stigmas of the flowers of the dwarf plants.

The anthers and stigma of a flower are shown in the sketch. They are easily recognized in trumpet-shaped flowers (petunia, morning glory, honeysuckle, azalea) or in bell-shaped flowers (tulip, daffodil). One might also observe in these flowers that the stigma is covered with a sticky substance. Its purpose is to hold any pollen grain that falls on the stigma and to provide nutrient for subsequent growth of the grain. The captured pollen grain, from which the sperm develops, sends a fine tube down the style to the ovary, where, eventually, the sperm fertilizes the egg in the ovule. A viable seed then develops. The seeds (peas in Mendel's experiment) of the hybrid contain both tallness (from the "father") and dwarfness (from the "mother").

Mendel found that the hybrid plants that grow from these seeds are not of intermediate height, but are all tall, like their fathers. If the pollen from the dwarf plants is applied to the stigmas of the tall plants, the result is the same—all the hybrid plants are tall. Mendel referred to tallness as a dominant trait, and to dwarfness as a recessive trait: If both parents are tall or dwarf, the plant will be tall or dwarf, respectively; but if the seed contains tallness from one parent and dwarfness from the other parent, the plant will be tall.

Now consider what will be observed when the seeds from the hybrid plants are sown and grow into plants the following year. Every cell in the main part of the hybrid plant contains the two characters, tallness and dwarfness. The reproductive cells, however,—the pollen and the ovule—are different. The sperm from a pollen grain that finally combines with an egg from an ovule to start a new seed contains either tallness or dwarfness, but not both; and similarly for the egg. The probability of tallness (T) in either a sperm or an egg is 1/2, and the probability of dwarfness (D) in either a sperm or an egg is $\frac{1}{2}$. Thus, P(T) = P(D) = $\frac{1}{2}$.

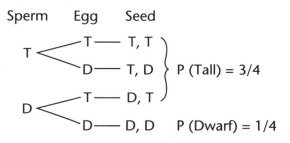

We can set up the tree diagram above for the seed that results from the combination.

Three-fourths of the seeds, on the average, contain tallness, and the plants grown from them will be tall; one-fourth contain only dwarfness and the plants grown from them will be dwarf. This result is precisely what Mendel found. In the second generation, after his original crossing, 3/4 of the plants were tall and 1/4 of the plants were dwarf.

Problem:
From this field of second-generation pea plants, we select a tall plant. What is the probability that it is purebred tall and what is the probability that it is hybrid?

In the preceding tree diagram there are three equally likely cases in which the plant is tall. Only one of them is T, T, and the other two are T, D, or D, T. Thus, P (purebred tall) = $\frac{1}{3}$ and P (hybrid) = $\frac{2}{3}$.

Stated differently, the odds against selecting a purebred-tall plant are 2 to 1.

Problem:
I plant one pea from the tall plant that we selected in the preceding problem (after isolating the plant to assure that it pollinates itself when it blooms). What is the probability that the plant which grows from it will be tall?

The desired probability is the sum of two probabilities, each of which can be expressed as a product:

1. (Probability that the tall plant from which the pea was taken was purebred tall) × (Probability that the pea from such a plant contains tallness) = $\frac{1}{3} \times 1 = \frac{1}{3}$.
2. (Probability that the tall plant from which the pea was taken was hybrid) × (Probability that the pea from such a plant contains tallness (see the tree diagram on the previous page)) = $\frac{2}{3} \times \frac{3}{4} = \frac{1}{2}$.

The total probability that our plant will be tall is then $\frac{1}{3} + \frac{1}{2} = \frac{5}{6}$.

Problem:
Suppose that the plant that grows from this pea actually turns out to be tall. What is the probability that the parent plant (and, of course, the pea) was purebred tall?

This is an inference problem.

$$P_2 \text{ (parent was purebred tall)} = \frac{P_1 \left(\begin{array}{c}\text{parent was} \\ \text{purebred tall}\end{array}\right) \times P\left(\begin{array}{c}\text{tall plant via} \\ \text{purebred tall parent}\end{array}\right)}{\left[\begin{array}{c} P_1\left(\begin{array}{c}\text{parent was} \\ \text{purebred tall}\end{array}\right) \times P\left(\begin{array}{c}\text{tall plant via} \\ \text{purebred tall parent}\end{array}\right) + \\ P_1\left(\begin{array}{c}\text{parent was} \\ \text{hybrid}\end{array}\right) \times P\left(\begin{array}{c}\text{tall plant via} \\ \text{hybrid parent}\end{array}\right) \end{array}\right]}$$

$$= \frac{\frac{1}{3} \times 1}{\frac{1}{3} \times 1 + \frac{2}{3} \times \frac{3}{4}} = \frac{\frac{1}{3}}{\frac{1}{3} + \frac{1}{2}} = \frac{2}{5} = 0.40$$

Thus, the fact that the pea produced a tall plant has increased the probability that the parent was purebred tall from 1/3 to 2/5.

Problem:
Suppose that we had planted three peas from the same parent plant and that all three produced tall plants. What is now the probability that the parent plant was purebred tall?

$$P_2 \text{(parent was purebred tall)} = \frac{P_1\left(\begin{array}{c}\text{parent was}\\\text{purebred tall}\end{array}\right) \times P\left(\begin{array}{c}\text{3 tall plants via}\\\text{purebred tall parent}\end{array}\right)}{\left[\begin{array}{c}P_1\left(\begin{array}{c}\text{parent was}\\\text{purebred tall}\end{array}\right) \times P\left(\begin{array}{c}\text{3 tall plants via}\\\text{purebred tall parent}\end{array}\right) + \\ P_1\left(\begin{array}{c}\text{parent was}\\\text{hybrid}\end{array}\right) \times P\left(\begin{array}{c}\text{3 tall plants via}\\\text{hybrid parent}\end{array}\right)\end{array}\right]}$$

$$= \frac{\frac{1}{3} \times (1 \times 1 \times 1)}{\frac{1}{3} \times (1 \times 1 \times 1) + \frac{2}{3} \times \left(\frac{3}{4} \times \frac{3}{4} \times \frac{3}{4}\right)} = \frac{\frac{1}{3}}{\frac{1}{3} + \frac{9}{32}} = \frac{32}{59} = 0.54$$

Comparison with the preceding result shows that the more tall plants we grow in this generation, the greater is the probability that their parent was purebred tall. If even a single dwarf plant appears, however, the probability that the parent was purebred tall immediately drops to zero.

Chromosomes and genes. This section will briefly review the basis for Mendelian heredity and for the inheritance of so-called sex-linked characteristics. This division of biological science has undergone wonderful development during this century, but what we give here is intended only to provide the information needed for understanding the problems.

In the nucleus of every cell (except a reproductive cell (or germ cell)) are a certain number of pairs of chromosomes, indicated in the sketches below by short lines. The number of chromosome pairs in cells is characteristic of the species. In man there are 23 pairs. The chromosomes are extremely long molecules, and various groups of atoms along them, known as genes, are responsible for various physical characteristics of the organism. For example, in every cell of a pea plant, the genes for tallness or dwarfness occur at a certain location along both chromosomes of some particular pair. If at least one of these genes is for tallness, the plant will be tall; otherwise it will be dwarf.

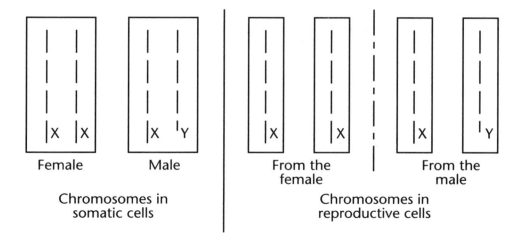

Female   Male   From the female   From the male

Chromosomes in somatic cells   Chromosomes in reproductive cells

The sex of the organism is determined by a particular pair of chromosomes, indicated as the bottom chromosomes in the sketches and labeled X or Y. If both are X chromosomes the organism is female; if one is X and the other is Y, it is male. The comparatively short Y chromosome contains relatively few genes.

The reproductive cells (or germ cells)—the sperm cell and unfertilized eggs—contain only one set of the chromosomes, as indicated in the sketches. The unfertilized egg, contributed by the female, always contains an X chromosome. The sperm cell, contributed by the male, contains an X chromosome or a Y chromosome, with equal probabilities, $P(X) = P(Y) = \frac{1}{2}$. If the sperm that enters the egg contains an X chromosome, the fertilized egg will then contain a pair of X chromosomes and will hence develop into a female; but if the sperm contains a Y chromosome, the fertilized egg will then contain one X and one Y chromosome and will hence develop into a male.

Certain genes are located in the X chromosome, and since the cells of a male contain only one X chromosome, inheritance of the corresponding traits does not quite follow the rules of Mendelian heredity. In particular, if a recessive trait is contained in a male's single X chromosome, the male will exhibit that trait because there is no opposing X chromosome to contain the corresponding dominant trait. The female, however, has two X chromosomes and hence would have to carry the genes for the recessive trait in both of them in order to exhibit the trait. Red-green color blindness, double thumbs, and hemophilia (excessive, long-continuing bleeding from even slight cuts) are three examples of such sex-linked characteristics.

Problem:
On the basis of the foregoing review, discuss the inheritance of red-green color blindness from a man who is color-blind and his wife who does not carry the trait, continuing as far as the grandchildren.

If the father is color-blind, he carries the trait (the color-blindness gene) in his X chromosome and therefore transmits it to his daughters. The daughters, however, also get an X chromosome from the mother, and since that one does not contain the gene, the daughters are not color-blind. The sons do not get the father's X chromosome; they get only the father's Y chromosome along with the mother's X chromosome. Thus, the sons are not color-blind and do not carry the trait; the daughters are not color-blind but each carries the trait in one of her two X chromosomes.

If a daughter marries a man with normal vision, each of her daughters (the granddaughters of the original source) gets a normal-vision gene from the father's X chromosome, along with an X chromosome from her mother, which has a probability of 1/2 of containing the color-blindness gene. On the average, then, half of these granddaughters carry the trait, and the other half do not. None of them is color-blind.

Each of the daughter's sons (the grandsons of the original source) gets a Y chromosome from his father, along with an X chromosome from his mother, which has a probability of 1/2 of containing the color-blindness gene. On the average, then, half of these grandsons are color blind.

But suppose that the daughter marries a man who is color-blind. Then each of her daughters (the granddaughters) has the color-blindness gene in the X chromosomes obtained from her father, and also has an X chromosome from her mother that has a probability of 1/2 of containing the color-blindness gene. Accordingly, on the average, half of these granddaughters have the gene in both chromosomes and will be color-blind; the other half have the gene in only one chromosome and, although not color-blind, will carry the trait, so in this respect they will be like their mother.

The sons (the grandsons) are not affected by the fact that their father is color blind, because they do not receive his X chromosome. However, since half of their mother's X chromosomes carry the color-blindness gene, each son's probability of being color-blind is 1/2.

Problem:
In the case discussed four paragraphs back, we found that each granddaughter had a probability of 1/2 of being a carrier. Suppose that a granddaughter marries a man with normal vision and they have a son. What is the probability that the son is color-blind?

$$P\left(\begin{array}{c}\text{Son is}\\\text{color-blind}\end{array}\right) = P\left(\begin{array}{c}\text{She is a}\\\text{carrier}\end{array}\right) \times P\left(\begin{array}{c}\text{Son is color-blind}\\\text{if she is a carrier}\end{array}\right)$$

$$= \frac{1}{2} \times \frac{1}{2} = \frac{1}{4}$$

Inference problem:
When the boy is old enough to be tested, he turns out not to be color- blind. That fact does not prove that his mother is not a carrier since even if she is a carrier his probability of being color-blind is only 1/2.   But the fact that he is not color-blind does reduce the probability that she is a carrier. What is the revised probability?

$$P_2(\text{Mother is a carrier}) = \frac{P\left(\begin{array}{c}\text{Son is not color-blind, via}\\\text{a mother who is a carrier}\end{array}\right)}{\text{Total } P\left(\begin{array}{c}\text{Son would not be}\\\text{color-blind}\end{array}\right)}$$

$$= \frac{P_1\left(\begin{array}{c}\text{Mother is}\\\text{a carrier}\end{array}\right) \times P\left(\begin{array}{c}\text{Son is not color-blind}\\\text{if mother is a carrier}\end{array}\right)}{P_1\left(\begin{array}{c}\text{Mother is}\\\text{a carrier}\end{array}\right) \times P\left(\begin{array}{c}\text{Son is not}\\\text{color-blind}\\\text{if mother is}\\\text{a carrier}\end{array}\right) + P_1\left(\begin{array}{c}\text{Mother is not}\\\text{a carrier}\end{array}\right) \times P\left(\begin{array}{c}\text{Son is not color-}\\\text{blind if mother is}\\\text{not a carrier}\end{array}\right)}$$

$$= \frac{\frac{1}{2} \times \frac{1}{2}}{\frac{1}{2} \times \frac{1}{2} + \frac{1}{2} \times 1} = \frac{\frac{1}{4}}{\frac{1}{4} + \frac{1}{2}} = \frac{1}{3}$$

Thus, our one piece of evidence has reduced the mother's probability of being a carrier from 1/2 to 1/3.

Problem:
Suppose that there are four more sons, making a total of five, and none of them is color-blind. What is now the probability that the mother is a carrier?

In the word equations of the preceding problem change "Son is not color-blind" to "Five sons are not color-blind." Then the numerical expression changes to

$$\frac{\frac{1}{2} \times \left(\frac{1}{2}\right)^5}{\frac{1}{2} \times \left(\frac{1}{2}\right)^5 + \frac{1}{2} \times 1} = \frac{\frac{1}{64}}{\frac{1}{64} + \frac{1}{2}} = \frac{1}{33}$$

Thus, after having five sons with normal vision, the mother's probability of being a carrier is reduced from 1/2 to 1/33. Furthermore, since the probability that a carrier's daughter is also a carrier is only 1/2, the probability that any particular daughter is a carrier is $\frac{1}{33} \times \frac{1}{2} = \frac{1}{66}$.

Probability May Depend on What You Know

How much do you already know about it? Different people may have different estimates of the probability of a particular event, depending on their knowledge of the matter. For example, when a shooter throws a pair of dice, the players may use the standard table (p. 104) to determine the probabilities of his getting the various numbers from 2 to 12; but if one of the players knows that the dice are loaded he will use a different set of probabilities.

Increased accuracy, however, need not imply dishonesty; it may result simply from deeper knowledge or understanding. For example, consider that someone has just arrived at a bus stop and wishes to estimate the probability that a bus will come within the next 10 minutes. He knows that the buses make a total of 48 round trips per day, so he calculates that the average time between buses is $\frac{24 \text{ hours}}{48} = \frac{1}{2}$ hour = 30 minutes. Accordingly, he considers that the probability is $\frac{10}{30} = \frac{1}{3}$ (sketch (a)). However, someone who has already been waiting at the bus stop for 10 minutes considers that the bus must come within the next 20 minutes, so his estimate of the probability is $\frac{10}{20} = \frac{1}{2}$ (sketch (b)). If someone else knows that the buses do not run at all between midnight and 6 a.m. he will calculate the average time between buses to be $\frac{18}{48} = \frac{3}{8}$ hr $= 22\frac{1}{2}$ min, and will then calculate a more accurate value for the probability. If someone else also knows that between 7 a.m. and 9 a.m. and between 4 p.m. and 6 p.m. the buses run three times as often as during the rest of the day, he will calculate a different, still more accurate value.

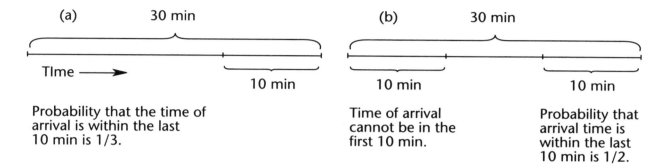

(a) 30 min

Time ⟶

10 min

Probability that the time of
arrival is within the last
10 min is 1/3.

(b) 30 min

10 min

Time of arrival
cannot be in the
first 10 min.

10 min

Probability that
arrival time is
within the last
10 min is 1/2.

Study the data. Suppose that a physician is studying a new treatment for a certain type of ailment. He finds that of 150 patients with this ailment, the treatment cured 120, so he considers that the probability of effecting a cure with this treatment is $\frac{120}{150} = \frac{4}{5}$.

But a more perceptive physician may notice that the treatment cured nearly all (say 95 out of 100, or $\frac{19}{20}$) of his light-skinned patients, but relatively fewer (say 25 out of 50, or $\frac{1}{2}$) of his dark-skinned patients. He then has two values for the probability—one for light-skinned people and one for dark-skinned people. But he might not yet be satisfied with this breakdown, important as it would be. He might want to know, for example, whether the different dark-skinned people from the different regions of the Earth—regions around the Mediterranean Sea, in Africa, in Asia, in America, in the far north—react differently to the treatment; and if so, whether the types of reactions are truly heritable or are related to diet or life style, which are matters of custom.

By such studies he may find several different values of the probability, depending on the kind of patient. Furthermore, such studies can lead to a clearer understanding of the scientific basis for the treatment.

Notes on Statistics

What fraction of the men who at age 25 appear to be healthy will still be alive at age 70? 71? 72? . . . 100? What fraction of 7th grade students can give an immediate answer to "11 × 12 = ?"? Statistics is the science of gathering the information needed to answer such questions, analyzing the information so as to reach plausible conclusions, and determining the probability that these conclusions are correct. (In spite of the final *s*, the word "statistics" is a singular noun, like the word "athletics;" however, a particular numerical item might be referred to as a statistic, and when used in that sense, "statistics" is a plural noun.) This interesting and challenging branch of science is somewhat beyond what we can usefully review here; our discussion will concern only a few relevant items, with emphasis on some pitfalls in the use of the numerical data.

How big must the numbers be? We have already given some examples of estimating probability by actually counting—namely the examples of the 2273 tacks and the 10000 flips of the coin. With such fairly large numbers of tests, we expect that the results give acceptable estimates of the probabilities. More precisely, suppose there are 20000 flips of a coin, from which, on the average, there should result 10000 heads. Take our measure of deviations as $\frac{1}{2}\sqrt{10000} = 50$. Then the probability is about 50% that the number of heads is between 9950 and 10050. The probability that the number of heads is between 9900 and 10100 is 0.774; between 9850 and 10150 is 0.930; between 9800 and 10200 is 0.985; and between 9750 and 10250 is 0.998.

With only 200 flips of the coin, there should be, on the average, 100 heads. Then, with $\frac{1}{2}\sqrt{100} = 5$, the probability is about 50% that the number of heads is between 95 and 105, 0.774 that it is between 90 and 100, and so on.

Unfortunately, the total number of trials is often quite small. For example, a physician would like to compare two different treatments for a certain ailment, but if he treats only about ten cases of this ailment per year, one treatment would have to be far superior to the other in order for him to be sure of its superiority after only a year or two. But even if a study involves quite large numbers it may nevertheless yield no conclusion. For example, a thousand residents of a town may be immunized against a certain disease in order to test the effectiveness of the immunization procedure. But even if none of them get the disease, if no one else in the town gets the disease either, nothing will have been learned. Incidentally, note how easily one might be misled by the enthusiastic statement "A thousand people were immunized and not a single one of them got the disease!"

How many fish in the lake? In order to determine, approximately, the number of fish in a lake, we might proceed as follows: By means of a seine, catch a fairly large number of fish, say, 200; tag them and throw them back into the lake. After several days—enough time for the tagged fish to mix themselves in among their fellows—again set out the seine and collect a fairly large number of fish, say 300. If 15 of these are found to be tagged, we conclude that about $\frac{15}{300} = \frac{1}{20}$ of the fish in the lake are tagged. Then the total number of fish in the lake is about $200 \times 20 = 4000$.

Can you think of any reason to question this method, other than that the samples are somewhat too small for good accuracy?

Suppose that the lake contains both trout and bass, but that the seine was spread around an area where the trout like to feed. Then both the initial catch of 200 and the final catch of 300 contained only trout, so that our experiment gave the number of trout in the lake but gave no information on the number of bass in the lake.

Suppose further that only the smaller trout feed in the place where the seine was spread, while the larger trout feed elsewhere in the lake. Then the experiment did not even give the entire trout population, but gave only the number of the smaller trout.

A fisherman or a marine scientist familiar with conditions in the lake could no doubt suggest other reasons why the experiment was faulty. But our brief discussion has already indicated how much prior knowledge and careful study must go into the design of a statistical experiment. Even costly and extensive statistical studies have been designed with so little insight that the final results yielded no believable conclusions, or only limited information. It is often desirable for an experimenter to consult a statistician while designing an experiment, but the experimenter must provide the statistician with information on all matters that he is aware of that might influence the result.

Where did they get those numbers? A physician wrote that jogging is "a dangerous fad" and that "The American Automobile Association reports that 8300 joggers in the U.S.A. have been killed by automobiles and over 100000 injured during 1977." But the American Automobile Association, when asked about these numbers, explained that the numbers did not refer specifically to joggers, but to all pedestrians; there were no separate data on joggers.

A New York publication carried the statement that there were 8 million rats in New York City. This statement was widely quoted, but someone soon changed the number to 9 million, which was then the approximate population of the city. The purpose of the change was apparently to enable people to say that there was a rat " for every man, woman, and child in the city," a favorite phrase of certain types of public speakers. When someone checked with the Health Department, which is the only organization that tries to ascertain such numbers, it turned out that they estimated the rat population to be 250000 at most.

An advertisement, seeking to point out excesses and absurdities of government regulations, stated that there was a regulation, using 26911 words, governing the sale of cabbages. This statement was also widely quoted, but when a reporter tried to find the regulation, he found that no such regulation had ever existed.

Questionnaires and polls—who gets them and who answers them? The Literary Digest was a respected weekly magazine, carrying national and international political news along with news items and articles in many other fields. It had developed a system for polling the public and used it from 1916 to 1936 to survey public opinion on various political questions, and also to predict the results of presidential elections, which it did correctly five successive times. In 1936, in an ambitious and costly undertaking it again tried to predict the outcome of the presidential election by means of a nationwide poll mailed out to 10 million voters. From the results of this poll the Literary Digest confidently predicted that the Republican candidate, Alfred M. Landon, would overhelm the Democratic candidate—the incumbent president, Franklin D. Roosevelt. Precisely the opposite happened—Landon carried only two states; the Digest had overestimated the percentage for Landon by 20 percent! Especially humiliating to the Digest was the fact that three other, far simpler, polls correctly predicted the Roosevelt victory.

In retrospect, the reasons for the misleading result of the poll were fairly clear:

1. The 10 million voters to whom the straw ballots were sent were selected from lists of the magazine's subscribers, telephone subscribers, and automobile owners. But such people did not represent the general population, for in 1936, in the midst of the Great Depression, it was mainly the wealthier people or the upper middle-class people who could afford telephones, automobiles, or subscriptions to the more expensive magazines, and the majority of such people were strongly anti-Roosevelt.
2. Fewer than one quarter of the questionnaires were returned. This fraction is rather small, but not surprisingly so—many people do not bother to respond to questionnaires, especially when they have nothing to gain by responding. Nevertheless, the fact that only a small fraction responded raises questions as to whether those who responded constituted a typical sample of the entire group. In this case, it was probably not typical: Many of those who were anti-Roosevelt hated him so bitterly that they would have eagerly grasped this opportunity to show their disapproval; while the pro-Roosevelt people had no such strong emotional stimulus to respond.

In general, when responses are received from only a small fraction of those who got the ballots or questionnaires, it would be well to ask yourself what kinds of people would have taken the trouble to respond, and whether their answers might be so biased that the results of the poll are useless. In the case of the Digest poll, for example, it might have been best to conclude that the respondents did not accurately represent the entire group polled (which was improperly chosen in the first place). Sometimes, however, the non-responders are simply those who have no interest in the subject. For example, a questionnaire concerning the service in the public library would not be returned by most of those who never use the library.

Questionnaires and polls—do people tell the truth? Trying to determine meaningful statistics when they concern behavior or sentiments of people can be especially difficult, and the results of a questionnaire can be very misleading. People are funny.

An automobile manufacturer asked his potential customers whether to minimize the external chromium and other elements of a flashy appearance and put the savings into making a sturdier car, less likely to need frequent repairs. The people responded as sensible people should—they responded overwhelmingly in favor of the sturdy unadorned car. But when the manufacturer built such cars, they sold very poorly, while the competitors' flashy cars continued to sell very well. The manufacturer had forgotten how readily good sense is overpowered by outward appearance or an appeal to vanity—something that every salesman knows.

Similar misleading results are obtained from questionnaires to which the responses would indicate income (people claim to make more money that they do), good taste in literature or art (people claim to read the best books and magazines when they actually read trash), freedom from racial or religious prejudice (the most bigoted people proclaim that they are unprejudiced), and so on. Curiously, they often are not quite aware that their answers to the questionnaires are untrue: They think "My salary will soon increase, when the boss sees how valuable I am," or "As soon as I finish reading this trash I shall go to the library and get a *good* book."

The more successful questionnaires are those that directly concern the respondent's needs or wants, as "Would you be in favor of con-structing a sidewalk along your block, if you would be assessed <u>XXX</u> dollars to help pay for it?" Also successful are questionnaires and polls conducted by means of trained interviewers in long and thor-ough personal interviews. Modern polls using this method for pre-dicting the results of presidential elections have been remarkably accurate, even though only a very few thousand voters are inter-viewed. In contrast, the Literary Digest's 10 million voters, thought-lessly selected and given only straw ballots, provided the wrong answer.

Question:
The president of Absynthia became increasingly autocratic, refused to permit elections, and crushed any dissent by means of a ruthless secret police. Eventually, believing that the people admired him, he agreed to allow a presidential election in which he ran against a more democratic opponent.

A poll conducted by a group from a neighboring country did, indeed, indicate that most of the electorate would vote for him. The result of the election, however, was quite the opposite—his opponent won by a large margin.

Why did the poll fail to correctly predict the result of the election?

Answer:
In this case it is easy to see why the poll was foolish: Any remarks made to a stranger might be reported to the secret police. Accord-ingly, if a voter wished to remain healthy, he would be sure to tell the pollster that he admired the president and strongly supported him.

Statistics cannot substitute for careful experiments. A scientist, trying to make a certain measurement, finds that the measurement varies considerably from one test to another. However, reassured by the "laws" of statistics, he makes the measurement a thousand times and supposes that the average of his thousand values is very accurate. He would do much better to try to determine the cause of the large variation of his data, and then try to improve his technique by eliminating this cause. A single measurement with an improved technique would be more trustworthy than the average of his thousand poor measurements.

Drawing conclusions from flimsy data. A newsboy is riding along the street on his bicycle, accurately tossing his newspapers onto his customer's porches. One newspaper, however, lands in a bush; he dismounts and goes to retrieve it and toss it onto the porch. As he returns to his bicycle, a motherly lady wags her finger at him and says "You see, young man, haste makes waste." The boy mounts his bicycle and continues as before. It was absurd for the lady to conclude from her one observation that hand-carrying all the newspapers to the customers' porches would save time.

In a health-food store, a salesman tells a customer "My mother-in-law took these pills three times a day and her arthritis was cured after only a month." Such a story is usually an outright lie. In any case, even if the salesman tells it in good faith, it is essentially hearsay and not useful as evidence. Such stories are sometimes referred to as "anecdotal evidence" and have dubious value. An appreciable amount of such evidence, however, may prompt a scientific study of the matter.

GEOMETRY

Simple Constructions in a Plane Using Straight Edge and Compass

Angles and triangles.

1. Given the three sides of a triangle, *a*, *b*, and *c*, construct the triangle.

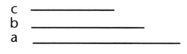

    With one end of the line *a* as center, draw an arc of radius *b*.
    With the other end of line *a* as center, draw an arc of radius *c*.
    Draw lines (of lengths *b* and *c*, respectively) from the ends of line *a* to the points where the two arcs intersect.

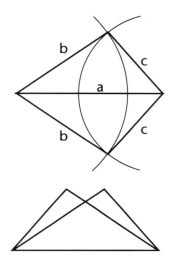

    As the sketch shows, the construction results in two different triangles whose sides have the desired lengths. They are different in the sense that, going clockwise around them, the order of the sides is *a*, *b*, *c* in the upper triangle and *a*, *c*, *b* in the lower triangle. If you slide and rotate the lower triangle in the plane of the paper until it is on the other triangle, it will not coincide with it. One triangle is the *mirror image* of the other, where, in the preceding sketch, the "mirror" is a plane through side *a* perpendicular to the plane of the paper. Stated differently, if the paper is folded along the line *a*, the two triangles will coincide. These last two sentences are equivalent because looking at a diagram from the backside is equivalent to looking at it in a mirror.

Problem:
Show that the length of one side of a triangle cannot be greater than the sum of the lengths of the other two sides.

2. At a given point *P* on a line construct an angle equal to a given angle *a*.

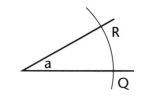

    With the vertex of angle *a* as center draw an arc of any convenient radius intersecting the two sides of the angle at points *Q* and *R*. With point *P* as center draw an arc of the same radius intersecting the line at point *S*. Set the compass radius equal to the distance from *Q* to *R*; then with this radius and with *S* as center draw an arc intersecting the first arc at *T*. The line through *P* and *T* will make the desired angle with the line.

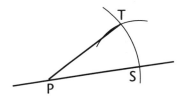

3. Through a given point *P* draw a line parallel to a given line *a*.

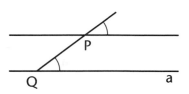

    From any point *Q* on line *a* draw a line through *P*. Using the procedure just described, construct an angle at *P*

equal to the angle at *Q*. The line that you draw through *P* to make this angle is parallel to line *a*.

When a line crosses two parallel lines, as in the sketch below, angles *a*, *b*, *c*, and *d* are all equal, and angles *e*, *f*, *g*, and *h* are all equal.

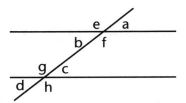

Show that the three angles of a triangle sum to 180°.

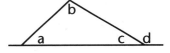

Draw a line through the apex parallel to the base. Then angles *a* and *d* are equal, and angles *c* and *e* are equal. Angles *b*, *d*, and *e* sum to 180°; that is, *b* + *d* + *e* = 180°. If, in this equation, *d* is replaced by its equal, *a*, and *e* is replaced by its equal, *c*, the equation becomes

$$b + a + c = 180°$$

as was to be shown.

Now show that in the sketch on the left

$$d = a + b$$

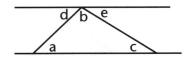

4. Given two sides of a triangle and the angle between them, draw the triangle. Are there more than one triangle containing the same two sides and included angle? (Compare construction 1.)

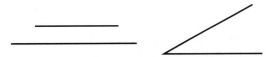

5. Given one side of a triangle and the angles at its two ends, construct the triangle.

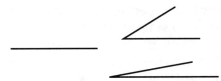

6. Given two sides *a* and *b* of a triangle and the angle *A* opposite side *a*, construct the triangle.

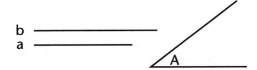

Since the angle is opposite side *a* it is at one end of side *b*. Put the side *b* along one side of the given angle. With the other end of *b* as center and with *a* as radius draw an arc that intersects the other side of the angle. The lines from this intersection point to the ends of *b* complete the triangle.

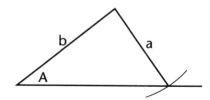

Are there more solutions to the problem?

If *a* is less than *b*, the arc will cut the side of the triangle at two points and thus give two triangles. In addition, of course, the mirror images of these two triangles also satisfy the conditions.

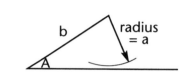

Why is there only one solution (other than the mirror image) if *a* is greater than *b*?

Are there any cases in which there is no solution? If *a* is so short that the arc does not even reach the other side of the angle there will not be a solution.

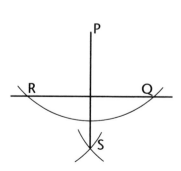

7. Given a line and a point *P* not on the line, construct the perpendicular from the point to the line.

   With *P* as center and with any radius that is more than enough to reach the line, draw an arc cutting the line at two points, *R* and *Q*. With *R* and *Q* as centers and with the same radius, or with any other radius greater than $\frac{1}{2}RQ$, draw arcs intersecting on the other side of the line, at *S*. The desired perpendicular is the line through *P* and *S*.

   Definitions:
   Perpendicular: At right angles (to a given line or surface).

   Vertical: Perpendicular to the Earth's surface. If you hang a weight at the end of a thread, the thread hangs vertical.

8. Construct the perpendicular bisector of a line *PQ* of given length.

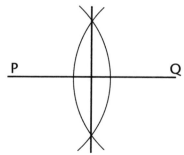

9. Bisect a given angle.

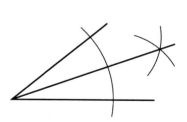

10. Inscribe a circle in a given triangle *ABC*. That is, construct a circle within the triangle that just touches all three sides.

Bisect angles *A* and *C*. At every point along the bisector of angle *A*, the distances to the two sides *AC* and *AB* are equal. Similarly, every point on the bisector of angle *C* is equidistant from the two sides *BC* and *AC*. Hence, point *O*, where the two bisectors meet, must be equidistant from all three sides. Then with *O* as center we can draw a circle that just touches (is tangent to) all three sides.

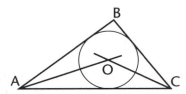

Furthermore, since point *O* is equidistant from sides *AB* and *BC*, it must lie on the bisector of angle *B*. In other words, the three angle bisectors of a triangle meet at a point that is the center of the inscribed circle.

Definition:
Where the line and the circle just touch, we say that they are tangent to each other. The word is also used as a noun: The line is a tangent of the circle. It would not be correct to define tangency as meeting at a point, because that could mean that they cross. We have to consider a line that cuts the arc in two nearby points, and define a tangent as the limiting position of the line as the two points come closer and closer to each other.

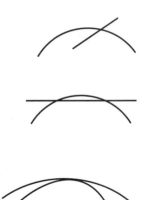

Curves may also be tangent to each other.

11. Circumscribe a circle about a triangle; that is, construct the circle that passes through all three vertices of the triangle. The point where two perpendicular bisectors meet is the center of the circumscribed circle. The three perpendicular bisectors meet at a point.

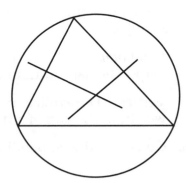

For both of these statements the reasoning is very similar to that in the preceding section on the inscribed circle.

Some Properties of Triangles

The medians of a triangle. Median: the line from a vertex of a triangle to the middle of the opposite side.

Show that the three medians of a triangle meet at a point that is one-third of the distance from each side to the opposite vertex:

In the triangle *ABC*, the three medians are *AF*, *BD*, and *CE*. Medians *BD* and *CE* cross at some point *O*; and we wish to show that *AF* also passes through *O*. Draw *ED*. Triangle *AED* has the same shape as (is "similar" to) triangle *ABC* but its sides are half as long. In particular, *ED* is half as long as *BC*. Also, since *ED* is parallel to *BC*, ∠*EDO* = ∠*CBO* and ∠*DEO* = ∠*BCO*; also ∠*DOE* = ∠*BOC*. Thus, the three angles of triangle *EDO* are equal to the three angles of triangle *CBO*, so the two triangles are similar; and since side *ED* is half as long as side *BC*, the dimensions of triangle *EDO* are half the corresponding dimensions of triangle *CBO*. Then *EO* is half of *OC* and *DO* is half of *OB*; that is, *O* is at one-third the distance from *E* to *C* and at one-third the distance from *D* to *B*.

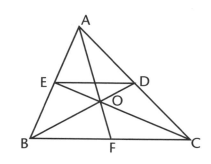

Now if we had used *AF* and *BD* as our two crossing medians, we would have found that they cross at a point that is one-third the distance from *F* to *A* and one-third the distance from *D* to *B*. But the point that is one-third of the distance from *D* to *B* has already been found—it is point *O*. Hence all three medians cross at point *O*.

A median passes through the centers (= centers of gravity) of all strips parallel to the base of the triangle. When the median is vertical, the elemental centers of gravity are all in the same vertical line (the median), so the net force of gravity lies along the median. The median thus passes through the center of gravity. Since the same reasoning applies for all three medians, we see that all three must pass through the center of gravity, which is thus the point *O* of the preceding discussion.

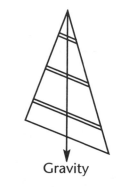

Gravity

Make a triangle of heavy cardboard and find point *O* where the medians cross. If you put a pin through the triangle near the edge, and let the triangle hang loosely from it, the point *O* (center of gravity) will be directly below the pin; or if you suspend the triangle by a light thread, the thread, which hangs vertical, will be aligned with point *O*.

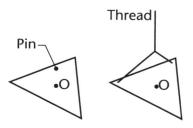

The altitudes of a triangle. Altitude: The perpendicular from a vertex to the opposite side.

Show that the three altitudes of a triangle meet at a point.

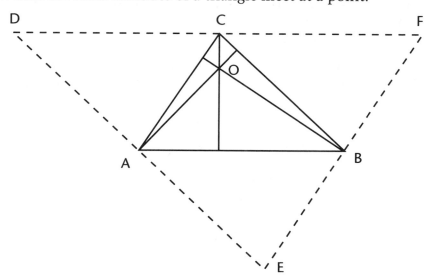

Given the triangle *ABC* and its three altitudes. Through the three vertices draw lines parallel to the opposite sides. These are the three dashed lines in the sketch. The figure now contains four equal triangles—the given triangle and three copies. (Prove that they are all equal.) Then, since *DC* = *CF*, *C* is the midpoint of the side *DF* of the large dashed triangle *DEF*. Similarly, *A* and *B* are the midpoints of the other two sides. The three altitudes are then the perpendicular bisectors of the three sides of the dashed triangle; and you have already shown that the three perpendicular bisectors of the sides of a triangle meet at a point (which is the center of the circumscribed circle).

Problem:
Draw the figure for the case of a triangle in which one angle is greater than 90° (called an obtuse angle). Using this figure, go through the proof that the three altitudes meet at a point.

Equilateral triangle; regular hexagon. A triangle with three equal sides is made as follows: Draw a circular arc with point *A* as center and with radius equal to the desired length of a side. Without changing the radius, put the compass point at any location *B* on this arc and draw an arc that intersects this arc at *C*. The triangle *ABC* is equilateral.

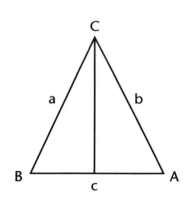

A regular hexagon can be made as follows: Draw a circle and, without changing the radius setting of your compass, lay off six equally spaced points around the circumference. Draw lines between pairs of adjacent points.

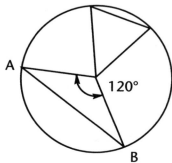

Two equal sides. A triangle with two equal sides is called an isosceles triangle. It is easy to show that the angles opposite the two equal sides are also equal: If, in the sketch, sides *a* and *b* are equal, draw the median from vertex *C* to side *c*, cutting the given triangle into two smaller triangles. In these two triangles, the sides of one are equal to the sides of the other, so the two triangles are equal (except that one is the mirror image of the other). Hence the two corresponding angles *A* and *B* are equal.

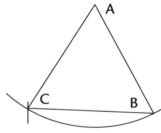

A triangle with two vertices on a circle and the third vertex at the center of the circle is of this type, as illustrated in the sketch below.

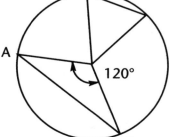

Definition:
A circular arc may be defined by its angle at the center of the circle. For example, the arc *AB* may be referred to as a 120° arc.

Three vertices on a circle. If the third vertex of the triangle is also on the circle, its angle is half of what it would be if it were at the center. That is, in the sketch, angle *A* is half of angle *B*.

Proof:
Draw the dashed line through *A* and *B*. In △*ABC*, ∠*BAC* = ∠*BCA*. Then, since ∠*CBE* = ∠*BAC* + ∠*BCA* (see item 3 in the preceding section, pp. 135 and 136), ∠*CBE* = 2∠*BAC*, or ∠*BAC* = $\frac{1}{2}$∠*CBE*.

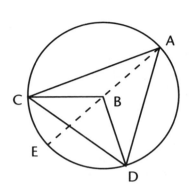

Similarly, ∠*BAD* = $\frac{1}{2}$ ∠*EBD*

Adding the two equations gives

∠*BAC* + ∠*BAD* = $\frac{1}{2}$ (∠*CBE* + ∠*EBD*), or

∠*CAD* = $\frac{1}{2}$ ∠*CBD*

This result holds no matter where vertex *A* is on the long arc *CD*; thus, angles *M*, *N*, *P*, and *Q* are all equal and measured as half the short arc *CD*. This fact applies even in the limiting case when *M* coincides with *C* and the line through *M* and *C* has become the tangent at *C*; that is, ∠*TCD* is measured as half the arc *CD*.

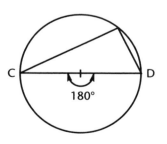

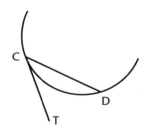

There is a useful special case in which the line *CD* is the diameter of a circle (and the arc *CD* is a semicircle): since the central angle of the semicircle is 180°, all inscribed angles are 90°, or right angles.

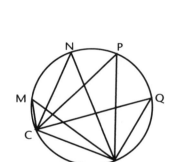

Problem:
Given a right triangle. Show that the median to the hypotenuse has half the length of the hypotenuse.

Suppose that you have to construct a circle through points *C* and *D* such that an angle inscribed in the circle, whose sides pass through *C* and *D*, is, say 73°. One procedure is as follows: Draw the line *CD* and from the ends draw lines *CO* and *DO* making angles of 90° − 73° = 17° with *CD*. The point *O* where they meet is the center of the circle. Draw the circle. Any angle such as ∠*CMD* inscribed in the long arc,

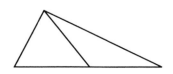

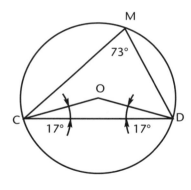

with its sides passing through *C* and *D*, is 73°. Why? How would the procedure be different if the desired angle is greater than 90°?

Problem:
Given any triangle *ABC*, and points *D*, *E*, and *F* located such that ∠*DAB* = ∠*DBA* = ∠*CBE* = ∠*BCE* = ∠*CAF* = ∠*ACF* = 30°. With *D*, *E*, and *F* as centers, 120° arcs are drawn through the vertices of the triangle. Prove that they meet at a point *G*.

First, suppose that *G* is simply the point where the two arcs *AGB* and *BGC* meet. Draw the lines *AG*, *BG*, and *CG*. Angles *AGB* and *BGC* are 120° (why?). Then *AGC* must also be 120°, since the three angles at *G* must sum to 360°. But if it is 120°, point *G* must lie on the 120° arc through *A* and *C*. Hence point *G* is the common intersection point of the three 120° arcs.

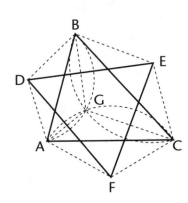

Problem:
In the preceding figure, prove that triangle *DEF* is equilateral.

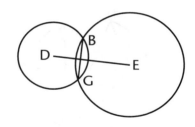

Line *DE* is perpendicular to line *BG* since it connects the centers of two circles that meet at *B* and *G*. Similarly *DF* is perpendicular to *AG* and *EF* is perpendicular to *CG*. Thus the three sides of triangle *DEF* are perpendicular to three lines that meet at angles of 120°, and hence they must meet at 60° angles. Accordingly triangle *DEF* is equilateral.

Problem of the rocking equilateral triangle. Given an equilateral triangle *PQR* with vertices *Q* and *R* on the sides of a 120° angle *O*. Prove that as the triangle rocks, with *R* and *Q* sliding back and forth along the sides of the angle *O*, the vertex *P* remains along the bisector of *O* (the dashed line).

From *Q* and *R* draw lines parallel to the sides of angle *O*, meeting at *V*. Draw line *SVT* perpendicular to the bisector of *O*. Note that triangles *SVQ* and *VTR* are both 30° – 30° – 120° triangles.

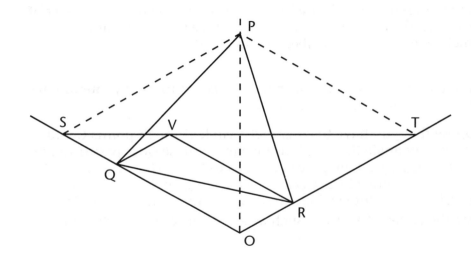

Consider the line *SVT* as a completely flattened triangle whose sides are *SV*, *VT*, and *ST*. Then, with reference to the preceding problem, points *Q* and *R* are two vertices of the equilateral triangle discussed there; so point *P*, which is the third vertex of the equilateral triangle, is at the vertex of the 30° – 30° – 120° triangle on side *ST* (sides *SP* and *PT* are shown as dashed lines). Accordingly, *P* lies above the middle of line *ST* and along the bisector of angle *O*; and *P* must slide up and down along the bisector as the triangle rocks.

Construction Problems

Square inscribed in a triangle. Given a triangle, construct within it the largest possible square whose base lies on the base of the triangle.

In the lower left corner draw a small square of any convenient size. Then through the lower left vertex of the triangle and the upper right corner of this small square draw a straight line and extend it to the right side of the triangle (point *O*). This intersection is the upper right corner of the desired square.

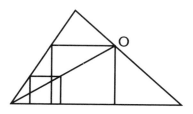

How would you proceed if the triangle looked like the one below?

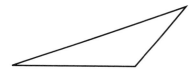

Oriented triangle inscribed in a triangle. Given two triangles *A* and *B*, construct within *A* the largest possible triangle whose sides are parallel to the sides of *B* and which is oriented like *B*.

Inscribe near the top of *A* a small triangle whose sides are parallel to the sides of *B*, and two of whose vertices touch the sides of *A*. Draw a line through the apex of *A* and the third vertex, and extend it to intersect the base (point *O*). This intersection point is the corresponding vertex of the desired inscribed triangle.

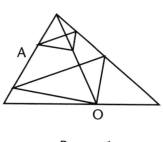

Three equal lengths, I. Given a triangle, *ABC*, find points *D* and *E* on sides *AB* and *BC*, respectively, such that *BD* = *DE* = *EC*. Take any point *F* along *BA* and, with a compass, locate point *G* along *BC* such that *FG* = *BF*; then locate point *H* along *BC* such that *GH* = *FG*. Draw *FH*. Draw *DC* parallel to *FH* and then *DE* parallel to *FG*.

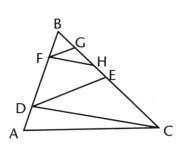

How can this problem be solved for a triangle like one of these two?

Point *D* would have to be located on the extension of line *AB*.

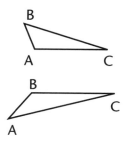

Three equal lengths, II. Given a triangle *ABC*, find points *E* and *F* on sides *AB* and *BC*, respectively, such that *AE* = *EF* = *FC*.

Take *MC* any convenient small length on *BC*. Locate *N* on *AB* such that *AN = MC*, and draw a line through *N* (shown dashed) parallel to *AC*. With *M* as center and with radius equal to *MC*, swing an arc cutting this line at *Q*. Draw *CQ* and extend it to intersect *AB* at *E*.

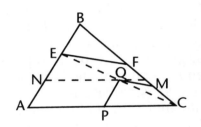

Through *E* draw *EF* parallel to *QM*. The line *PQ*, parallel to *AN*, has been drawn in order to help you see the proof of the construction.

Two equal lengths. Given lines *A* and *B* and point *P* between them. Find the point on line *A* that is equidistant from point *P* and line *B*.

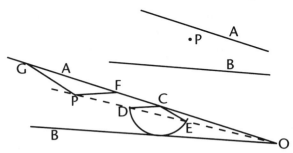

Extend lines *A* and *B* until they intersect at *O*. Draw line *OP*. From any point *C* on line *A* as center, draw an arc tangent to line *B* and cutting *OP* at points *D* and *E*. Draw lines *CD* and *CE*. From *P* draw *PF* parallel to *CD* and *PG* parallel to *CE*. The points *F* and *G* both satisfy the requirement that they be equidistant from point *P* and line *B*.

Solve this problem for the case when point *P* lies above line *A* rather than between lines *A* and *B*.

Problem:
Given an angle *A* and a circle *O* within it. Construct a circle that is tangent to the given circle and to both sides of the given angle.

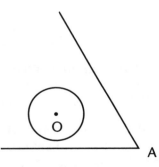

Solution:
Since the desired circle is tangent to both sides of the angle, its center lies along the angle bisector. Accordingly, we seek a point *P* that lies along this bisector and is equally distant from either side of the angle *A* and from the circle *O*. In the preceding problem we desired a point that is equally distant from a given line and a given point, but now we desire a point that is equally distant from a given line and a given circle. Although we do not yet know which point on the given circle is to be the point of tangency, we do know that the line from the desired point *P* to the point of tangency goes to the center *O* of the given circle. We can thus restate our problem as follows: Find a point *P* on the bisector such that its distance to *O* exceeds its distance to the line *AB* by *r*, the radius of the circle. Our problem is now like the preceding problem except that the two distances are not equal. This difficulty is easily eliminated. We draw a line *CD* parallel to line *AB* and distant *r* from it, and we require that point *P* be equally distant from point *O* and line *CD*.

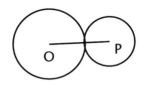

The solution is now like the solution of the preceding problem. Extend the angle bisector to meet line *CD* at *C*. Draw a line through *O* and the intersection point *C*. From an arbitrary point *Q* on the

bisector draw a perpendicular *QS* to the line *CD* and then locate
points *M* and *N* along line *OC* such that *QM* = *QN* = *QS*. Draw lines
through *O* parallel to *QM* and *QN*. The two points *T* and *P* where
these lines intersect the bisector are the centers of two circles that are
solutions to our problem.

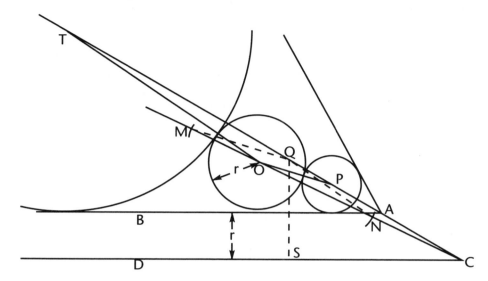

Directed line between circles. Given two circles *P* and *Q* and a line,
shown above them, of given length and direction. Find a line connecting the two circles having the same length and direction as the
given line.

From the center, *O*, of circle *P*, draw a line *OA* having the
desired length and direction. With *A* as center, and with
radius equal to that of circle *P*, draw a circle (shown
dashed) intersecting *Q* at *B* and *C*. Now any line connecting the two equal circles and parallel to *OA* will have
the desired length and direction, but only the lines to
points *B* and *C* will also connect the two given circles *P*
and *Q*. These two lines are shown as *BD* and *CE* on the
sketch.

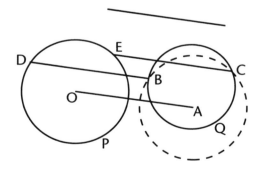

Would you get different answers if you started by drawing the line to
the left from the center of circle *Q* instead of to the right from the
center of circle *P*? Can you solve the problem if you are given two
arbitrary curves instead of two circles?

Quadrilateral with given sides. On the basis of the problem just
studied, show how to construct a quadrilateral, given the lengths of
the four sides, *a*, *b*, *c*, and *d*, and the angle between the pair of
opposite sides *a* and *c*.

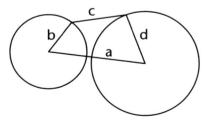

Do the preceding construction, with the radii of the two circles
equal to *b* and *d*, and with the distance between their centers equal
to *a*. The fourth side of the quadrilateral is the line connecting the
two circles, having the desired length *c* and having the desired direction relative to *a*. As before, there are two different solutions; and
their mirror images may be considered as two additional solutions.

Problem:
Given an angle and a point *O* within it. Draw a circle that is tangent to both sides of the angle and that passes through point *O*. (There are two answers.)

A matter of viewpoint—intersecting sets of lines (Desargues' theorem).

1. Given (sketch (a)) three lines that meet at point *O*, and a pair of points on each line: *A* and *D*, *C* and *F*, and *B* and *E*. Draw lines *AC* and *DF*, and extend them to their intersection at *J*; draw lines *CB* and *FE*, and extend them to their intersection at *G*; and draw lines *AB* and *DE*, and extend them to their intersection at *H*.

Prove that *G*, *H*, and *J* lie on a straight line.

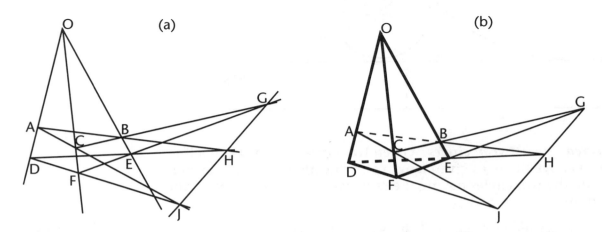

Perhaps the main part of the proof consists of (1) using an eraser to remove the lower extensions of the three intersecting lines, (2) using a pen to darken some of the lines, and (3) changing lines *AB* and *DE* to dashed lines (sketch (b)). The main part of the figure is now viewed as a pyramid resting on its base *DEF*, and intersected by a plane in the triangle *ABC*. Furthermore, the three pairs of lines that meet at *G*, *H*, and *J* lie in the three side faces (extended) of the pyramid. Now in each of the three pairs, one line lies in the plane of the base *DEF* and the other lies in the plane of the triangle *ABC*; hence each of the three intersection points *G*, *H*, and *J* must lie in the intersection of these two planes. Finally, since two planes intersect in a straight line, the three points lie along that straight intersection line.

Thus by viewing the drawing in a three-dimensional context the proof is simple.

2. Given a point *O* within a triangle *DEF*, with lines from *O* to the three vertices, and an inner triangle *ABC* whose three vertices are on these three lines. Extend the sides of both triangles so that the corresponding three pairs of lines meet. Prove that the points *G*, *H*, and *J* where they meet lie on a straight line.

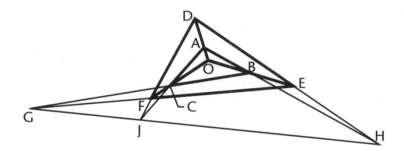

A proof is not actually needed. The result follows from the previous result in either of the following two ways:

 (a) The figure is merely the top view of the pyramid, etc., shown in the preceding figure of problem 1.

 (b) In the preceding figure the three lines meet at *O* at fairly small angles. If the three angles are made so large that they sum to 180°, the result is the figure shown above.

3. Show that the figure below is another variation of the figure of problem 1, with the same letters used at corresponding points.

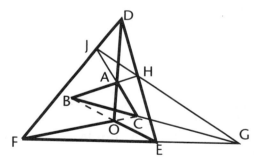

Like the preceding figure, it is the top view of the pyramid; however, for this case, two of the edges of the pyramid have been extended beyond the apex *O*, as shown by the dashed lines in the sketch on the right. The triangle *ABC* is actually outside of the pyramid.

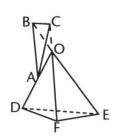

4. Given three circles of different sizes and six tangent lines that "enclose" them in pairs, as in the sketch on the right. The three pairs of tangents meet at points *A*, *B*, and *C*, respectively. Prove that *A*, *B*, and *C* lie on a straight line.

Consider that the three circles are actually the outlines of three spheres lying on a table, and that the three pairs of spheres are tight inside of three (intersecting) cones

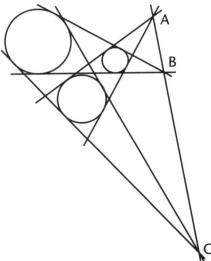

Element

outlined by the three pairs of tangents. Then the three cones are also lying on the table, and their vertices *A*, *B*, and *C* are on the table. If you now rest a plane on top of the three spheres it will also rest on top of the cones, tangent to each cone along the line of contact, which is a straight line passing through the vertex. (Such a line is called an "element" of the cone.) Thus the plane and the tabletop make contact at points *A*, *B*, and *C*; and since the plane and tabletop must intersect along a straight line, *A*, *B*, and *C* must lie on that line.

5. In this sketch, two pairs of tangents cross *between* the circles, but the third pair does not. Prove that in this case the three intersection points *A*, *B*, and *C* also lie along a straight line.

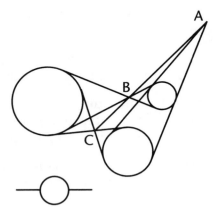

For this case consider the spheres to be half embedded in the tabletop instead of lying on it.

Show that the reasoning will not apply when all three pairs of tangents cross between their circles.

Soap-Film Problems

How three films meet. Where three soap films meet, the angle between every pair of films must be 120° in order that the tensions in the three films balance each other. A simple experiment would be useful for demonstrating how soap films meet. Take a piece of thin sheet aluminum about 40 cm long and 1.5 cm wide and bend it to form a U that will fit tight around the inside of a small plastic sandwich bag. Put a little dilute soap or detergent solution into the bag, and with a long narrow rubber tube blow into the solution until the bag is filled with bubbles. The bubbles form a very irregular honeycomb but it is easy to see that all intersections are made by groups of three films meeting at angles of 120°.

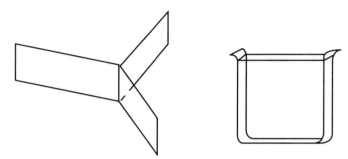

In order to show the honeycomb to a large class, it may be projected onto a wall or screen by an overhead projector. The projector must be turned on its side in order that the bag may remain vertical (so as not to spill the soap solution).

One might suppose that, say, four films meeting at right angles or in an X would also have their tensions in equilibrium. And so they would, but the equilibrium is not a *stable* equilibrium. In particular, if the intersection point should spread out into a short line, as shown in sketch (b), the combined tensions of *m* and *n*, and of *p* and *q* would overbalance the tensions in the short piece and continue to pull it out until the configuration of sketch (c) is reached. By contrast, the three-film configuration is stable because any imaginable small deformation would cause the forces to become unbalanced in such a way that the deformation is corrected.

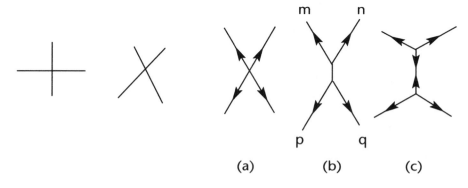

m   n

p   q

(a)   (b)   (c)

Three anchor pins. Given the locations *A*, *B*, and *C* of three parallel wires or pins that anchor the ends of three soap films, find the locations of the films.

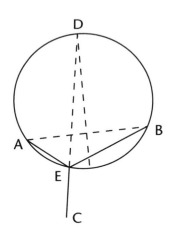

Draw a circle through *A* and *B* such that the short arc *AB* is 120°. Find the midpoint *D* of the long (240°) arc *AB*. Draw *CD*, intersecting the short arc *AB* at *E*. The lines *AE*, *BE*, and *CE* locate the three films.

Prove that the three lines meet at angles of 120°.

The quadribubbler. In some bubble pipes, the bowl is divided into four sections so that blowing produces four bubbles simultaneously. One might suppose that the four would merge into a symmetrical group of four equal parts, as in sketch (a). As just explained, however, the crossed film + arrangement is unstable. The most symmetrical arrangement that can be obtained is of the type indicated in sketch (b).

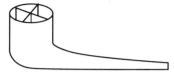

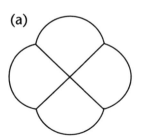

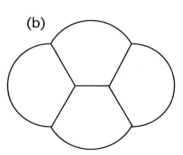

(a)   (b)

Problems:
Consider that these two sketches represent two-dimensional symmetrical arrangements of soap films, in which the arcs are parts of circles and three films must meet at 120° angles.

1. How would you construct the sketches, using only a compass and a 30°-60°-90° triangle?

2. Show that in sketch (a) the arcs are 150°; show that in sketch (b) two of the arcs are 120° and two are 180°.

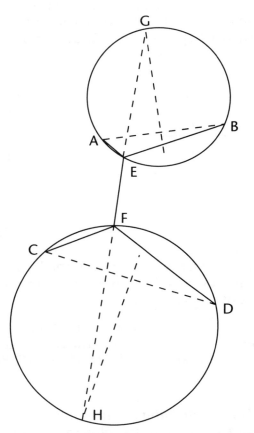

Four anchor pins. Given the locations of four pins *A, B, C, D* that anchor the soap-film system, locate the soap films.

Proceed as before, drawing one circle through *A* and *B* and another circle through *C* and *D*. Then find points *G* and *H* that bisect the long arcs *AB* and *CD*, respectively. The line *GH* intersects the short arcs at *E* and *F*, where the nodes (or branch points) are located.

Find another set of locations for the film segments by putting one circle through *A* and *C* and another through *B* and *D*. This problem thus has two solutions. How must *A, B, C,* and *D* be located so that only one solution is possible? How must they be located so that no solution of this type is possible?

If the two 120° arcs *AB* and *CD* intersect and the line *GH* passes through the overlap (sketch (a)), the corresponding solution is impossible. In such a case, one might put one circle through *A* and *C* and the other circle through *B* and *D* (sketch (b)). If the line *GH* does not cross both 120° arcs, the corresponding solution is also impossible. If the points *A, B, C, D* are all relatively close to a straight line, no solution of this type is possible.

Five anchor pins. Given the locations of five pins, *A, B, C, D,* and *E* that anchor the soap-film system, locate the soap films.

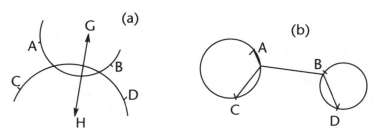

Draw the circles through *A* and *B* and through *C* and *D* as before, and locate *G* and *H*, the centers of the long arcs. Then similarly draw a circle through *G* and *H* and locate *J*, the center of its long arc. The line from *E* to *J* meets this circle at node *F* and the lines from *F* to *G* and from *F* to *H* meet the first two circles at the other two nodes.

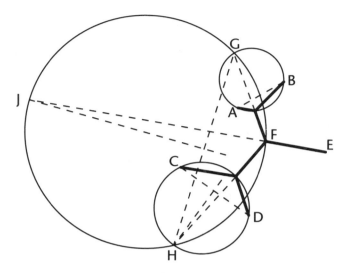

Road systems of minimum length.

Road systems of minimum length. As mentioned previously, soap films are in tension—they tend to contract to the least area compatible with other conditions, such as remaining attached to the pins. Accordingly, if points *A*, *B*, *C* . . . of the preceding problems represent the locations of, say, cities, the soap-film patterns that have been derived represent the road systems of least total length connecting these cities. However, in the preceding two problems, there was some arbitrariness in the choice of pairs of pins through which to draw the initial circles. For example, in the four-anchor problem, the circles were put through *A* and *B*, and through *C* and *D*, although they might have been put through *A* and *C*, and through *B* and *D*. The results that were obtained showed short roads, with only one break, between *A* and *B* and between *C* and *D*. If it were desired that the roads between *A* and *C* and between *B* and *D* be as short as possible, the other solution would represent the minimum-total-road-length system for that case.

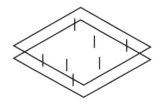

Sometimes a "beltway," in which the road passes through the cities consecutively (for example, in our four-anchor problem, the road would go from *B* to *A* to *C* to *D*), is actually the shortest road that links the cities. However, this approach discriminates against people who wish to travel between the end cities (that is, from *B* to *D* in the four-anchor case), because their route would not only be long and roundabout but would also encounter the traffic of all the intermediate cities.

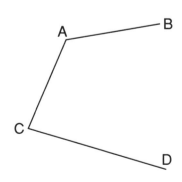

Experimental solution. The experimental approach to these problems is to actually use soap films. Get two sheets of plastic about 15 cm square and separate them with pins about 1.5 cm long located at the desired points. When this contrivance is dipped into a dilute soap solution and withdrawn, there will be a system of films connecting the pins—but it will not always be the desired system, as just discussed.

The Square Through Four Points

Construct a square whose four sides, extended if necessary, pass through four given points, A, B, C, and D.

Method I. Construct circles with AB and CD as diameters, and find the points E, F, J, and K that bisect the four semicircular arcs AB and CD. Draw the line EF and extend it to meet the opposite sides of the circles at G and H. Draw the lines AG, BG, DH, and CH.

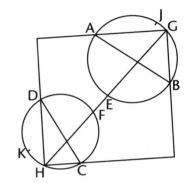

Since arcs AE and EB are each 90°, angles AGE and EGB are each 45°; similarly, angles DHF and FHC are each 45°. Accordingly, GH is the diagonal of the square whose sides lie along AG, BG, DH, and CH.

Instead of putting the diagonal through E and F, you might have put it through J and F, through E and K, or through J and K, thereby obtaining three more squares. Try one of these cases. The construction for the J-K case is shown below; but try to do it yourself before referring to the sketch.

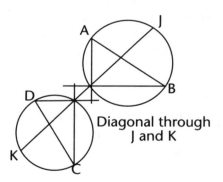

In addition you might have put the two circles through A and D and through B and C, or even through A and C and through B and D, thereby getting additional squares.

Instead of proceeding with these possibilities, however, we shall describe a simpler approach to solving this problem.

Method II. The second method is based on a very simple construction: Given a line MN with a pair of parallel lines through the end points. Superimpose an identical arrangement of lines at right angles to this given arrangement. The two pairs of parallel lines form a square.

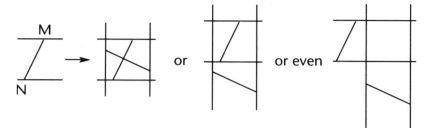

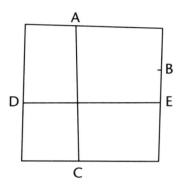

We apply this construction as follows: Draw the line *AC* between two of the given points, and from a third point, *D*, draw a line *DE* perpendicular to *AC* and of the same length. Draw a line through *B* and *E*. A line through *D* parallel to *BE* and lines through *A* and *C* perpendicular to *BE* complete the square.

Instead of drawing line *DE* to the right of *D*, you might have drawn it to the left of *D*, as in the second sketch. The remainder of the procedure is as before, but the resulting square is quite different. Furthermore, instead of starting with line *AC* you might have started with line *AB* (thereby assuming that *A* and *B* are on opposite sides of the square), or with line *AD* (thereby assuming that *A* and *D* are on opposite sides of the square), and for each of these, two different squares would have been obtained. Thus there is a total of six different squares that satisfy the requirement that four given points lie along four different sides of the square.

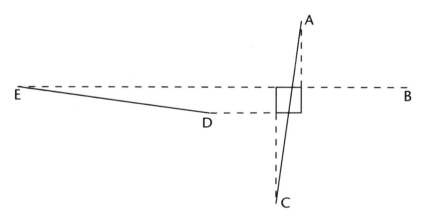

Problems:

1. Construct a 2:1 rectangle whose four sides, extended if necessary, pass through four given points, *A*, *B*, *C*, *D*. Do this problem by both method I and method II.

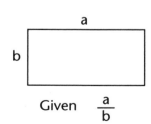

Given $\dfrac{a}{b}$

2. Construct a parallelogram of given shape whose four sides, extended if necessary, pass through four given points.

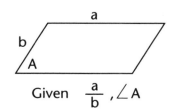

Given $\dfrac{a}{b}$, $\angle A$

The Pythagorean Theorem

Proof. The sketches show three similar triangles with a square on the long side of each. The area of each square is 3.2 times the area of its triangle. The triangles were drawn such that the area of the large triangle is the sum of the areas of the two smaller triangles. Then,

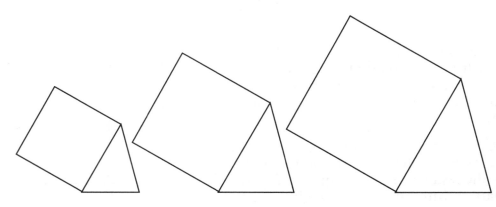

since the three diagrams are similar, we conclude from the preceding facts that the area of the large square is the sum of the areas of the two smaller squares. This reasoning has an important application in the case of a right triangle (a triangle in which one of the angles is a right angle). The next sketch shows a

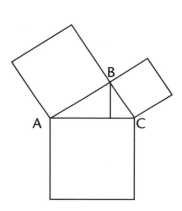

right triangle *ABC* with an altitude drawn from the right angle *B* to the long side *AC* (called the "hypotenuse"), cutting the triangle into two smaller triangles. These two triangles are similar to each other and to the big triangle because (1) each contains a right angle and (2) each has an angle in common with the big triangle. (If two angles of one triangle are the same as two angles of another triangle, the third angle must also be the same for both (because the three angles of a triangle must sum to 180°), and the triangles are similar.) Thus, all three triangles are similar and, furthermore, the area of the large triangle is the sum of the areas of the two smaller triangles. Then, as previously discussed, if a square is put on the hypotenuse of each of the three triangles, the area of the large square equals the sum of the areas of the two smaller squares. Or, as commonly stated, the square of the hypotenuse equals the sum of the squares of the other two sides.

This theorem was given in about 500 B.C. by Pythagoras, a Greek philosopher and mathematician; however, it was probably known before then. It has been called the most important theorem in geometry, since it is frequently used in all branches of engineering and physics.

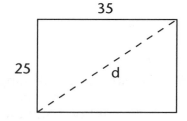

As a simple example of its use suppose you wish to go from one corner of a rectangular lot to the diagonally opposite corner. The lot is 25 meters by 35 meters. How much distance do you save by going diagonally, compared with going around the edge?

The length of the diagonal *d* is given by

$$d^2 = 25^2 + 35^2 = 625 + 1225 = 1850$$

$$d = \sqrt{1850} \approx 43$$

Thus, the diagonal distance is about 43 meters, while, if you walk around the edge, the distance is 25 + 35 = 60 meters, or 17 meters longer.

As another example, consider the common 60°–30° right triangle. What is the ratio of the height h to the base b in such a triangle?

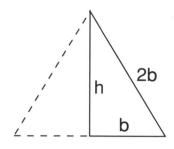

The triangle is half of an equilateral triangle, as shown in the sketch, so the base is half the hypotenuse, which is therefore $2b$. Then

$$h^2 = (2b)^2 - b^2 = 4b^2 - b^2 = 3b^2,$$

from which

$$h = \sqrt{3b^2} = \sqrt{3}\, b \approx 1.732b$$

Given a square whose side is 1, show that the length of the diagonal is $\sqrt{2} \approx 1.414$.

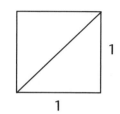

Given a rectangular parallelepiped with edges a, b, and c, show that the length of the diagonal (shown dotted in the sketch) is $\sqrt{a^2 + b^2 + c^2}$.

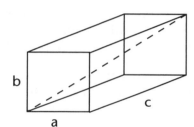

Given a circle of radius 5 cm, with a chord AB located 3 cm from the center. How long is AB?

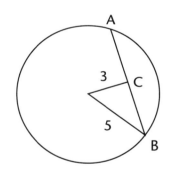

Determine the length of CB, which is half of AB:

$$(CB)^2 = 5^2 - 3^2 = 25 - 9 = 16$$

$$CB = \sqrt{16} = 4$$

Therefore

$$AB = 2 \times CB = 8 \text{ cm}$$

In the sketch, O is the center of the circle. Two dimensions of the rectangle are shown. What is the radius of the circle?

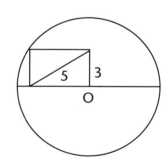

Problem:
(a) Given a circle inscribed in a square, and a small circle inscribed between a corner and the large circle. If the radius of the large circle is 1, what is the radius of the small circle?

(b) Given a sphere inscribed in a cube, and a small sphere inscribed between the corner and the large sphere. If the radius of the large sphere is 1, what is the radius of the small sphere?

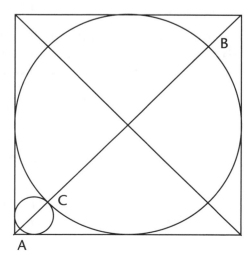

Answer:
(a) The distance from the center of the square to the corner A is

$\sqrt{1^2 + 1^2} = 1.414$. Then the distance from the corner to the farthest point B on the large circle is $1.414 + 1 = 2.414$. The distance from the corner A to the nearest point C of the large circle is $1.414 - 1 = 0.414$. But this point is the *farthest* point on the small circle; that is, the distance from A to C for the small circle corresponds to the distance from A to B for the large circle. Accordingly

$$\frac{\text{Radius of small circle}}{0.414} = \frac{\text{Radius of large circle} = 1}{2.414}$$

from which

$$\text{Radius of small circle} = \frac{0.414}{2.414} = 0.1716.$$

Altitude of the regular tetrahedron. Given a regular tetrahedron, that is, a solid having four faces, all equal equilateral triangles. The length of every edge is 2. What is the altitude of the tetrahedron?

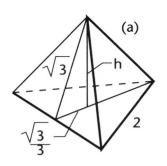

Because of the symmetry of the tetrahedron, the altitude is the distance from the top vertex to the center of the bottom face, which is at one-third of the face altitude from the edge. The length of the face altitude, as previously shown, is $\sqrt{3}$. The needed dimensions are shown in sketch (a), from which the altitude h of the tetrahedron is found:

$$h^2 = \left(\sqrt{3}\right)^2 - \left(\frac{\sqrt{3}}{3}\right)^2 = 3 - \frac{3}{9} = \frac{8}{3}$$

$$h = \sqrt{\frac{8}{3}} \approx 1.6330$$

Now prove that a point on this altitude at distance $h/4$ up from the base is equally distant from all four vertices.

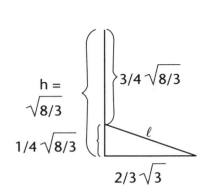

Again, because of symmetry, it will suffice to compare the distance to the top vertex with the distance to any of the three vertices at the base. The distance to the top vertex is (see sketch (b))

$$\frac{3}{4}\sqrt{\frac{8}{3}} = \sqrt{\frac{9}{16}\sqrt{\frac{8}{3}}} = \sqrt{\frac{9}{16} \times \frac{8}{3}} = \sqrt{\frac{3}{2}} \approx 1.2247$$

The distance to the bottom vertex is

$$\ell^2 = \left(\frac{1}{4}\sqrt{\frac{8}{3}}\right)^2 + \left(\frac{2}{3}\sqrt{3}\right)^2 = \frac{1}{16} \times \frac{8}{3} + \frac{4}{9} \times 3 = \frac{1}{6} + \frac{4}{3} = \frac{9}{6} = \frac{3}{2},$$

from which

$$\ell = \sqrt{\dfrac{3}{2}}$$

the same as the distance to the top vertex.

A different proof of this result is as follows: The center of gravity of any pyramid or cone lies one-fourth of the altitude above the base. For a tetrahedron, any one of the four faces may be taken as the base of a pyramid, so the center of gravity is one-fourth of the altitude from every face, or three-fourths of the altitude from every one of the four vertices.

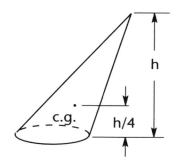

Miss Muffet and the spider. The sketch shows a $12 \times 12 \times 30$ room. Peacefully eating her curds and whey, Miss Muffet is seated on her tuffet at point M, at distance 1 above the center of edge CB. A spider is on the opposite wall at point S, at distance 1 below the center of edge HE. It desires to crawl along the wall to point M in order to sit beside Miss Muffet. Find the shortest path.

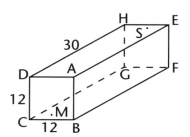

The obvious path goes straight up from S to the middle of edge HE, then straight along the ceiling to the middle of edge DA, and then straight down to point M, a total distance of $1 + 30 + 11 = 42$. But is that the shortest path?

Suppose that the room were unfolded so that its six surfaces lie on a flat surface. The unfolding can be done in various ways; three ways are shown here. In all three, the four long surfaces are unfolded the same way, but the end walls are attached to them along different edges. In each sketch the line from S to M shows the shortest path for that particular way of unfolding the room.

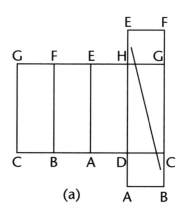

(a)

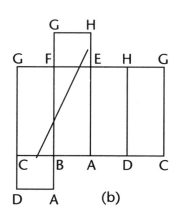

(b)

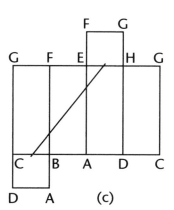

(c)

In sketch (a) the distance from S to M is

$$\sqrt{(30+6+6)^2 + 10^2} = \sqrt{42^2 + 10^2} = 2\sqrt{21^2 + 5^2} = 2\sqrt{466} = 2 \times 21.587 = 43.17$$

This path is thus longer than the obvious path previously considered. In sketch (b) the distance from S to M is

$$\sqrt{(30+6+1)^2 + (11+6)^2} = \sqrt{37^2 + 17^2} = \sqrt{1369 + 289} = \sqrt{1658} = 40.72$$

In sketch (c) the distance from S to M is

$$\sqrt{(30+1+1)^2 + (12+6+6)^2} = \sqrt{32^2 + 24^2} = 8\sqrt{4^2 + 3^2} = 8 \times 5 = 40$$

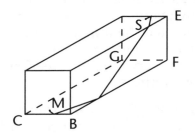

The paths in sketches (b) and (c) are both shorter than the obvious path, and the shortest path (c) is a full 2 units shorter. This sketch shows this shortest path along the surfaces of the room after they have been folded together.

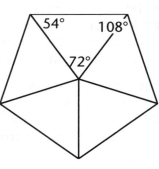

The regular pentagon. The equilateral triangle, the square, and the regular hexagon have already been discussed. The regular pentagon is shown on the right. The five radial lines divide it into five equal isosceles triangles. Each angle at the center is 360°/5 = 72°; so each angle at the base is $\frac{180° - 72°}{2}$ = 54°, and each angle of the pentagon is 2 × 54° = 108°.

Problems:
For a regular polygon of n sides,

(a) If it is divided into n equal isosceles triangles, as in the preceding sketch, what is the angle of the apex of each triangle?
(b) What is the base angle of each triangle?
(c) What is the polygon angle (the angle between adjacent sides)?

Answers:
(a) 360°/n

(b) $\dfrac{180° - \dfrac{360°}{n}}{2} = 90° - \dfrac{180°}{n} = 90°\left(1 - \dfrac{2}{n}\right)$

(c) $180° - \dfrac{360°}{n} = 180°\left(1 - \dfrac{2}{n}\right)$

Problems:
Draw a regular pentagon *ABCDE* and then draw the two diagonals *AC* and *BD*.

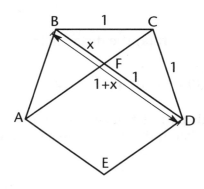

(a) Show that the two large triangles *ABC* and *BCD* are isosceles and that the small triangle *BCF* is similar to the two large ones.

(b) Show that triangle *CDF* is isosceles.

(c) Let the length of each side of the pentagon, as *CD*, be 1. What is the length of the diagonal *BD*? (This problem requires some algebra.)

Answers:
(a) They are isosceles because their two sides are sides of the regular polygon and are therefore equal. The two base angles of the small triangle, $\angle CBF$ and $\angle BCF$, are the same as the base angles of the two large isosceles triangles; hence the small triangle is isosceles and similar to the large triangles.

(b) The diagonal *AC* is parallel to side *ED*, and the diagonal *BD* is parallel to side *AE*. Hence *AFDE* is an equal-sided parallelogram (rhombus), so *FD = AE = 1*. Therefore triangle *CDF* has *FD = CD = 1* and is isosceles.

(c) Let the sides *BF* and *CF* of the small triangle be *x*. By comparing the small triangle with the similar large one, we have

$$\frac{x}{BC} = \frac{BC}{BD}, \text{ or } \frac{x}{1} = \frac{1}{x+1}, \text{ whence } x^2 + x = 1.$$

Solving for *x* gives $x = \dfrac{\sqrt{5}-1}{2} = 0.6180$. Finally, the length of the

diagonals, 1 + *x*, is $1 + \dfrac{\sqrt{5}-1}{2} = \dfrac{\sqrt{5}+1}{2} = 1.6180$.

Problem:
Draw a right triangle whose sides are 1, 2, and $\sqrt{5}$. Using these lengths, construct a regular pentagon with the aid of a straight edge and a compass (no ruler, no protractor).

In the preceding sketch the location of *F* along the line *BD* is of special interest because *BF/FD = FD/BD*. This ratio, 0.6180 has, since antiquity, attracted the attention of artists and mystics, who have referred to it as the golden section, golden mean, magic ratio, or other such fanciful term. It is postulated to have special aesthetic appeal in, for example, the width/length ratio of a picture frame, or the location of a tie clip along a necktie. (Shown on the right are two locations for the tie clip, corresponding to including or omitting the knot in defining the length of the necktie.)

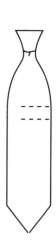

The 36°-54°-90° triangle. Drop a perpendicular from point *C* to the middle point *G* of the diagonal *BD*. In the triangle *GCD*, angle *C* is 54° (see the sketch at the beginning of the preceding section) and angle *D* is 90° – 54° = 36°. The length *GD* is

(1 + *x*)/2, or $\dfrac{\sqrt{5}+1}{4} = 0.8090$.

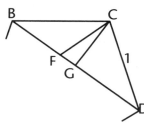

Then by the Pythagorean theorem,

$$CG = \sqrt{1 - (GD)^2} = \sqrt{1 - \left(\frac{\sqrt{5}+1}{4}\right)^2} = \frac{\sqrt{10 - 2\sqrt{5}}}{4} = 0.5878$$

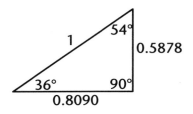

The sketch on the left shows these results for the 36° right triangle.

The triangle *FCG* is an 18°-72°-90° triangle. Its three sides are *FC* = 0.6180, *CG* = 0.5878, and *FG* = *BG* − *BF* = 0.8090 − 0.6180 = 0.1910. Increase these numbers by the factor 1.6180 in order to make the hypotenuse equal to 1. The results are shown in the sketch.

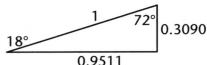

Exercise:
With a strip of paper tape (or a strip cut from a sheet of paper) make a tight flat overhand knot. The knot is in the form of a regular pentagon.

Areas

Rectangles and parallelograms. A rectangle is a 4-sided figure whose four angles are all right angles. Its area is the product of its length and its width—or of its base and its altitude. That is, if its base is *b* and its altitude is *h*, the area is *hb*. In this sketch, if each little square is a unit of area, the area of the rectangle is 8 × 5 = 40. The figure makes it clear that 5 rows of 8 units each is the same as 8 columns of 5 units each—which is one way of showing that 5 × 8 = 8 × 5.

A parallelogram is a 4-sided figure whose opposite sides are parallel (and therefore equal). The following sketch shows how a parallelogram can be transformed to a rectangle by cutting off a right triangle from one end and attaching it to the other end. In this way it becomes apparent that the area of the parallelogram is also the product of its base and its altitude.

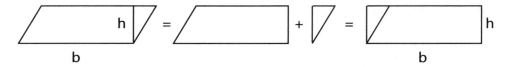

Triangles. A triangle is half of a parallelogram having the same base and altitude, as can be seen in the sketch. Therefore the area of a triangle is one-half of the product of its base and its altitude,

Area = $\frac{1}{2}$ *bh*. For a sketch like this one, the bottom line is usually called the base; however, either of the other two sides of the triangle can be considered as the base if that would be more convenient. In all three cases shown here the product of base and altitude must be the same since $\frac{1}{2}\,bh$ must be the area regardless of which side is chosen as base. That is, $\frac{1}{2}\,b_1h_1 = \frac{1}{2}\,b_2h_2 = \frac{1}{2}\,b_3h_3$.

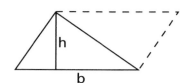

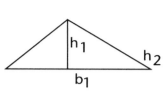 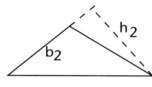 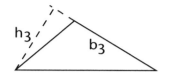

Two other ways of showing that the area of a triangle is half the product of its base and its altitude are indicated in these sketches. The triangles are cut up and the pieces rearranged to form rectangles. The method on the left shows that the area of the triangle is equal to base $\times (\frac{1}{2}$ altitude), and the method on the right shows that it is equal to $(\frac{1}{2}$ base$) \times$ altitude.

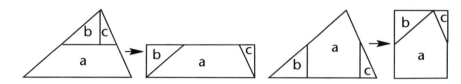

Problem:
Given a square cake with icing on both the top and sides. Cut it into 7 equal pieces so that all pieces have the same amount of cake and the same amount of icing.

Locate 7 points equally spaced along the perimeter, and make straight cuts from the center to these 7 points. Every piece now consists of one or two triangles, all with the same altitude and total base length and thus all with the same area. The inner pieces—cake plus top icing, but without the side layer of icing—have the same shapes as these 7 pieces but are slightly smaller, and similarly all have the same area. The seven sections of side icing, being the differences between equals, are then also all equal.

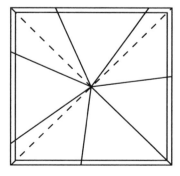

Problem:
Given a point O inside of an equilateral triangle, and perpendiculars from O to the three sides. Prove that the sum of the lengths of the three perpendiculars is a constant, and equal to the altitude of the triangle.

This property of equilateral triangles has important applications. Suppose, for example, that we have several different mixtures of three

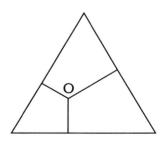

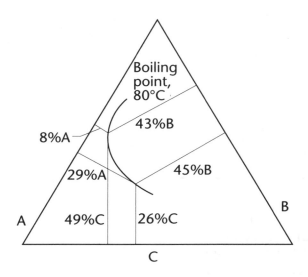

components, *A*, *B*, *C*. (These might be, for example, water, methyl alcohol, and ethyl alcohol, respectively.) We can represent the relative proportions of the three components in each mixture by a point on an equilateral triangle; for if we let the altitude of the triangle represent 100%, the three perpendiculars can represent the percentages of the three components. The sketch shows an equilateral triangle containing a curve labeled "boiling point, 80°C," which signifies that mixtures whose compositions are represented by points on the curve all have boiling points of 80°C. Example compositions are indicated for two points on the curve. The mixture represented by the upper point contains 8% *A*, 43% *B*, and 49% *C*; and the

mixture represented by the lower point contains 29% *A*, 45% *B*, and 26% *C*.

Other curves would correspond to other boiling points. The figure might appear like that shown in this sketch, which shows curves for three different boiling points.

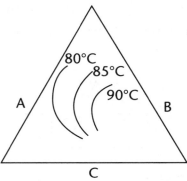

Perspective

Oblique viewing, parallel rays. In this section we suppose that the objects viewed are so small and so far away that the rays from the object to the eye are essentially parallel.

Draw two triangles of different shapes on separate sheets of paper (a fairly stiff paper, preferably). Now see if you can hold the second sheet in such a way that the triangle on it appears to have the same shape as the triangle on the first sheet (as viewed perpendicular to the sheet).

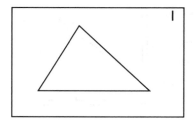 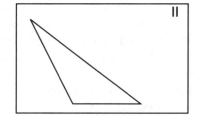

This can always be done—with a little experimentation you can find how to hold sheet II so that the triangle on it appears to have the desired shape. In this case, viewing the sheet from the lower right, as shown by the arrow, at an angle of about 15° with the sheet, will make the sheet look like the sketch on the right. Looking down from the opposite direction (dashed arrow) will accomplish the same result except that it will correspond to viewing the drawings upside down.

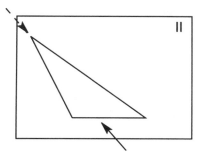
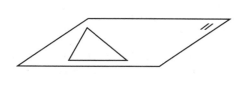

How could you have predicted the direction of the arrow in the left sketch?

Suppose that, instead of a triangle, each sheet has a pair of lines meeting at a point. Can you always determine how to hold either sheet so that its pair of lines will appear similar to the pair on the other sheet? Yes, for this problem is essentially the same as the problem of the two triangles—you have only to connect the ends of each pair of lines with a third line in order to convert the pairs of lines to triangles.

Suppose that, instead of a pair of lines on a triangle, each sheet has three lines meeting at a point. Can you now hold the second sheet so that its set of three lines will appear similar to the set of three lines on the first sheet?

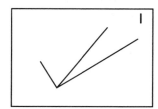
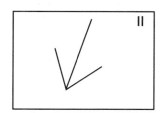

In general it is not possible, and it is easy to see why. For the pairs of lines, a particular viewing direction will make the second pair look like the first. But there is no reason why this viewing direction should make an arbitrary third line on II correspond similarly with a third line on I.

But now consider these two arrangements on which have been added dashed lines connecting the tips of the pairs of outer lines. The two

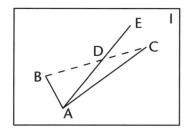
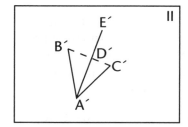

arrangements have been constructed so that

$$\frac{BD}{DC} = \frac{B'D'}{D'C'} \text{ and } \frac{AD}{DE} = \frac{A'D'}{D'E'}$$

Since all four fractions remain the same when the arrangements are viewed from various directions, it is now possible to view II from such a direction that it will be similar to I.

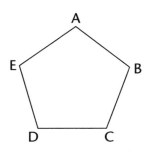

Problem:
The first sketch shows a regular pentagon as viewed from a direction perpendicular to its plane. The second sketch shows two adjoining edges of such a pentagon, as viewed obliquely. Complete this oblique view by drawing the other three edges.

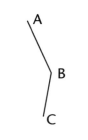

Answer:
In the first sketch, we see that the diagonal *EC* is parallel to edge *AB*. This parallelism is retained in the oblique view. Also, the length of *EC* is 1.618 times the length of *AB* (see the section on the regular pentagon) and this ratio is also retained in the oblique view. Accordingly we can locate point *E*. In order to locate point *D* we similarly construct the diagonal *AD* parallel to the edge *BC*. As a check, we may verify that ED is parallel to the diagonal *AC*.

Problem:
It is easy to show that the three medians of an equilateral triangle meet at a point that is one-third of the distance from each side to the

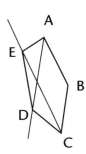

opposite vertex. Show that it then directly follows that the three medians of *any* triangle meet at a point that is one-third of the distance from each side to the opposite vertex.

Answer:
As already discussed, the equilateral triangle looks like any desired triangle if viewed from the correctly chosen direction. In this perspective view, medians remain medians and a point one-third of the distance along a median will remain one-third of the distance along the median.

The next problem of this group concerns three lines that meet at a point but are not all in the same plane. They might be considered as

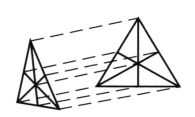

the three edges of a parallelepiped that diverge from a vertex, as shown by the heavy lines in sketch I. In sketch II is shown a set of three diverging lines on a sheet of paper, like the sets in the previous problems. You already know that, in general, there is no way to hold II so that its set of three lines is similar to the set of three lines on the drawing in I. But can you move *both* the parallelepiped and sketch II so that the set of three edges of the parallelepiped appears similar to the set of three lines in sketch II?

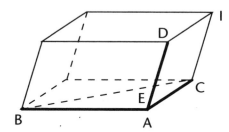
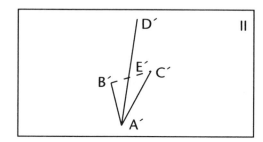

Yes, you can. Draw the base diagonal *BC* in the parallelepiped and the line *B′C′* in II. Move the parallelepiped until, as it appears to you (sketch III),

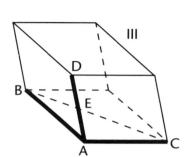

$$\frac{BE}{EC} = \frac{B'E'}{E'C'} \text{ and } \frac{AE}{ED} = \frac{A'E'}{E'D'}$$

Now you can move II until its set of three lines appears similar to the corresponding set of three lines in sketch III.

Note that *E* is not actually a point in space, because the lines *AD* and *BC* do not actually intersect. It is only a point on sketch III (or a point on a photograph of the parallelepiped, or a point on the retina of the eye).

Using a length of wire, make a stiff model of the three edges *AB*, *AD*, and *AC* and the diagonal *BC*, and move it about until the arrangement resembles, first, sketch I, and then, sketch III.

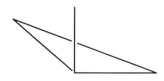

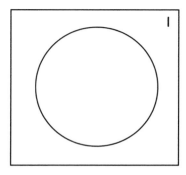
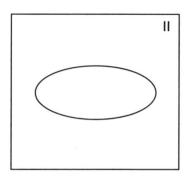

Given a drawing of a circle (I) and a drawing of an ellipse (II):

(1) How can you hold I so that it looks like II?
(2) How can you hold II so that it looks like I?

An ellipse may be considered as a flattened circle or as an elongated circle. Further discussion of ellipses is given in a later section.

Problems:

(a) Given a circle inscribed in an equilateral triangle, show that

$$\frac{\text{Area of circle}}{\text{Area of triangle}} = \frac{\pi}{3\sqrt{3}} = 0.6046$$

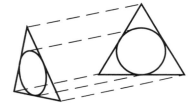

(b) We may view the equilateral triangle from such a direction that it looks like any desired triangle. Show that the inscribed circle then appears like an inscribed ellipse that is still tangent to the three sides at their midpoints and that has an area that is 0.6046 times that of the triangle. Such an ellipse is the largest ellipse that can be inscribed in a triangle.

(c) As viewed from point *A* (left-hand sketch), three posts in a distant group *O* appear to be uniformly spaced, as in the middle sketch. From point *B*, 30° to the left, they appear as in the right-hand sketch. (The spacings shown are in arbitrary units.) Just how are the three posts arranged?

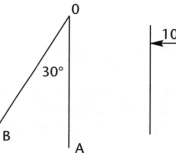

Answer:
Draw one set of three lines equally spaced as in the view from *A*. Draw a second set at 30° to the first set, spaced as in the view from *B*. The three inter-section points *P*, *Q*, and *R* show the arrangement of the three posts.

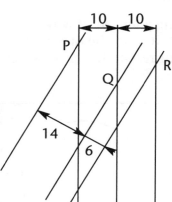

Question:
A spacecraft is flying around the moon at an altitude of about 60 km, continu-ally photographing the surface. A cliff appears on two successive photographs, approximately perpendicular to the direction of flight. How can one determine the height of the cliff from the two photographs? We know the locations of the spacecraft at the times that the pictures were taken.

Stereoscopy. Do the following experiment: Hold your fists in front of you at arm's length, side by side except that one fist is about 3 cm closer than the other fist. If you shut one eye and look at them, you cannot see that one is closer than the other, but if you look with both eyes you can easily see that one fist is closer than the other. This experiment and the preceding problem exemplify the basis for any stereoscopic observation by your eyes (or in general, for any stereo-scopic observation, as by a pair of cameras, in order to get the effect of solidity, or depth).

Shown here is a pair of stereo views of a trio of balls. You see the three-dimensional arrangement by looking at the left view with your left eye and looking at the right view with your right eye. That, however, is more easily said than done, for you cannot separately manipulate your two eyes as easily as you can your two hands.

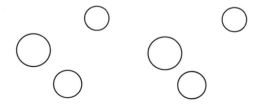

There are two approaches: 1. Look at the space between the two views and then let your eyes relax, as if you were day-dreaming. 2. Look over the top of the page at some distant object—perhaps something on the opposite wall, and then, without changing focus, lower your eyes to the pair of views. In either method you will, at first, see four views, since each eye sees both views. With a little effort you can make the middle two converge and give the stereo-scope effect. (If one of the middle two appears above or below the other, rotate the paper, or bend your head to the side in order to get them to the same level.)

Such a stereoscopic view has an interesting characteristic: When you move your head, say, to the left, the object appears to move to the right. Explain.

Answer:

In the sketch, *A* and *B* are your two eyes, *C* and *D* are the views of the object on the paper, and *E* is the imaginary object located about 40 cm behind the paper. Suppose that *E* were a real object. Then when you moved your head to the left, your eyes would move with it, to *A'* and *B'*, and the two lines of sight would move to *A'E* and *B'E*, still converging at *E* (short-dashed lines). However, in the stereoscopic view, the lines of sight (long-dashed lines) must go through the two views *C* and *D*, so when you move your head to the left, they converge to *E'*, which is to the right of *E*.

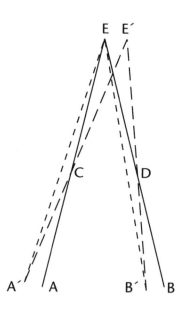

A reversed object, in which front and back are interchanged, is seen by looking at the left view, *C*, with your right eye and looking at the right view, *D*, with your left eye. This reversed object is seen at *F*, where the two lines of sight cross. For this case, when you move your head to the left, the imaginary object *F* also appears to move to the left. Why?

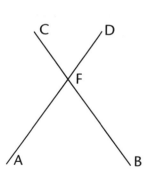

Any surface with a simple, small periodic design will show the stereo effect—for example, a sheet of ruled paper (turned sideways, with the lines vertical), a red-checked gingham tablecloth, the backs of a set of encyclopedia volumes on a table or bookshelf, or even the teeth of a comb. Thus, on staring vacantly at the tablecloth, you may suddenly perceive that it has receded from you; and moving your head to the side will verify that different checks have merged to give you a stereo image.

Problem:
On February 5, 1979, the spacecraft Voyager I photographed the planet Jupiter from a distance of 28.4 million kilometers. Sketch (a) shows the planet and three of its four large moons, as they appear in the photograph. Given that

The moons have nearly circular orbits with radii as shown,

The orbits are almost exactly in the plane of the planet's equator,

The equatorial radius is as shown,

The spacecraft was so far away that the light rays from Jupiter and the moons to the camera were nearly parallel,

Locate some points along the planet's equator and sketch the equator.

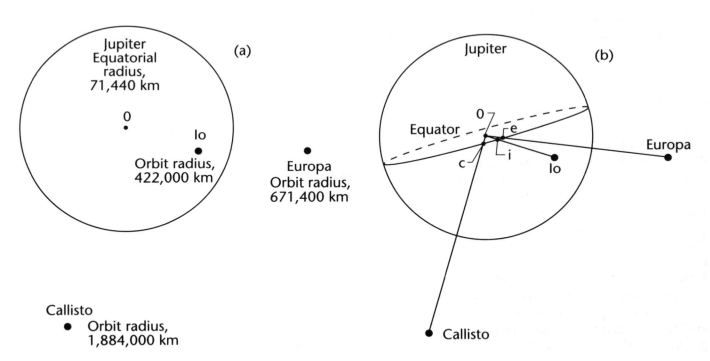

Procedure:
Draw lines from the center of the planet, *O*, to the three moons (sketch (b)). Along the line from *O* to Callisto, locate the point *c* such that its distance from *O* is

$$\frac{71440}{1884000} \times \text{length of the line from } O \text{ to Callisto on the sketch}$$

Similarly spot the points *i* and *e* on the lines from *O* to *Io* and to Europa. These three points must lie on the equator, so we draw an ellipse through them, with *O* as its center, representing the equator.

The planet *Io* is seen against the face of Jupiter, so it is obviously between the camera and the planet; and the point *i* must then be on the near side of the planet. With regard to Callisto and Europa, however, we cannot tell directly from the photograph whether they are closer or farther than Jupiter; correspondingly, the point *c* or the point *e* might be on either the near side or the far side of the equator. However, the only equator ellipse that we can manage to draw through the three points is the one that is shown on the sketch; that is, all three moons are closer to the camera than Jupiter is.

Nearby viewing, nonparallel rays. In the preceding problems, we considered the appearance of an object when the eye is so far away that the rays from the object to the eye are practically parallel. We now consider the appearance of an object when the eye is fairly close, as when an artist is painting a still life.

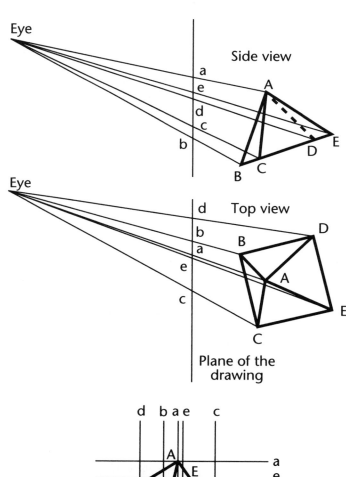

The object to be considered is a square-based pyramid. The back edges of the pyramid could, of course, not be visible unless the pyramid were transparent; however, for completeness, we include them as dashed lines in the drawing.

In the sketch the artist's canvas is supposed to be perpendicular to the plane of the paper, and is designated in the sketch as "Plane of the Drawing." The pyramid is supposed to be in the lower right part of the scene. Then the artist's eye is above and to the left of the pyramid; and it is from that viewpoint that he will draw it.

The upper part of the figure is a side view of the arrangement, and just below it is a top view. (These are ordinary draftsman's drawings, made as if the object is viewed with parallel rays.) In both views, straight lines go from the eye to the five corners, *A, B, C, D,* and *E*. The points where these lines pass through the canvas are designated *a, b, c, d,* and *e*, respectively.

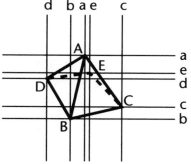

You can now proceed to make the drawing shown in the bottom part of the figure: Draw a set of horizontal parallel lines spaced exactly like the points *a, b, c, d,* and *e* in the side view; and a set of vertical parallel lines spaced like the same five points in the top view. Then where the two *a* lines cross is where the apex *A* of the pyramid will be on the drawing; where the two *b* lines cross is where the bottom corner *B* will be on the drawing; and so on. Connecting the points with straight lines finally gives the desired drawing of the pyramid on the canvas.

The base of the pyramid is square, so opposite edges are equal and parallel. However, you may have noticed that in the final drawing they do not appear to be either equal or parallel. As a similar case consider a drawing showing two railroad tracks crossing each other at right angles and going off into the distance. Where they cross, the rails actually form a perfect square; but the drawing shows

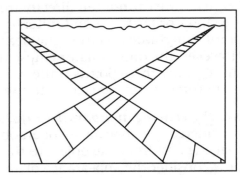

each pair of rails converging in the distance and hence cannot show the square as two pairs of equal and parallel lines.

Return to the drawing of the pyramid. If the viewer looks at the canvas from the point marked Eye, he will see the pyramid just as the artist saw it when he drew it. If the viewer looks at the drawing from any other point, the pyramid will appear more or less distorted. That is, the pyramid as seen on the drawing will not appear like the actual pyramid as viewed from *any* location. Similarly a person watching a movie will see everything grossly distorted if he is seated far to the side of the screen. Such distortion may be very disturbing at first, but the viewer usually adapts to it after a few minutes.

Pascal's theorem. Given two lines that pass through point *O*, with points *A, E,* and *C* on one of the lines and points *F, B,* and *D* on the other line. Extended lines *EF* and *CB* meet at *P*, extended lines *BA* and *DE* meet at *Q*, and extended lines *FA* and *DC* meet at *R*. We can show that the three intersection points *P, Q,* and *R* lie along a straight line.

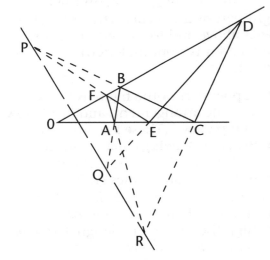

As illustrated in the preceding sketch, a picture of a pair of parallel lines (as railroad tracks) shows the lines converging to a point on the horizon; and if the landscape contains more than one pair of parallel lines, all the pairs converge to points along the same horizon. Suppose we consider our sketch to be such a picture, with lines *FA* and *DC* representing one pair of parallel lines, lines *BA* and *DE* representing another pair of parallel lines, and line QR representing the horizon where the two pairs of parallel lines appear to converge. We must now show that lines CB and EF represent another pair of parallel lines in the same landscape.

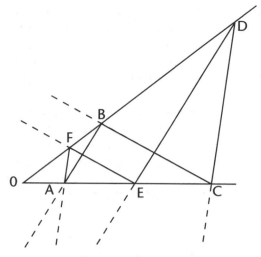

This sketch shows the landscape as in an engineering drawing (or as viewed from a high-altitude airplane). In this drawing, lines FA and DC are parallel and lines BA and DE are parallel. Then triangles OFA and ODC are similar, and triangles OBA and ODE are similar. Then

$$\frac{OF}{OA} = \frac{OD}{OC} \text{ and } \frac{OB}{OA} = \frac{OD}{OE}$$

Dividing the first equation by the second gives

$$\frac{OF}{OB} = \frac{OE}{OC}, \text{ or } \frac{OF}{OE} = \frac{OB}{OC}$$

which shows that triangles OFE and OBC are similar. Lines FE and BC must then be parallel so that in the picture (the first sketch) they must meet at some point P that is on the same horizon as points Q and R.

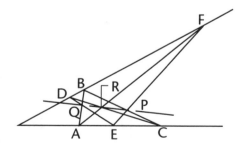

In this sketch we have interchanged the labels of points F and D. The three pairs of lines, EF and CB, BA and DE, FA and DC, now all cross within the angle; nevertheless the three intersection points, P, Q, and R, still appear to lie on a straight line. Thus, although we proved the theorem by the device of assuming that the sketch represents a photograph of a landscape, the theorem seems to apply in cases in which the same device seems inapplicable. We would not really be justified in assuming that our previous proof applies to this case; so we proceed with the following proof for this case in which the intersection points Q, R, and P lie *between* the two lines DBF and AEC.

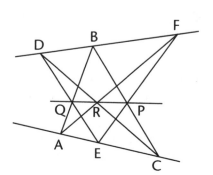 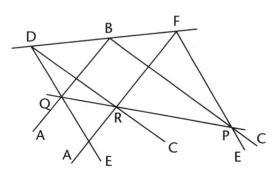

We have the "hexagon" *ABCDEFA* (left-hand sketch) inscribed between two lines, which we interpret as a picture of three pairs of parallel lines going off to *A, E,* and *C* on the infinitely distant horizon. The three pairs of parallel lines are shown in the right-hand sketch. Now in the previous proof we had such a group of six lines intersecting at three points along a straight line,and we showed that if the group included two pairs of parallel lines, the remaining two lines were also parallel. We now have the converse problem: Given that the group consists of three pairs of parallel lines, show that the three intersection points *Q, R,* and *P* lie along a straight line. More specifically show that if we draw a line through two of the intersection points, say *Q* and *P,* the third intersection point *R* will be on the same line.

For the present we shall say that line *DR* intersects line *QP* at point *N,* and line *FR* intersects *QP* at point *M.* Extend the lines *DBF* and *QP* of the right-hand sketch to meet at point *O.* By comparing similar triangles, we get

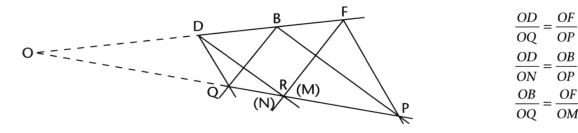

$$\frac{OD}{OQ} = \frac{OF}{OP}$$

$$\frac{OD}{ON} = \frac{OB}{OP}$$

$$\frac{OB}{OQ} = \frac{OF}{OM}$$

Divide the first equation by the second equation and get

$$\frac{ON}{OQ} = \frac{OF}{OB}, \text{ or } \frac{OB}{OQ} = \frac{OF}{ON}$$

Comparing this last equation with the third equation shows that points *N* and *M* are identical—that is, the lines from *D* and from *F* both intersect the line *OQP* at the same point. In other words, the intersection point *R* lies on *QP,* which is what we wished to prove.

Problems:
(1) Using the techniques described, make a drawing of a set of three mutually perpendicular lines of equal length crossing each other at their midpoints. Assume the eye to be in about the same location as for the pyramid—above and to the left.

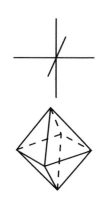

Then, on this drawing, connect pairs of adjacent ends of the lines (corresponding to equilateral triangles), thus getting a drawing of a regular octahedron.

(2) Suppose that, using a wide-angle lens, you photograph a scene containing a sphere far to the side. Will the image of the sphere on the film be a circle?

No, it will be an ellipse, the intersection of a circular cone with a plane oblique to its axis (see p. 175). If you look at the ellipse from the direction of the lens (or the sphere) it will appear circular. If, however, you project your picture onto a screen and view the scene perpendicularly from the back of the room, the image will appear elliptical, and a viewer who is unaware that you used a wide-angle lens might conclude that you have a low-quality camera.

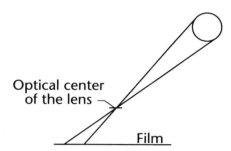

Optical center of the lens

Film

(3) You are given a drawing and told that it accurately represents a cube; however, you suspect that it is just an arbitrarily drawn six-sided figure. How might you verify your suspicion?

(a) A cube has three sets of four parallel lines. If the drawing represents a cube, each set of four lines, when extended, should meet at a point that represents infinity in that direction (sketch (a)).

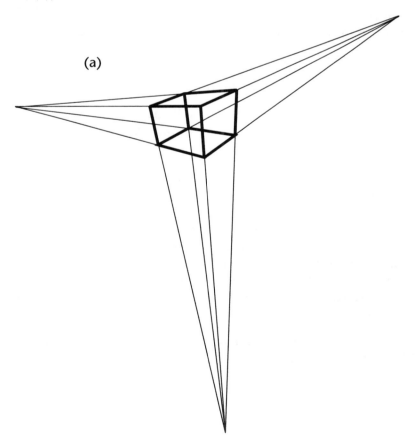

(a)

(b)

(b) If the drawing represents a cube, the four cube diagonals in the drawing would have to meet at the same point (sketch (b)).

Note that if the figure satisfies these two criteria, that fact does not prove that the figure represents a cube or even a parallelepiped; but it does indicate that the figure was not arbitrarily drawn.

(4) Suppose the figure of problem (3) does represent a cube. Within the figure sketch a smaller cube having the same orientation and the same center.

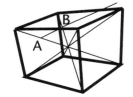

Draw the cube diagonals. From any of the three points at infinity (sketch (a) of problem (3)) draw a line connecting two diagonals, as shown in the sketch. From the two end points *A* and *B* of this line draw lines to other diagonals, similarly aligned with the other two points at infinity. Continue in this way until all edges of the little cube have been drawn.

The Conic Sections

Ellipses. As already mentioned, an ellipse is a flattened circle, in which every point of the circle has been brought closer to a given diameter by the same fraction. For example, the sketch shows a circle with a number of chords like *EAD* drawn perpendicular to a diameter. On each of these lines, points like *B* and *C* are located at one-fourth and one-half of the distance from the diameter to the boundary ($AB = \frac{1}{4} AD$; $AC = \frac{1}{2} AD$). The curves through the two sets of points are ellipses. This definition tells us immediately that if we look at a circle obliquely we see it as an ellipse, since all of a set of parallel lines are foreshortened by the same fraction.

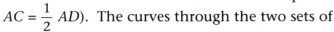

A second definition of an ellipse is that it is the path of a point that moves in such a way that the sum of its distances to two fixed points is constant. For example, in the ellipse of this sketch, *MA* + *NA* = *MB* + *NB* = *MC* + *NC*. The two points *M* and *N* are called the foci of the ellipse. (Foci is plural of focus.) Compare this definition of an ellipse with the definition of a circle: (1) For a circle, the point moves such that its distance from a given point (the center) is constant. (2) For an ellipse, the point moves such that the sum of its distances from two given points (the foci) is constant.

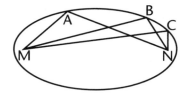

The ellipse as a section of a cone. When a plane passes through a right circular cone, the intersection is an ellipse. Following is a simple proof.

First consider sketch (a), where two tangents *PA* and *PB* are drawn to a circle from point *P*. It is easy to see that the two tangents are equal: Draw the line *PO* to the center of the circle, and draw the radii to the two tangent points *A* and *B*. The two right triangles *OPA* and *OPB* are equal since the two radii are equal and *OP* is common to both; hence the corresponding sides *PA* and *PB* are equal. Now consider sketch (b), where several tangents are drawn from a point *P* to a sphere. We can again draw radii to the tangent points, and show that the triangles *POA*, *POB*, . . . are equal, hence that the tangents *PA*, *PB*, . . . are equal.

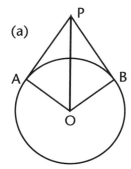

(a)

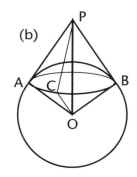

(b)

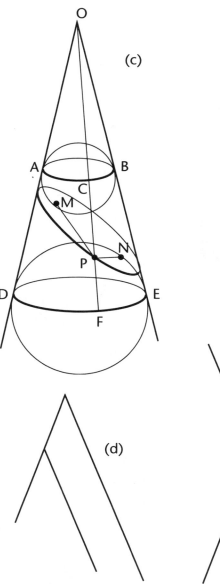

(c)

Now consider sketch (c), which shows the intersection of a plane with a right circular cone, which we shall prove is an ellipse. We insert into the cone two spheres that are tangent to the cone along the circles *ABC* and *DEF*, and are tangent to the plane at points *M* and *N*. Through an arbitrary point *P* of the intersection we draw the cone element *OCPF*. The lines *PM* and *PC* are tangent to the same sphere and are therefore equal; similarly, the lines *PF* and *PN* are tangent to the same sphere and are therefore equal. Then $PM + PN = PC + PF = CF$, the distance along a cone element from the upper circle to the lower circle. Finally, since all such distances between the two circles are equal, the sum $PM + PN$ must be the same for all points *P* around the intersection. Hence, by definition, the intersection is an ellipse and the two points *M* and *N* are its foci.

Parabola and hyperbola. As the inclination of the intersecting plane increases, the ellipse gets longer and relatively narrower until, finally, the plane is parallel to one of the cone elements, as in sketch (d). The intersection is then a parabola. If the inclination increases further, the plane intersects the extension of the cone through its vertex, as in sketch (e). The complete intersection thus consists of two branches, which together constitute a hyperbola. The three types of curves—ellipses, parabolas, and hyperbolas are known as the conic sections.

(d)

(e)

The standard definitions of the parabola and the hyperbola are as follows:

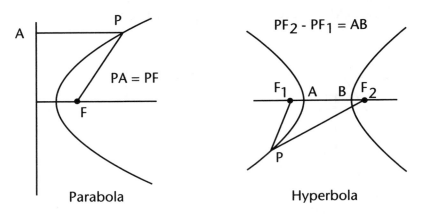

Parabola	Hyperbola

Parabola: A plane curve, the path of a point whose distances from a fixed point and a fixed line are equal. (In the sketch, $PA = PF$.)

Hyperbola: A 2-branch plane curve, the path of a point such that the difference between the distances to two fixed points is constant. (In the sketch, $PF_2 - PF_1 = AB$.)

Problem:
The sketch shows the two branches of a hyperbola formed by a plane that intersects the double cone. F_1 and F_2 are the points where the two spheres touch the plane, and B is an arbitrary point along the hyperbola. Prove that $BF_2 - BF_1$ is the same for all points B along this branch of the hyperbola.

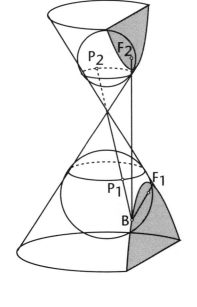

An ordinary flashlight may be used to demonstrate that the ellipse, the parabola, and the hyperbola are sections of a cone. The flashlight produces not only a strong central beam but also a weaker conical beam having a half-angle of about 45°, indicated in the sketches by dashed lines. In a darkened room, shine the light against the wall from a distance of about 15 cm. Then the conical beam represents the cone, and the wall represents the plane that passes through it. If the flashlight is at an angle of about 70° to the wall (sketch (a)), the outline of the conical beam on the wall is an ellipse. If the angle is

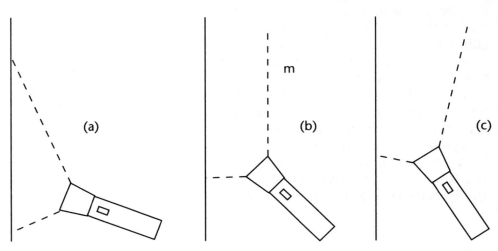

reduced about 25° so that the wall is parallel to the opposite edge of the beam (line *m* in sketch (b)) the outline of the beam is a parabola. If the angle is reduced further (sketch (c)) the outline on the wall is a branch of a hyperbola.

Perspective characteristics. When a drawing of a conic section is viewed obliquely, it appears different, of course; however, it still appears as the same type of conic section. For example, if the parabola in the sketch is viewed obliquely from the lower left, it will appear as a narrower parabola, and its vertex, initially at *M*, will have moved up along the curve; and when the viewing direction makes only a small angle with the plane of the paper, the vertex will appear to be at point *N*. Similarly, if an ellipse or hyperbola is viewed obliquely, it will still appear as an ellipse or hyperbola, but it will appear wider or narrower, and its vertices will appear to have moved to different locations on the curves.

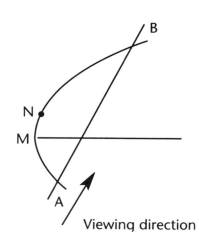

Unlike ellipses and hyperbolas, all parabolas are geometrically similar. Although we just referred to a "narrower" parabola, if we view this narrower parabola through a magnifying glass it will appear like the original; that is, the "narrower" parabola is just a smaller parabola. Stated differently, if we view a parabola through a cylindrical lens, which magnifies in only one direction, it appears the same (except for orientation) as if we viewed it through an ordinary lens that magnifies in both directions. The magnification ratios of the two lenses are different, however.

Problem:
Show that a one-dimensional n-times magnification in the direction perpendicular to the parabola axis gives the same result as a two-dimensional n^2-times magnification. If you can handle the analytical geometry, you might also consider one-dimensional magnification in other directions.

The Königsberg Bridges

In the eighteenth century the city of Königsberg,* on the Pregel River near where it opens into the Gulf of Danzig, had seven bridges, as shown schematically in sketch (a). The problem associated with the city and its bridges is: Can one walk through the city in such a way as to pass over every bridge once, and return to the starting point? Try various routes on the sketch and see if you can come to a conclusion as to whether it is possible.

It was then in East Prussia. Now in Soviet Russia, it is called Kaliningrad and its river is called the Pregolya River; and it has nine bridges.

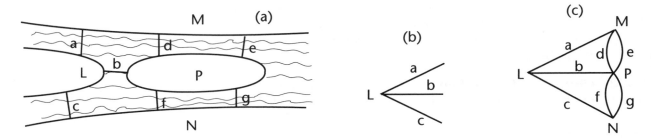

In order to solve the problem we first simplify the arrangement. The three bridges *a, b*, and *c* on the left, all of which go to the area *L*, we consider as meeting at a point (sketch (b)). That simplification does not alter the problem, since in both sketches if we get to *L* by one of the three bridges we can leave by either of the other two. Similarly we represent the island *P* by a point to which five bridges are attached and we represent each of the areas *M* and *N* by points to which three bridges are attached (sketch (c)). Our map has thus been simplified to a network in which points *L, M*, and *N* are each attached to three bridges and point *P* is attached to five bridges. Points like *L, M, N, P* to which several bridges are attached are called nodes. If the number of bridges attached to a node is even, it is called an "even node;" if the number is odd, it is called an "odd node." We see in sketch (c) that all four nodes are odd.

We now reason as follows: If one starts out from an odd node, say *L*, and goes along, say *a*, he must later return to *L* along, say *b*. In order to traverse *c*, he must again leave *L*, going along *c*. But now, having traversed all three bridges, there is no way to return to *L* without passing over one of these three bridges a second time. We see, then, that the *starting* node must be even.

A similar reasoning applies to every other node (other than the starting node). If one enters, say, a three-bridge node along one bridge, he may leave along a second bridge, and eventually return along the third bridge, after which he is unable to proceed further. Thus, not only the starting node but also every other node must be even. A compromise is possible if the network has exactly two odd nodes: One might start out at one of the odd nodes and end at the other odd node. But if there are more than two odd nodes, even this type of compromise is impossible.

If all the nodes are even, there is no way for a route to end at a node other than the starting node. For: (a) Whenever a route goes through a node, it traverses one bridge when arriving and one bridge when leaving, so an even number of untraversed bridges remain at the node. (b) Hence, when the traveler traverses a bridge to reach a node, that node must have another bridge along which he can leave (unless it is the starting node). This bridge, in turn, reaches another node that has another bridge along which he can leave. In this way, he continues from node to node, for his progress can never be blocked until he returns to the starting node.

As just shown, if all the nodes of a network are even, the traveler will never be stranded—he must be able to continue until he returns to the starting node. The fact that he returns to the starting node, however, does not assure that he has transvered every bridge of the network. Nevertheless, if any bridges were omitted, it will always be possible to expand his route so that it will include them. The proof of this statement will be the answer to the first problem.

Problems:

1. Prove that an even-node network can always be traversed completely.
2. For the networks shown in the sketches, determine:

    (a) Which can be traversed completely, with return to the starting node.
    (b) Which can be traversed completely, starting at one node and ending at another.
    (c) Which cannot be traversed completely.

3. Show that the number of odd nodes in a network is even.

 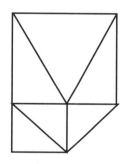 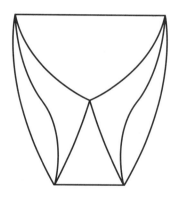 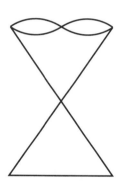

4. Consider the edges and corners of a cube as a network of 12 bridges and 8 nodes. All the nodes are odd.

    (a) Find a shortest route that goes through all the nodes and returns to the starting node.
    (b) Find a route that goes over the maximum number of bridges (not traversing any bridge more than once) and passes through all the nodes but does not return to the starting node.

5. Consider the edges and vertices of a regular dodecahedron (next page) as a network of 30 bridges and 20 nodes. Do parts (a) and (b) of problem 4 for this case too.

Answers:

1. Suppose that the network is so extensive and confusing that when you have traced a path through it, finally returning to your starting node *S*, you leave part of the network untraversed. Such a route is shown by the solid lines in the sketch. Now trace a route through the untraversed part (shown by the dashed lines in the sketch), starting at some node, as *N*, where it joins the first route. Then the desired complete route is as follows: Follow the first route as far as *N*, then traverse the second route completely, returning to *N*, and then complete the first route from *N* back to *S*.

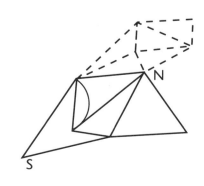

3. Every bridge is attached to a node at both ends, so the total number of attachments is twice the number of bridges and is therefore an even number. The total number of attachments on the even nodes is an even number, because each even node has an even number of attachments. Then the total number of attachments on the odd nodes must also be even, since the sum of the two numbers must be even. Then, since each odd node has an odd number of attachments, there must be an even number of them.

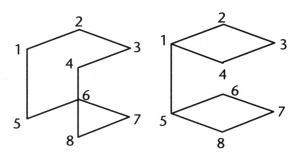

4. (a) 1-2-3-4-8-7-6-5-1

   (b) 1-2-3-4-1-5-6-7-8-5

5. (a) 1-2-3-4-. . .-18-19-20-1

   (b) 1-2-3-4-5-1-20-19-18-17-16-15-14-13-12-11-10-9-8-7-6-5

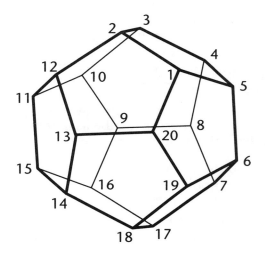

The Labyrinth Problem

The labyrinth problem (or the catacombs problem) is related to the problem of the Königsberg bridges: A person starting at any node (crossroad) in the labyrinth must traverse every path in the labyrinth, once in each direction, and finally return to the starting node. Requiring that every path be traversed twice, once in each direction, is comparable to doubling every bridge in the Königsberg-bridges problem; it assures that every node is even. The other main difference between the two problems is that, for the Königsberg-bridges problem, the traveler has a map of the city with its bridge system, whereas the labyrinth explorer does not have a map of the labyrinth.

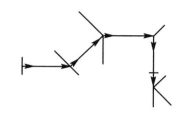

The solution given by G. Tarry in 1895 is essentially as follows: (1) As you pass along a path from one node to the next, draw an arrow on the wall, showing your direction of travel, at each end of the path— that is, at the entry and exit of the path (see the sketch). (2) When you come to a node and find that you have not been there before (that is, no arrows can be seen at the entrances of any of the other paths), make a special mark on your exit arrow to indicate that this was the first path by which you arrived at this node—the "discovery path." Such a mark is shown on the final arrow of the sketch. (3) Proceed along any paths you like from node to node (if you come to a dead end, simply return to the node and try another path) but (a) do not go along a path a second time in the same direction, and, above all, (b) *do not leave a node along the path by which you first arrived there (the discovery path, marked by the special arrow) unless no other unused exit path from that node remains.*

This italicized restriction is the essence of Tarry's rule. To repeat: Proceed through the labyrinth in any way you like but (1) do not go along any path twice in the same direction and (2) do not leave a node by its discovery path unless you have no other choice. Then, when you finally return to your starting point and find no unused exit paths there, you will have passed twice, once in each direction, along every path in the labyrinth.

To justify this assertion we first note that in your route through the labyrinth the number of arrivals at a node equals the number of departures from it (except, of course, the starting node and any other node when you have just arrived there). It is impossible to be left stranded at a node; that is, when you arrive at a node there will always be a permissible (unused) exit path, even if you have to leave along the same path by which you just arrived; and not until you have finally left the node along its discovery path will all of the entrance and exit paths at that node be used up.

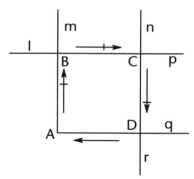

The fact that you cannot be left stranded at a node assures that you can continue until you finally return to the starting node and find no permissible (unused) exit paths there. But is it possible by this procedure to return to the starting node and leave some of the labyrinth unexplored? Consider the simple labyrinth portion shown in the sketch. If your path is *ABCDA*, as indicated, does that complete your route and yet leave the six dead-end side branches unexplored? No, your task is not yet finished, for the exit path *AD* is still available at *A*. Hence you turn and go back from *A* to *D*. And now, since *CD* was a discovery path, you may not continue from *D* to *C* before exploring both of the side branches *q* and *r*. Similarly, when you get to *C* you will have to explore both of the side branches *n* and *p* before continuing to *B*, and so on. Thus, (a) having to take an available exit path, but (b) avoiding the discovery path until it is the only available exit path assures that no parts of this labyrinth remain unexplored.

Is this conclusion applicable to all labyrinths? Consider the route shown in the following sketch, which represents a part of a labyrinth near the starting node. Let *A* be the starting node, *B* the first node

Chapter 6

discovered from *A*, and *C* the first node discovered from *B*. When the route eventually ends at *A*, all paths meeting at *A* have been used twice, including the discovery path *AB*. But the route would not have returned to *A* along this discovery path unless all the other paths meeting at *B* have been used twice; and the path between *B* and *C* would not have been used twice unless all the other paths meeting at *C* have

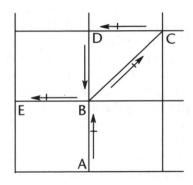

been used twice. We may not continue this simple reasoning, how-ever, for we may not assume that from each node we proceed directly to discover the next one. In this sketch, for example, the route goes from *D* to *B*, which has already been discovered, before proceeding to discover *E*. In any case there is a central group of two or more nodes (*A*, *B*, . . .) all of whose paths will have been traversed twice before the route ends at *A*. Adjacent to this central group is at least one node that was discovered by a path from one of the central groups, just as node *E* in the sketch was discovered from *D*. Then all of this node's paths must also have been traversed twice (just as, in the sketch, the route could not have returned to *B* from *E* unless all of *E*'s paths were used twice). Then this node may be added to the central group. By this reasoning we continue to enlarge the central group, taking in one node after another, until all the nodes are in the group. Accordingly we conclude that every path in the labyrinth has been used twice before the route ends at *A*.

Problem:
Traverse this labyrinth, starting at node *A*. Number your paths be-tween nodes, indicate directions of travel by arrows, and mark the arrows of discovery paths. Note that the four corners of the labyrinth need not be considered as nodes—they are merely bends in the paths.

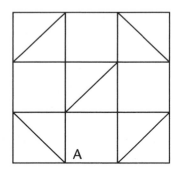

Answer:
This sketch shows one of the many possible routes.

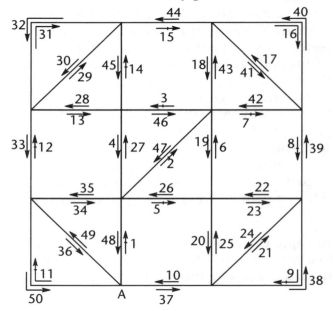

The Möbius Band

Cut a strip of paper about 30 cm long and 3 cm wide. Use a paper that is lined on only one side or that has some other way of distinguishing between the two surfaces; or, if both sides of your paper are alike, color one side or put marks over it with your pencil (sketch (a)). Twist the strip through 180° (sketch (b)) and paste together the ends to form a twisted belt (sketch (c)). The letters *m, n, p, q* designate corresponding points in sketches (a) and (c).

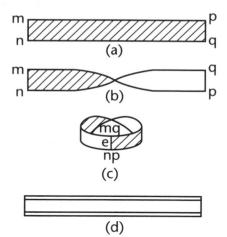

The twisted belt, or *Möbius band*, is a surface with only one side—you may move your finger along the surface from any point to any other point without having to go around an edge. For example, you may start at point *e*, move left along the center of the band, come to the point directly under point *e* after going once around, and continue around once more to return to the starting point, having thereby traversed both of the original sides of the strip shown in (a).

The Möbius band has not only a single surface but also a single edge. You may start at any point on the edge, run your finger tip twice around the band and return to the starting point, having thereby traversed both of the original edges of the strip shown in (a).

Get another strip like the one in sketch (a) and draw two lines along it at distances of 6 or 7 mm from the two edges (sketch (d)).

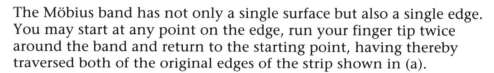

Convert the strip into a Möbius band as before; the two lines now run along beside the double-length edge that was just mentioned. Using your scissors, cut along the lines until you return to the starting point, and examine the result. You now have

(1) The edge band, twice as long as the Möbius band from which it was cut. It has a 720° twist, and is thus not a Möbius band—it has two separate surfaces. Note that in order to have only one surface, a band must have an odd number of half-twists (an odd number × 180°).

(2) The central part is still a Möbius band, but narrower than the original one because its edge has been trimmed off. It is not free of the edge band, however, for the two are linked together.

Exercises:
Make another Möbius band with lines near the edge, just like the one that you just cut into two parts. Study it and try to see if you might have predicted the results of cutting along the edge lines.

Suppose you have a Möbius band and cut it along the center. What would be the result? The result is merely the limiting case of the edge band, when the edge band becomes so wide that the central Möbius band is squeezed down to nothing. That is, the result is a band twice as long as the Möbius band, with a 720° twist.

What will be the result if you cut this band along the middle?

Since the band has two surfaces and two edges, cutting it along the middle merely makes two bands that are like it except that they are narrower; also, the two are linked together.

Compact Möbius bands. The bands for the preceding studies were made of strips that were 30 cm long and 3 cm wide. Maintaining the same width, see how short a strip you can use to make the band. Note how the band seems to approach something like a twisted cone as your strip becomes short.

Make a compact band as follows: Cut a piece of paper in the shape shown, with three equilateral triangles (numbered 1, 2, and 3 in the sketch) and a tab on the edge of triangle 3 (sketch (a)). Fold triangle 1 under triangle 2 (sketch (b)); then fold triangle 3 under triangle 1 (sketch (c)). Smear adhesive on the side of the tab that faces us in sketch (c), fold it up, insert it between triangles 1 and 2, and attach it to the edge of triangle 1. This last step connects the uncolored surface with the colored surface.

Verify that this compact arrangement has only one surface. (Note that the crease at the fold in the paper is not an edge; it is merely a highly curved part of the surface.)

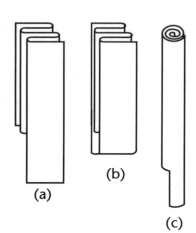

Other types of compact one-sided sheets are shown in these sketches. Sketch (a) shows an accordion-pleat arrangement. It has an odd number of sections, so that when the tab is folded under and attached to the back section (sketch (b)), one surface becomes continuous with the other.

Another arrangement is a spiral, as in sketch (c). The tab at the outer end of the spiral must be folded under and attached to the inner end of the spiral in order to complete the construction.

The Klein bottle. If a bottle is made of thin sheet, the opening at the top has a sharp edge, and one cannot move along the surface from the inside of the bottle to the outside without passing over this sharp edge. The Klein bottle, like the Möbius band, has only one surface—one may go along the surface from any point to any other point without having to go around a sharp edge. In fact, unlike the Möbius band, it has no edge at all.

Twists in a Rubber Band

Rubber band on a pencil. Hang a wide rubber band near the end of a pencil, as in sketch (a) on the next page. Take the back part (m) and wind it once around the pencil. Does sketch (b) represent the result? No, for your rubber band now has a 360° twist, as indicated in sketch (c). If you now take the back part (n) and wind it once more around the pencil, the rubber band will have a total twist of 720°. Instead, take the *front* part (*l*) and wind it once around the pencil. By using the front part, you add a 360° twist in the opposite direction, thereby canceling the first twist and yielding an untwisted band (sketch (d)). Each additional winding either adds or subtracts a 360° twist; and only an odd number of loops around the pencil can result in an untwisted rubber band.

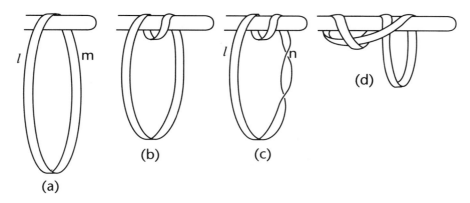

(a)   (b)   (c)   (d)

Following is an alternative procedure that may help to clarify the geometry. After putting the rubber band on the pencil (sketch (a) below), twist the hanging loop to the right (looking up), as in (b) and put the lower loop over the end of the pencil (c). Twist this loop to the left (looking down) as in (d) and put the upper loop over the end of the pencil (e). By following this procedure you can see that putting the second loop on the pencil requires a twist. The twist that changed (a) to (b) is only 180°; but this twist is contained in both section *p* and section *q*, so the total twist along the hanging part of the rubber band is 360°.

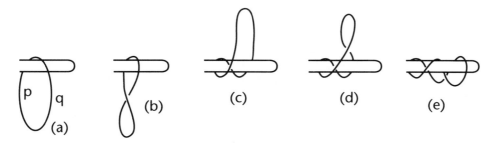

(a)   (b)   (c)   (d)   (e)

In changing (c) to (d) you added an equal and opposite twist, so there is no twist in the final result (e). If, in this step, you had turned the loop to the right, you would have increased the total twist to 720°; and every additional turn of the loop to the right would add 360° more.

Exercise:
Show how sketch (e) would change if the total twist were 720°; 1080°.

Another approach is as follows: Lay the rubber band on the table (a) and turn over the right end to form a figure-8 (b). If you weave the end of the pencil through the two loops of the figure-8, the 360° twist is retained. Now start again with sketch (a) and lift the middle part of the lower section over the upper section to form three loops (c). Obviously no twist is introduced in this step. Weave the end of the pencil through the three loops in order—down through 1, up through 2, down through 3—to get the untwisted three-loop arrangement of the preceding sketch (e). More complex weaving through the three loops may introduce twist. If the third loop is made by turning the right end of the figure-8 (sketch (b)) to the right, the arrangement of sketch (d) is obtained. It has 720° of twist, and weaving the end of the pencil through the three loops in the same order as before—down through 1, up through 2, down through 3—gives a doubly twisted arrangement of three loops.

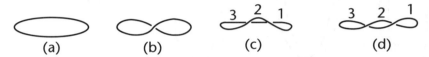

(a)	(b)	(c)	(d)

We must now acknowledge a degree of superficiality in our discussion of twist, because manipulating a rubber band cannot really introduce a net twist in it. But how, then, have we apparently introduced twist along an untwisted rubber band?

In order to answer this question, make the 2-loop arrangement shown in sketch (c) of the first paragraph, hold together the front and back of the hanging part just below the pencil, and slip the two loops off of the pencil. Pull out the upper double loop into a single loop and note that it has a 360° twist, opposite to the 360° twist of the hanging loop. The total twist is thus seen to be zero, as it must be. We see that every loop that is wrapped around the pencil, although it may appear to be smoothly wrapped, contains an inherent 360° twist.

Exercise:
1. Make a Möbius band and cut it along its center line to make the 720° twisted band. Show that this band can be wrapped around your pencil to give three loops with no apparent twist anywhere along the band.

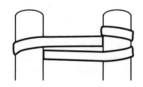

2. Wrap a rubber band around two fingers (or two pencils) as shown in the sketch, so that it has no twists.

Questions:
(1) The Möbius band has only a 180° twist. The edge band, which goes around the Möbius band twice, might then have been expected to have 2 × 180° = 360° twist. Instead, its total twist is 720°. Whence came the additional 360°?

(2) In the first paragraph we saw that after (c) had been made, if the back part *n* was wrapped around the pencil once more, an additional 360° twist would be added, giving a total twist of 720°. However, if *n* was moved to the left of the front part *l* before it was carried around the pencil, 360° would be subtracted and a

smooth untwisted 3-loop arrangement would result. How does this little change in technique cause such a basic change in the result?

Answers:

(1) In cutting out the edge band, you went around the Möbius band twice, as if going around a double loop, and thereby acquired the additional 360° of twist that was inherent in the second loop. Conversely, if you wrap the edge band smoothly twice around your pencil, as if making (c) of the first paragraph, you will either (a) conceal 360° of twist in the second loop and leave only an apparent 360° of twist along the band (as in (c), except that the twist is in the opposite direction), or (b) add 360° of twist, making a total twist of 1080° along the band. These two possibilities exist because your original Möbius band could have been made in either of two ways: its 180° of twist could have been either to the right or to the left, and the 720° of twist in the edge band is, correspondingly, either clockwise or counterclockwise, respectively.

(2) To make the arrangement of sketch (c), the first step was essentially a twist of the hanging part to the left (shown here in (a)). Then, in moving *n* to the left before carrying it around the end of the pencil, you essentially twist the hanging part to the right (shown here in (b)), thereby canceling the twist produced in the first step.

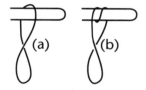

Band around a package. If a rubber band is looped twice around a small box (sketch (a)), it must have a 360° twist along it, as previously discussed. If the two loops are at right angles to each other (sketch (b)), the twist is retained. If a third loop is added (sketch (c)), the twist is either doubled or eliminated. However, you may tie up your box with a narrow ribbon, using three loops as in (c), so that the ribbon appears untwisted while on the box, but shows a 720° twist like the Möbius edge band when it is slipped off of the box. Also, the ribbon may contain an overhand knot (sketch (d)) that is not apparent when the ribbon is around the box.

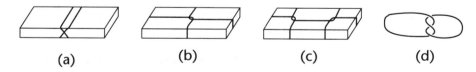

| (a) | (b) | (c) | (d) |

Show that there are eight different ways of putting the rubber band around the box so that one loop is along the middle of the box and two loops are across it, as in (c). (Instead of boxes, use eight small rectangles of cardboard, perhaps 2 cm × 3 cm.)

The Philippine Wine Dance

In the Philippine Wine Dance the dancer holds a glass of wine on the palm of her hand and turns her hand continuously about the vertical axis, turning it always in the same direction without spilling the wine and without moving her feet. Now if you hang your arm with the palm up and rotate it about the vertical axis, you will find it impossible to rotate it more than about 360°. How does the dancer manage to continue rotating it indefinitely?

The main elements of the dance, very oversimplified, are indicated in these sketches. The sketches represent front views of a right-handed dancer turning her palm clockwise. At the beginning, the arm hangs with the hand turned toward the inside (the pulse side) of the wrist, and the arm twisted backward (counterclockwise) about its axis so that the hand points outward with the thumb pointing toward the rear of the body (sketch (a)). If the arm is now twisted clockwise, the hand can be rotated nearly 360° about the vertical axis (sketch (b)), which in these simple sketches looks like sketch (a)). The arm is now raised to shoulder height, with the hand and arm aligned (sketch (c)), and continued up (sketch (d)) as the hand is bent outward (away from the pulse side) at the wrist. It is now possible to continue rotating the hand clockwise while gradually lowering it to the starting position (sketch (a)). The cycle may be repeated indefinitely.

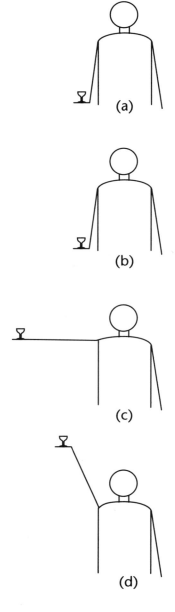

As mentioned earlier, the sketches greatly oversimplify the basic dance positions. In sketch (d), in particular, only a little rotation of the hand is possible, and the dancer must complete the rotation while lowering the hand and twisting the body. Movements of the body are, in fact, usually necessary if the palm is to remain quite horizontal throughout the cycle. These movements, however, are by no means detrimental—the twisting and swaying of the body, along with the sinuous motions of the right arm and the balancing motions of the left arm, all combine to make up a graceful dance.

On the other hand, some people are very supple and can perform the basic motions without twisting and swaying the body. In one variation of the dance, the performer holds a lighted candle in each hand and has a third candle on top of her head. She rotates both hands simultaneously, alternately moving them between low and high positions, while the head candle shows only a slight swaying.

Problem:
How do the movements outlined in the preceding description avoid continuous clockwise twisting of the arm?

Consider a disc with a loop of string on each side, as shown in the sketch (a). If the disc is turned clockwise (looking down) through 360° while the ends of the loops are held fixed, the two loops will become twisted as shown in sketch (b): the upper one is twisted like an ordinary right-handed screw, and the lower one is twisted like a left-handed screw. Suppose now that there is only the upper loop (c)

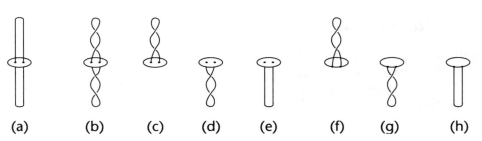

| (a) | (b) | (c) | (d) | (e) | (f) | (g) | (h) |

twisted as after a 360° clockwise turn. If this twisted loop is detached from the top of the disc and attached, without untwisting it, to the bottom of the disc (d), it retains, of course, its right-handed twist. A further 360° clockwise turn of the disc, however, will add a left-handed twist to it, as at the bottom of sketch (b), which cancels the right-handed twist and leaves an untwisted loop (e).

If the loop is attached to the edge of the disc, the discussion is not essentially altered: After the 360° clockwise rotation the loop has a right-handed twist as before (f), but after the loop is swung around to the bottom (g), a further 360° clockwise rotation will untwist it (h).

Furthermore, it is not necessary for the loop to extend at right angles to the disc. The reasoning remains unaffected if the loop extends at even a small angle to the rotating disc (sketches (i) to (l)). If the loop extends a little above the disc it acquires a right-handed twist; if it is then put a little below the disk (k), further turning of the disk untwists it.

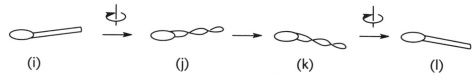

| (i) | (j) | (k) | (l) |

In the preceding two paragraphs the disc corresponds to the dancer's hand, and the loop of string corresponds to the arm that extends from the shoulder to the edge of the hand.

Photographs of the dance accompany an article on Fiber Bundles and Quantum Theory, by Herbert J. Bernstein and Anthony V. Phillips, in *Scientific American*, July 1981, pp. 122 et seq. Further discussion is given in a letter to the editors by Rosemarie Swanson, in *Scientific American*, September 1981, pp. 10–11.

Experiment:
Start with a disc and supporting string hanging from a rod or from your finger as in sketch (a). Write *T* at the top of the side that faces you. This side, always with the *T* at the top, must remain facing you during the following steps:

1. Swing up the disc in a counter-clockwise semicircular arc so that it will have a pair of strings in front of it and a pair of strings behind it. The pair of supporting strings are in front, as in sketch (b). Verify that the strings are arranged as in the sketch.
2. Move the disc through the remaining semicircle to return

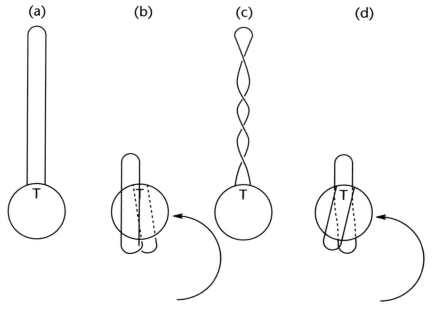

(a)   (b)   (c)   (d)

the disc to its original location. The hanging pair of strings will now be twisted through 720°, as in sketch (c).

3. Again swing up the disc through a counterclockwise semicircle, but with the supporting strings in the *back*, as in sketch (d).
4. Move the disc through the remaining semicircle. The strings will now be untwisted, as in sketch (a).

Try to see how the 720° of twist in sketch (c) develops, and how it is removed in steps (3) and (4).

The fact that you obtained configuration (c) without either twisting the supporting pair of strings or rotating the disc has been interpreted as showing that 720° of twist is equivalent to no twist at all. A twist of 360° is different: There is no way to obtain it without either twisting the supporting pair of strings or rotating the disc.

Knots and Tangles

The study of knots and tangles is useful and interesting, and of special value for developing finger dexterity and ability for geometrical visualization. Here included are only a very few arbitrarily selected items concerning them. A number of books, including the *Boy Scout Fieldbook* and books on sailing and seamanship, discuss knots and methods of tying them. An elementary one that also discusses some peripheral subjects, as magic knots, games, stunts, and history is *Knotcraft: The Art of Knot Tying* by Allen and Paulette MacFarlan. An article by Jearl Walker in *Scientific American*, vol. 249, no. 2, pp. 120–127, Aug. 1983, considers how friction is involved in knot design, and cites a more basic reference.

The square knot. The square knot is the most common knot, used, for example, in wrapping packages. The inexperienced often make it incorrectly, producing what the experts call a granny knot.

In the first step, put the end held by your right hand *behind* the end held by your left hand (sketch (a)) and bring it around one time (sketch (b)). In the next step put the end held by your right hand *in front of* the end held by your left hand (sketch (c)) and bring it around once (sketch (d)). Finally, pull on the free ends in order to tighten the knot. If, in the second step, the right-hand end is again placed *behind* the left-hand end (sketch (e)), the final result is the granny knot (sketch (f)). The granny knot has two drawbacks relative to the square knot:

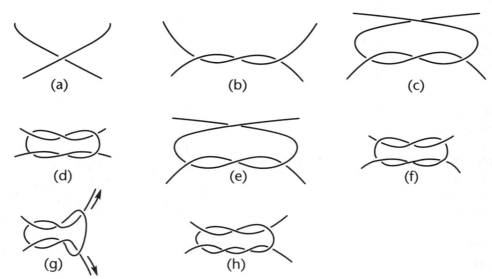

(1) It is more likely to slip.
(2) When drawn tight it is difficult to loosen. The square knot is
    more easily loosened, when desired, by pulling apart either pair of
    adjacent cords, as indicated in sketch (g).

The shoe-string bow is (or should be) made like a square knot.

If, in the first step, the cord is brought around *twice*, the final result is
a "surgeon's knot" (sketch (h)). If, then, in the second step, the cord
is again brought around twice, the resulting knot is very unlikely to
slip even if the cord has a very smooth surface.

The bowline. Sketch (a) shows the construction of a bowline. The
loop may be made about a tall post, a tree trunk, or any similar object
for which the ends are inaccessible, or it may be made in advance and
dropped over a pile at the end of the pier (sketch (b)).

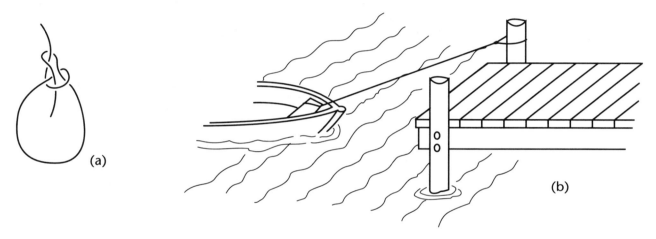

(a)

(b)

The bowline on a bight. A bight is part of a slack rope or cord. When
the ends of a cord are not available and the cord is sufficiently slack
that part of it can be made into a long double cord (sketch (a)), a knot
can be made with that part. The bowline just described can be made
with a doubled cord just as with a single cord. However, such a loop
is not quite the same as the loop known as a "bowline on a bight," the
construction of which is shown in sketch (b). How is it made?

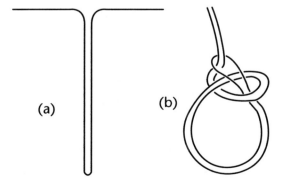

(a)

(b)

One procedure is shown in the following sketches. After (a) has been
made, spread apart the end of the doubled cord and bring it down
and around to the back (sketch (b)). Finally, bring it up (sketch (c)) to

(a)   (b)   (c)

fit around the back of the "standing part" (the cord beyond the knot).

The loop may be dropped over a pile at the end of a pier; but can you make the loop around the trunk of a tree?

Experiment:
Since the bight is essentially a double cord, one might expect that the bowline on a bight is twice as strong as a plain bowline. However, there is one part where the bowline on a bight has only a single cord; namely, the part that fits around the back of the standing part. "A chain is only as strong as its weakest link," but in this knot, the tension in this single cord should be alleviated by the friction at the point where it goes through the small loop. Make a bowline on a bight with a length of sewing thread. Put the loop around a pencil or other convenient object, and pull on the standing part until the thread breaks. Comment on the location of the failure.

The slip knot. There are several ways of forming a knot for a noose—a loop that binds more closely the more tightly the cord is drawn. Such knots are called "running knots" because they slip or "run" along the cord.

The standard slip knot is like an ordinary overhand knot made near the end of a cord (sketch (a)), except that the little loop is made around the standing part (sketch (b)). The large loop at the right on sketch (b) is the noose. If the noose is to be around a tree (or a tall post), the cord must be put around the tree before the knot is made; otherwise the complete arrangement (sketch (b)) may be made in advance. Pulling on the standing part tightens the noose around the object; pulling on the end loosens it.

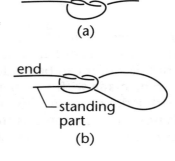

For some applications, friction in the small loop may interfere with the movement of the cord sliding through it. The problem can be avoided by changing the overhand knot to a tight square knot; the small loop will then remain large enough to let the cord slide easily through it.

A simple procedure for making the slip knot is as follows: Double the string (sketch (a)); bring the end back over the string (sketch (b)), thereby forming a pair of loops; take the loop of the standing part and pull it through the loop beside it (sketch (c)); and continue pulling it to form the noose (sketch (d)). Compare sketch (d) with sketch (b) of the preceding paragraph and verify that they are the same knot.

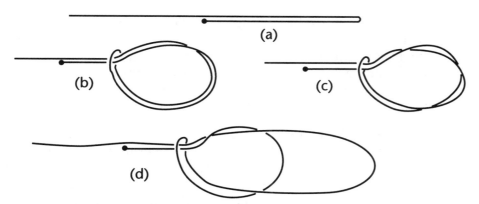

(a)

(b)   (c)

(d)

The running bowline. The running bowline is another form of noose. It is essentially a small bowline in which the main loop was made around the standing part.

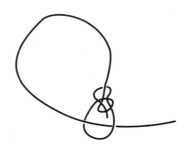

Running bowline

Party trick A. You can hold a straight piece of string between your hands and tie an overhand knot in it without letting go of the ends. The method is as follows: Fold your arms before grasping the ends of the string, which should be about 45 cm long. Then, when you unfold your arms, the string will have a knot in it. Whence came the knot?

Your two arms and your body can be compared with a length of string, and folding your arms puts an overhand knot in it (sketch (a)). Picking up the string with your two hands *A* and *B* (sketch (b)), gives an arrangement that is equivalent to two loops with the overhand knot between them (sketch (c)). Now either loop of such an arrangement can be enlarged at the expense of the other. By unfolding your arms, you bring hand *A* to the right and hand *B* to the left (sketch (d)), thereby enlarging the lower loop and at the same time shrinking the upper loop until it combines with the crossover to make a knot.

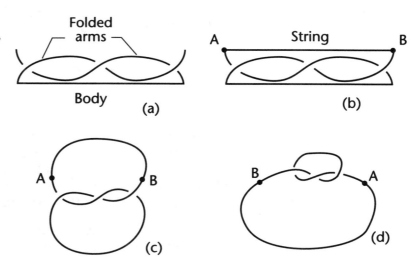

Party trick B. A 60-cm length of string connects the two wrists of each of two people, and each person's string passes between the string and body of the other person (sketch (a)). The problem for the two people is to separate from each other without cutting either string. (In the sketches, the hands are represented as knobs at the ends of the arms.)

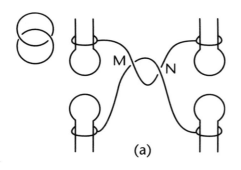

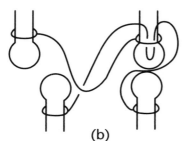

(a)

(b)

The two people are linked together like two links of a chain, and unless they recognize that fact they may perform the most ludicrous maneuvers in their efforts to separate from each other. But each link has two open spaces—the spaces between the wrists and the loops that encircle them; and you make use of these spaces in effecting the separation.

First note in sketch (a) that the lower person's string passes under the other string at *M*, and passes over it at *N*. In order to separate the two links you must take this right-hand part of the string and make it also pass under the other string. The procedure is as follows: Take a section of the right-hand part of the string and pass it down under the wrist loop of the opposing hand (sketch (b)). Then pull this piece of the string around the end of the hand (sketch (c)). When the string is now pulled up and out of the wrist loop (sketch (d)), the two people will be free of each other.

Problem:
In sketch (b) the section of string that is passed down through the wrist loop is on the side of the wrist toward us. Obviously, if it were a little to the side (sketch (e)), the final result would be the same. We must be careful, however, if we move the location all the way to the back. Of the arrangements in the two sketches (f) and (g), only one will serve to separate the two links. Which one is it?

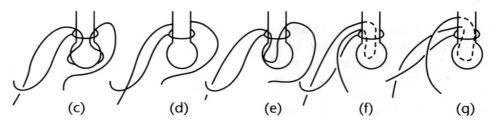

(c) (d) (e) (f) (g)

Knots along a cord. Use a length of cord about 1 meter long. Hold it as shown in sketch (a). The left end *A* is held between the second and third fingers of the left hand, with the thumb holding down the cord a few centimeters away. The right hand holds the cord about 20 cm away, with the rest of the cord hanging over the back of the hand.

Twist your right hand to the left and put a loop over the two fingers of the left hand. If you correctly twisted your hand, the loop should appear as in sketch (b). If your finger tips now pull end *A* to the left through the loop, you regain the unknotted string; but if you grasp end *A* between the thumb and the fourth finger, and pull it through the loop to the right, the cord will have a knot on it (sketch (c)).

Start again and put four loops on the two fingers, all by using the same technique of twisting the wrist to the left (sketch (d)). The first loop, marked 1 in the

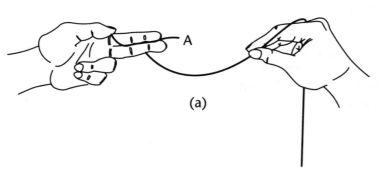

(a)

A

sketch, is closest to the finger tips, and loops 2, 3, and 4 are successively closer to the palm. Do not pull the loops too tight, and try to put all four in front of the finger knuckles. If you now pull end *A* to the left through the loops, you regain the unknotted string; but if you grasp end *A* between the thumb and the fourth finger and pull it through the loops, the string will have four knots on it (sketch (e)). The essential difference between the two cases can be seen by comparing sketches (f) and (g). The procedures are sometimes presented as a magician's trick in which, if the magician is sufficiently dexterous, the audience cannot distinguish between his techniques for obtaining the different results.

The doubly linked figure-8's. This section presents essentially a visualization exercise. You must try to see just why each step in the procedure produces the resulting configuration.

Start with two pieces of cord about 25 to 50 cm long. Interweave them and tie together their ends to form the linked figure-8's of sketch (a). Starting with this configuration, transform it to the configuration shown in (b). Then go from (b) to (c), and then from (c) to (d). Then return through the same steps from (d) to (a).

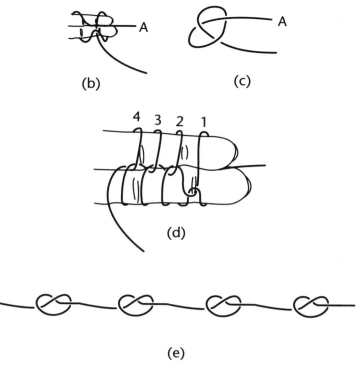

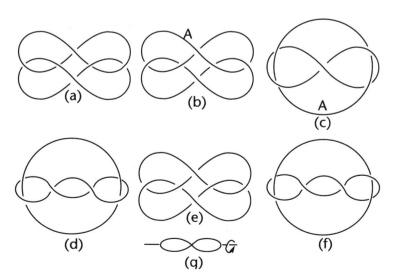

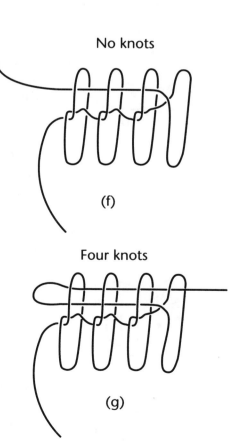

In order to go from (a) to (b), either (1) turn the lower figure-8 180° about its horizontal axis, as indicated in the small sketch (g) or (2) rotate the whole arrangement 180° in its plane (the plane of the table). (If, instead of turning the lower figure-8 as shown in (g), you turn it in the opposite direction, what do you get?) In order to go from (b) to (c), start by lifting the section of cord near *A* and bringing it down to the location marked *A* in (c). In order to go from (c) to (d), twist the right-hand end 180° about its horizontal axis.

Go directly from (a) to (c).

Make the configuration shown in sketch (e) and proceed to (f). Then return from (f) to (e). Note that (e) and (a) cannot be made from each other. Note also that (e) does not change its appearance if you rotate it 180° in the plane of the table.

Is it not a knot? In this section we discuss six cases of tangled cords, of which all but one are not knots at all, for they can be disentangled to form either straight unknotted string or a loop.

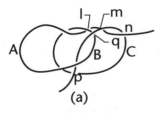

(a)

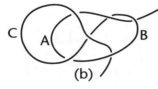

(b)

1. A cord arranged as in sketch (a) is not a knot, since it all straightens out when the two ends are pulled apart. (Tangling must be avoided.) This fact is not obvious, but the arrangement does look suspicious, because there are three instances in which the cord passes either under at two successive crossings (*l* and *m*, *n* and *p*) or over at two successive crossings (*q* and *m*).

If you take the section *C* between crossings *n* and *p* and swing it down (below the plane of the paper) and up again on the left side, you get the arrangement in sketch (b). In order to help show the relation between these two arrangements, corresponding points in the two sketches are marked with the same capital letters (*A*, *B*, *C*).

In sketch (b) you can see that pulling on the lower end of the cord will straighten out the whole arrangement, leaving a straight cord. The arrangements in the two sketches are equivalent to each other (and to a straight cord) in the sense that each is merely a distortion of the other.

The transformations (a) → (b) → straight cord can be demonstrated to a class by doing them on the glass platform of an overhead projector.

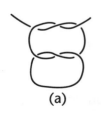

(a)

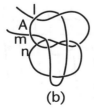

(b)

2. Make two loops in a piece of string about 60 cm long, as shown in sketch (a) and then weave the right-hand end through them, as shown in sketch (b). This "knot" will also disappear when the two ends are pulled apart. As in the preceding example, this fact is not obvious, but will become so after a little rearrangement.

Observe that there are three successive crossings, *l*, *m*, and *n*, where section *A* crosses over. Lift section *A*, carry it to the right, down and around the bottom, and finally up to its original location (sketch (c)). You can now see that pulling at end *B* will complete the unraveling. It seems almost enigmatic that all the twists of the square knot (sketch (a)) are undone so simply (sketch (b)).

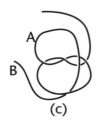

(c)

Problem:

Using a piece of string about 25 cm long, make the open square knot of sketch (a) and then tie together the two free ends. Transform the result to the arrangement shown here.

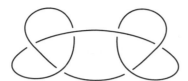

3. The arrangement shown in sketch (a) is included in this section because, without the rod through it (sketch (b)) it is not a knot at all. With the rod, however, it is a useful knot known as a "clove hitch" or "builder's hitch." It is often used for tying a cord to a rod at a desired location on the cord, as when the distance from the rod to a previously attached rod must be accurate. For that purpose, put an ink mark on the cord at the desired location and hold the mark on the rod with your thumb while you complete the knot and tighten it. The two loops may be put on the rod with a left twist of the right wrist, as in making the four knots along a cord.

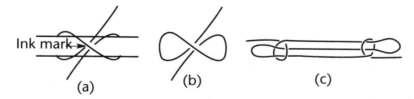

In sketch (a) the knot is shown spread out along the rod, in order to help show the construction. In an actual clove hitch, the two loops are in tight contact.

Sketch (c) shows an arrangement known as a sheepshank; it is used for shortening a cord. It is an organized tangle rather than a knot, for it easily comes apart when it is not in tension. The previously discussed slipknot is another example of an arrangement that, when loose, can easily come apart to restore the plain unknotted cord when the ends are pulled apart. In fact, any arrangement that can be formed on a bight should have the same characteristic; however, the bowline on a bight will require a bit of help before it can so easily come apart. Why?

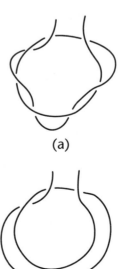

4. Examine sketch (a). Does it represent a knot?

Sketch (b) is offered as a first step in showing that it is not a knot.

5. First examine sketch (a) and determine whether it represents a knot. Then examine sketch (b) and determine whether the four intertwined loops will come apart when you pull apart the ends.

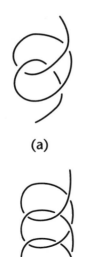

(a)

Suppose that you hold the upper part with one hand while you pull down with the other hand. You should be able to see that the lowest loop will come apart, leaving a similar series of three intertwined loops. As you continue to pull down, the lowest loop of this 3-loop column will come apart in the same way, leaving a similar series of only two loops. At this point the arrangement will be as in sketch (a), and further pulling will create an overhand knot.

The two ends of the column are not different: if you hold the *lower* end and pull up at the *upper* end, the upper loops will come apart, one after the other, and finally leave the bottom two loops to form the knot. In fact, if you flip over the column end for end, so that the upper and lower ends exchange places, the column will appear the same as before. But, then, just why do not the final two loops disintegrate like the others?

6. Show that this arrangement can be untangled to form a simple loop.

(b)

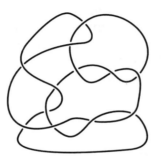

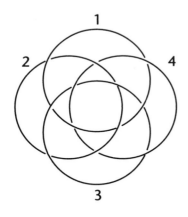

The four rings. Examine this arrangement of four intertwined rings. Note that ring 1 is linked with every other ring, but none of the other pairs are linked; ring 4 is over ring 3 and under ring 2, and ring 3 is over ring 2. If ring 1 is removed, will the remaining three rings come apart?

The doubled string. Start with a length of string about 70 cm long, fold it double, and put the fold over the string as shown in sketch (a). The result is obviously not a knot; if you pull apart the two ends you regain the straight string. If you now put the (double) end through the loop (sketch (b)), do you get a knot? No, for you can easily see that the arrangement in sketch (b) is essentially equivalent to the arrangement in sketch (a); and if you pull apart the two ends you regain the straight string. In fact, you may continue winding the double end of your string in and out of loops, making as complicated a tangle as you wish, without making a knot: if you slowly pull apart the two ends, carefully loosening tangles as they begin to tighten, you will recover the straight string. The reason is simple: Since the two ends of the doubled string are always

end

(a)

(b)

together, the doubled string is effectively equivalent to a closed loop ⊂⎯⎯⎯⎯⎯⎯⎯⎯⎯⎯⎯⎯⎯⊃ ; and it is impossible to make a knot in the string of a closed loop because making a knot in a string requires manipulating the end of the string.

Exercise:
Make a bowline on a bight and then pull apart the two ends of the bight to recover the straight string.

Through the Eye of a Needle

How many threads can be passed through the eye of a needle? If the ends of the threads can be cut neatly with sharp scissors, one might put as many as six or seven threads, one by one, through the eye of a sewing needle. The later threads can be inserted more easily if the earlier threads are pulled down tight along the side of the needle, as indicated in the sketch.

Perhaps twice as many threads can be put through by the following procedure:

1. Thread an ordinary sewing needle or, preferably, a quilting needle with a length of sewing thread about 1 meter long. Bring the needle to about the middle of the thread.
2. Put the point of the needle through the thread at a point about 4 or 5 cm from the eye of the needle. Untwisting the thread at this point will help. It may be difficult, however, to keep it untwisted while you put the needle point into it; perhaps a friend can keep it untwisted while you guide the needle point. Sketch 1 shows the untwisted part as a loop, although it actually closes down around the needle as soon as you let it go; and this fictitious open loop is shown in all the subsequent sketches in order to help explain the process.
3. Push the loop up the needle (sketch 2) and over the top (sketch 3).

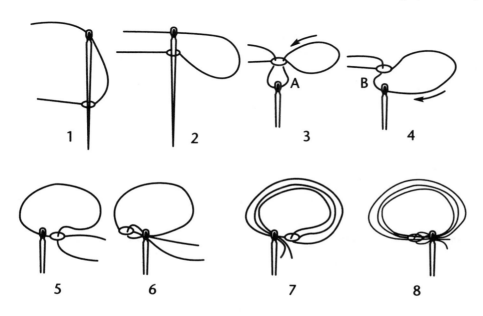

4. Pull down at *A* until the entire right-hand part in sketch 3 has been pulled through the small loop to form the large loop shown in sketch 4.
5. Pull left at *B*, just beside the eye of the needle, until the small loop has come around to the eye (sketch 5).
6. Pull the small loop through the eye (sketch 6). Note that three threads have come through the eye behind it.
7. Continue to pull until the small loop has again come around to the eye (sketch 7).
8. When the small loop is pulled through the eye, five threads now follow it through (sketch 8).

With each repetition, two more threads are pulled through. Eventually the eye is so full that the friction makes pulling difficult; and the process stops when the small loop, because of its slight extra bulk, can no longer be pulled through.

The Polyhedron Formula

There is an important formula that relates the number of vertices, *V*, the number of edges, *E*, and the number of faces, *F*, of a polyhedron:

$$V - E + F = 2$$

As an example, consider the polyhedron in the sketch. It has

9 vertices	$V = 9$
16 edges	$E = 16$
9 faces	$F = 9$

so

$$V - E + F = 9 - 16 + 9 = 2$$

in agreement with the formula.

In order to show the general applicability of the formula we first consider the network in sketch (a). Begin by drawing diagonals wherever needed in order to convert polygons with more than three sides into triangles (sketch (b)). Wherever we draw one of these diagonals (dashed lines) we increase the number of faces *F* by 1 and also increase the number of edges by 1. Hence the value of $V - E + F$ remains unchanged by thus making the network consist exclusively of triangles. Now start reducing the number of triangles by erasing the outermost lines of the network. If we erase an edge like *p*, we reduce the number of faces by 1 and also reduce the number of edges by 1 (sketch (c)); hence the value of $V - E + F$ remains unchanged. If

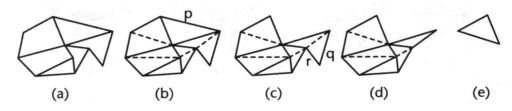

(a)   (b)   (c)   (d)   (e)

we erase edges *q* and *r*, we reduce the number of faces by 1, the number of vertices by 1, and the number of edges by 2 (sketch (d)); so again the value *of V – E + F* remains unchanged. We continue erasing edges in this way, $V - E + F$ always remaining unchanged, until there remains only a single triangle (sketch (e)). For this triangle it is easily seen that $V - E + F \ (= 3 - 3 + 1)$ is 1. Then since the value of $V - E + F$ remained unchanged throughout the procedure, it must have been 1 at the start.

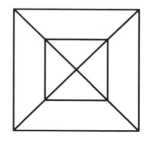

Now we return to the polyhedron of our first sketch. Suppose that the faces are of rubber sheet, so that they can stretch, and suppose also that we temporarily remove one of the faces—say, the bottom face. Then we can imagine that we take hold of the bottom edges and stretch them apart sufficiently that we can lay the whole surface of the polyhedron flat upon a table, as in the sketch.

For this stretched surface the formula $V - E + F = 1$ applies, and hence it applies to the surface before it was stretched, since stretching did not change *V*, *E*, or *F*. We had removed the bottom face, however, before we stretched the surface; when we reattach it in order to regain our original polyhedron, we increase *F* by 1 without changing *V* or *E*. Hence our formula for the complete polyhedron is

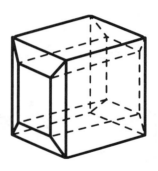

$$V - E + F = 2$$

Question:
Would our formula still apply to a polyhedron with a tunnel through it, as in the sketch?

As before, we may suppose that our polyhedron surface is made of rubber sheet, and that we temporarily remove one of the faces. But there is no way then to stretch out the polyhedron surface and lay it out flat on a table. Hence the procedure that we used before cannot be used for this case, so our method of proof would not apply. That fact does not tell us that our formula cannot be used for this case; it merely tells us that our method of proof would not have been valid for this case.

Problem:
Derive a formula for this case of a polyhedron with a tunnel.

Consider the surface to be made up of two parts:

1. The inner polyhedron, or tunnel. We apply the polyhedron formula but omit the 2 because of the missing faces at the ends of the tunnel:

$$F_t + V_t - E_t = 0$$

where the subscript *t* signifies tunnel.

2. The outer part, to which we again apply the polyhedron formula but omit the 2 because of the two missing faces:

$$F_o + V_o - E_o = 0$$

where the subscript *o* signifies outer part.

Add the two equations in order to get the formula for the entire surface:

$$F + V - E = 0$$

In this derivation, however, the vertices and edges of the two missing faces have been counted twice. But the number of edges of a face equals the number of vertices of a face, so $V - E = 0$ for each missing face. Hence, counting them twice does not invalidate the resulting formula.

Problem:
Show that, in general, 2 is subtracted from the right side of the polyhedron formula for every tunnel that the polyhedron contains. For example, if a polyhedron has three tunnels through it, the applicable formula is

$$V - E + F = 2 - 6 \text{ or } V - E + F = -4$$

The Regular Polyhedra

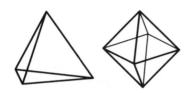

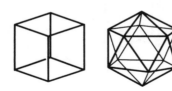

On a regular polyhedron,

1. All faces are equal regular polygons; that is, all edges are equal and all face angles are equal.
2. All dihedral angles (at the edges, where pairs of adjacent faces meet) are equal.
3. All vertices (where three or more faces meet) are equal.

No more than five. We can easily show that there can be no more than five regular polyhedra.

First, suppose the faces to be the simplest regular polygons, namely, equilateral triangles. At a vertex we may put together three, four, or five equilateral triangles, as shown in the sketches. We may also put together six equilateral triangles, but the group must be flat, so the point where they meet is not a vertex of a polyhedron. We conclude that there are no more than three regular polyhedra whose faces are equilateral triangles.

A systematic way of arriving at this conclusion is to recognize that the angles of equilateral triangles are 60° and that 3 × 60°, 4 × 60°, and 5 × 60° are all less than 360°, so that three, four, or five equilateral triangles can form a vertex; but that

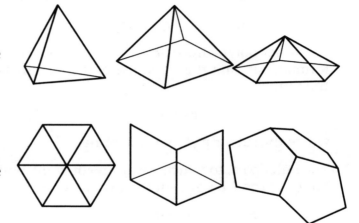

$6 \times 60°$ is not less than $360°$, so that six equilateral triangles do not form a vertex.

Next, suppose that the faces are squares, in which the angles are $90°$. Since $3 \times 90°$ is less than $360°$, but $4 \times 90°$ is not, they can form only one type of vertex where the edges of squares meet.

Next, suppose that the faces are regular pentagons, in which the angles are $108°$. Since $3 \times 108°$ is less than $360°$ but $4 \times 108°$ is not, there is only one type of vertex where the edges of pentagons meet.

For regular hexagons the angles are $120°$, and since $3 \times 120°$ is not less than $360°$, regular hexagons cannot form a vertex. For regular heptagons, octagons, . . ., the angles are even larger, so they similarly cannot be considered.

Thus, there are only five cases that cannot be ruled out merely by considering possible vertices.

Do all five exist? The fact that we cannot rule out these five cases does not prove that a regular polyhedron exists corresponding to each case. We proceed then to see if they can be constructed.

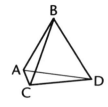

1. The regular tetrahedron: If three equal equilateral triangles *ABC*, *CBD*, and *DAB* are joined at vertex *B*, their three bases form a fourth equilateral triangle *ADC* that is equal to the first three. The four triangles form a regular tetrahedron.
2. The regular octahedron: On the three perpendicular axes *X*, *Y*, and *Z*, lay off six points, such as *A*, *B*, *C*,. . ., all equally distant from the origin *O*. The lines connecting nearest pairs of these points are the edges of eight equilateral triangles. They meet in groups of four at the six points, which are the vertices of a regular octahedron.

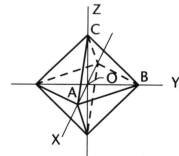

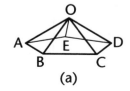

(a)

3. The regular icosahedron: First construct the 5-sided pyramid *O-ABCDE* of sketch (a) and then hang a triangle from each of the five edges (sketch (b)), making the dihedral angles *AB*, *BC*, . . . equal to the dihedral angles *AO*, *BO*, . . . of the pyramid. Then the four triangles *ABF*, *AOB*, *BOC*, and *BCG* are arranged around *B* just as four triangles of the top pyramid are arranged around *O*. Accordingly, a fifth triangle will fit into the opening and complete a pyramid *B-AOCGF* (sketch (c)) exactly like the top pyramid. Equilateral triangles will fit similarly into the remaining four openings. The bottom edges of the structure will then form an opening in the shape of a regular pentagon and a pyramid (sketch (d)) just like the top one can be fitted up against it.

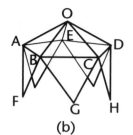

(b)

4. The cube: For a cube, we might start with a square base, attach the four vertical square sides, and finally close over the top opening with a sixth square.
5. The regular dodecahedron: The top face is a regular pentagon. From its five edges hang five regular pentagons meeting along

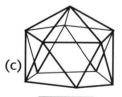

(c)

(d)

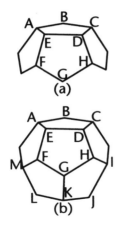

(a)

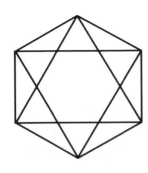

(b)

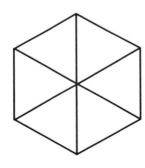

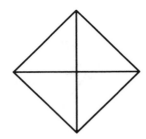

their edges (sketch (a)). Since there is only one way that three 108° angles can be fitted together, all the vertices *A,B,C,D,E* must be alike and all the dihedral angles *AE, ED, EF, DH, . . .* must be equal. Hence you can insert pentagons into the five V's at *F, H, . . .* with assurance that they will fit into the V's and also fit together along the edges *ML, GK, . . .* (sketch (b)). Note also that in sketch (b) five pentagons are attached around the pentagon *EDHGF* just like the five pentagons that hang from *ABCDE*.

The bottom edge of the structure in sketch (b) forms a pentagonal opening into which the twelfth pentagon fits to complete the dodecahedron.

Problems:

1. These three figures are views of regular polyhedra, including those edges (hidden) that would normally be shown as light lines or broken lines. Identify the polyhedra.

2a. The number of faces of a dodecahedron equals the number of edges of a cube. In fact, a correctly chosen set of face diagonals of the twelve pentagons will be the twelve edges of a cube. In the sketch on page 180, let the face diagonal 12-1 be a cube edge and identify the other eleven cube edges.

2b. The number of faces of a cube equals the number of edges of a regular tetrahedron. In fact, a correctly chosen set of diagonals of the six squares will be the edges of a regular tetrahedron. Identify such a set of diagonals.

3a. The number of faces of a cube equals the number of vertices of a regular octahedron. Sketch a cube and then sketch an enclosed regular octahedron with its vertices at the centers of the cube faces.

3b. The number of faces of a regular octahedron equals the number of vertices of a cube. Sketch a regular octahedron and then sketch an enclosed cube with its vertices at the centers of the octahedron faces.

3c. The number of faces of a regular icosahedron equals the number of vertices of a regular dodecahedron. Show how to connect the centers of the icosahedron faces to outline a regular dodecahedron.

4. Suppose that there is a sphere centered at the center of the regular icosahedron, of such size that it just touches the middle points of the thirty edges. The thirty contact points are all equivalent with regard to the relative locations and arrangements of their neighboring contact points. If I now imagine planes tangent to the sphere at all of these points, I should have a 30-face polyhedron in which all the faces are equal and similarly arranged relative to their neighbors. Is it a regular polyhedron?

5. The regular dodecahedron also has thirty edges. Answer the same question for this case.

6. Answer the corresponding questions for the other three regular polyhedra.

7. You will occasionally see a picture of a geodesic dome. It appears to be part of a regular polyhedron with a large number of

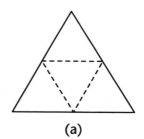

(a)

triangular faces, and, typically with six faces around every vertex. Could it really be part of a regular polyhedron?

8a. Cut an equilateral triangle 10–15 cm high out of a sheet of cardboard and draw the three dashed lines that divide it into four equal smaller triangles. Cut partly through the cardboard along these broken lines in order to facilitate bending. Finally form the piece of cardboard into a regular tetrahedron, fastening together the edges with transparent adhesive tape. An alternative method is to leave small flaps along the edges of the triangle when it is cut, and use them to paste together the pairs of edges.

8b. Here is a complete set of patterns for the five regular polyhedra. Determine how to form them into the polyhedra and indicate by pairs of letters or numbers which edges must be joined. The three pairs for the tetrahedron are indicated by the letters *a, a, b, b, c, c*. (If you construct any of these patterns, you may wish to leave a tab on one of each of these pairs, as shown in the sketch.)

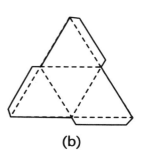

(b)

Tetrahedron

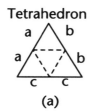

(a)

Octahedron

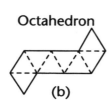

(b)

Cube

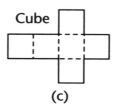

(c)

Icosahedron

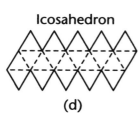

(d)

Dodecahedron

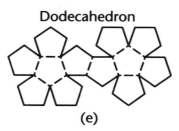

(e)

8c. These patterns are not the only ones that can be used to form the regular polyhedra. For example, here is an alternative pattern for the tetrahedron. Devise alternative patterns for the other four regular polyhedra.

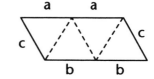

Similarly, prepare cardboard shapes for the other four regular polyhedra and form them into the polyhedra.

9. Assume that:

   (a) All the faces of the regular polyhedra are rigid polygons.
   (b) All the edges are hinges, and the attached faces can swing freely about them.
   (c) All the edges can swing freely about the vertices.

Show that the regular polyhedra are rigid structures.

10. Show from the polyhedron formula that a polyhedron with 60 hexagonal faces (we have already seen that they may not be perfect regular hexagons) is impossible.

11. Show that a polyhedron with 20 hexagonal faces and 12 pentagonal faces is consistent with the polyhedron formula.
12. Consider a polyhedron on which the faces have various numbers of sides, but on which only three edges meet at every vertex. Let

n_3 = the number of triangular faces,

n_4 = the number of tetragonal faces,

n_5 = the number of pentagonal faces, and so on.

Show that

$3n_3 + 2n_4 + 1n_5 + 0n_6 - 1n_7 - 2n_8 - \ldots = 12$

Answers:
2a. The twelve edges of the cube (on the sketch on page 180) are
12-1, 1-4, 4-10, 10-12, 14-19, 19-7, 7-16, 16-14, 12-14, 1-19, 4-7, 10-16.

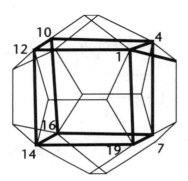

2b. The tetrahedron is shown in this sketch.

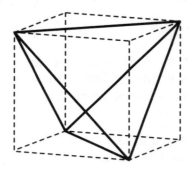

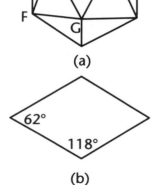

4. We have already learned that there is no regular polyhedron of thirty sides. In this case it is obvious that all vertices would not be the same. The three tangent planes through edges *AB*, *OB*, and *AO* meet at some point above the triangle *AOB*. This point is then a vertex where three faces (and three edges) meet. At point *B*, however, we have a vertex where five tangent planes meet (the five through the edges *BA*, *BO*, *BC*, *BG*, and *BF*). Hence the polyhedron has two different kinds of vertices.

In addition, the polygons, although all equal, are not *regular* polygons—they are lozenges with angles of about 62° and 118°.

7. First, we know that the five regular polyhedra that we have discussed are the only possible regular polyhedra. Second, it is obvious that the faces cannot all be equilateral triangles, because if every vertex had six equilateral triangles around it, the surface would have to be *flat*. Finally, if you carefully examine pictures of geodesic domes, you will see that they all show some irregularities.

8(c) Here is a set of alternative patterns. On these patterns or on your own patterns, identify the edges that have to be joined.

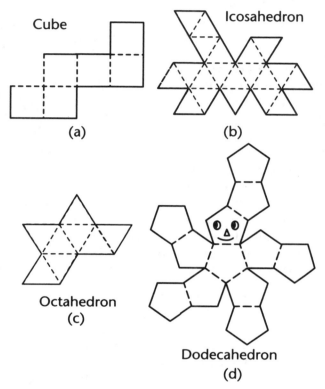

Cube
(a)

Icosahedron
(b)

Octahedron
(c)

Dodecahedron
(d)

9. As has already been noted, where only three faces meet to form a vertex, the vertex is rigid. It follows that the regular tetrahedron, the cube, and the regular dodecahedron are rigid structures. We have to consider, then, only the regular octahedron and the regular icosahedron.

Consider, first, the regular octahedron (sketch (a)). Separate the upper pyramid and place it on a table (sketch (b)). If points m and n are brought closer together while points l, m, and n all remain on the table, then point p must rise off of the table (sketch (b)). The same reasoning would apply for the lower pyramid. Thus, on the complete octahedron, if vertices l, m, and n remain intact, bringing together m

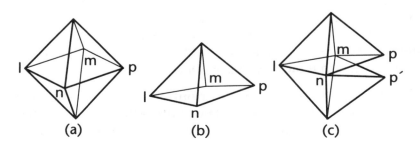

(a)

(b)

(c)

and *n* requires that edges *mp* and *np* split, with part going up and part going down (sketch (c)). Stated differently, as long as the edges and vertices remain intact, points *m* and *n* cannot be brought closer together. Since *m* and *n* represent any pair of opposite vertices, we conclude that the regular octahedron is stiff.

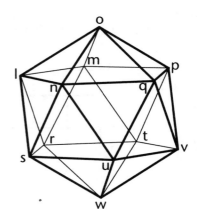

For the icosahedron, consider the pentagonal pyramid that forms its cap. If vertices *m* and *n* are brought closer together, points *p* and *q* must rise above the plane of *mln*. The same points *m* and *n* belong to the pyramid on the left, and we similarly conclude that points *r* and *s* must move to the left of the plane of *omn*. With the pairs of points *p,q* and *r,s* thus moving farther apart, points *t* and *u* must come closer together. But consider the pyramid at the bottom: If *t* and *u* are brought closer, point *v* must move down out the plane of *rstu*. But when *p* and *q* rose, they pulled *v* upward. Hence the edges *tv* and *uv* must split so that the upper part of *v* can rise while the lower part drops. If, however, all the edges and vertices remain intact, points *m* and *n* cannot be brought closer together.

In the preceding paragraph we conclude that changing the *m-n* distance in our icosahedron is not possible. Does it follow that no distortion of any kind is possible? Yes, it does: Note on the sketch all (nonadjacent) vertices except *u*—that is, *n, q, s, v, w*—are situated relative to *m* just as *n* is situated, so changing their distances from *m* is just as impossible as it is for *n*. Then can we change the distance from *m* to this remaining vertex *u*? Any displacement of *u* relative to *m* would change its distance to one of the other vertices, which is just as impossible as changing the *m-n* distance. And finally, since all vertices are equivalent, any discussion centered around *m* applies equally to all the other vertices. Thence we conclude that our icosahedron is rigid. (Actually it can be shown that any convex polyhedron with rigid faces is rigid.)

10. Consider the number of edges and the number of vertices of such a polyhedron: Each face has six edges, each of which is shared with an adjoining face; hence, there are $60 \times 6 \times 1/2 = 180$ edges. Each face has six vertices, each of which it shares with two adjoining faces; hence, there are $60 \times 6 \times 1/3 = 120$ vertices. The polyhedron formula is $F + V - E = 2$, but here we have $F + V - E = 60 + 120 - 180 = 0$. We see then that a 60-face polyhedron with all hexagonal faces is impossible; in fact, any polyhedron with exclusively hexagonal faces is impossible.

11. We have just seen that the contribution of any number of hexagonal faces to $F + V - E$ is zero. The contribution of 12 pentagonal faces to $F + V - E$ must be 2, for we already know that the regular

dodecahedron (which has 12 pentagonal faces) exists. Or we can easily calculate it by the method used in problem 10: $F + V - E = 12 + 12 \times 5 \times 1/3 - 12 \times 5 \times 1/2 = 12 + 20 - 30 = 2$. Thus, a polyhedron with 20 hexagonal faces (or any other number of hexagonal faces) and 12 pentagonal faces satisfies the polyhedron formula.

Problem 11 is of interest with regard to recent studies of large carbon molecules. Under appropriate conditions, the carbon that forms as soot from a flame, or that is formed by condensation from carbon vapor in a laboratory, contains a prominent fraction of 60-atom molecules, or clusters. It has been suggested that the 60 carbon atoms are arranged like the vertices of a polyhedron with 12 pentagonal faces and 20 hexagonal faces. (Prove that such a polyhedron has 60 vertices.) Sketch (a) shows the polyhedron and sketch (b) shows how you might visualize its construction: If you refer back to the sketch of the regular icosahedron you will see that it consists of 12 overlapping 5-sided pyramids. If we cut off the top third of every pyramid, there remains a polyhedron with 12 regular pentagons (one for each of the original 12 vertices) and 20 regular hexagons (one on each of the original 20 faces).

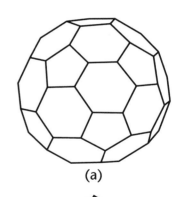

(a)

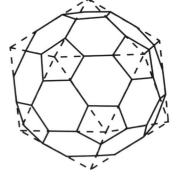

(b)

Reference: Harold Kroto: Space, Stars, C_{60}, and Soot. *Science*, vol. 242, pp. 1139–1145, November 25, 1988.

Problem:
In these two lattices the lines represent rigid rods and the heavy dots represent joints about which the rods can rotate freely in the plane of the paper. Of the 16 small squares in each lattice, 7 contain diagonal rods. Obviously, an isolated square can be deformed to a rhombus, but if a square contains a diagonal rod it is rigid. In one of the two lattices the

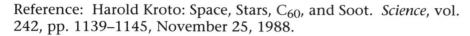

seven diagonal rods are so located that they make the whole lattice rigid. In the other lattice the seven diagonal rods are so located that the lattice remains deformable. Study the two lattices and determine which one is deformable. The answer (the deformed lattice) is shown in the lower sketch.

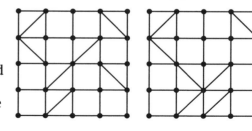

(This problem is contained in an article by A. K. Dewdney in *Scientific American*, May 1991, pp. 126–128.)

Symmetry. The regular icosahedron has a five-fold axis of symmetry through each vertex, a three-fold axis of symmetry through the center of each face, and a two-fold axis of symmetry through the center of each edge. That is, it has:

(1) An axis through each vertex, passing through the center of the icosahedron, which has the property that when the icosahedron is rotated 72° (= 360°/5) about the axis, it will appear the same as before the rotation.
(2) An axis through the center of each triangle face that is similarly defined except that the rotation angle is 120° (= 360°/3).

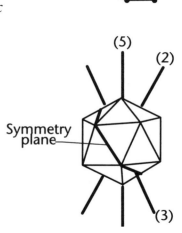

(3) An axis through the center of each edge that is similarly defined except that the rotation angle is 180° (= 360°/2).

In addition, each edge of the regular icosahedron lies in a plane of symmetry (a plane that splits the icosahedron in such a way that each half is a reflection of the other half, as if the plane were a mirror).

The five-fold axis through each vertex is also a ten-fold "alternating axis." That is, if you rotate the icosahedron 36° about the axis and then reflect it in the plane at right angles to the axis, it will appear the same as before the rotation.

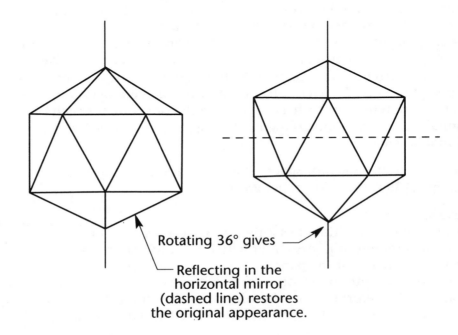

Rotating 36° gives

Reflecting in the
horizontal mirror
(dashed line) restores
the original appearance.

There is also a center of symmetry: A straight line through a center of symmetry intersects the figure or surface at two equidistant equivalent points.

Problems:
1(a) Show that the regular icosahedron and the regular dodecahedron have the same symmetry; that is, each has 6 five-fold axes, 10 three-fold axes, 15 two-fold axes, and 15 planes of symmetry.
(b) Show that the cube and the regular octahedron have the same symmetry; that is, each has 3 four-fold axes, 4 three-fold axes, 6 two-fold axes, 3 symmetry planes of one kind, and 6 symmetry planes of another kind.
(c) Show that the regular tetrahedron has 4 three-fold axes, 3 two-fold axes, and 6 symmetry planes.
2. What other alternating axes can you find among the regular polyhedra?
3. Cut a sheet of aluminum foil (preferably heavy duty foil) about 15 cm square. Fold it in two along the centerline, fold it again at right angles to the first fold, and then fold it along the 45° line. Put it on a pad of paper and, with the tip of your ballpoint pen, inscribe a simple design on it. Unfold it and examine the resulting pattern. Identify its symmetry elements. (You may also use a

thin paper, as wax paper, origami paper (in arts-and-crafts shops), or gift wrapping, and cut out your design with small sharp-pointed scissors.)

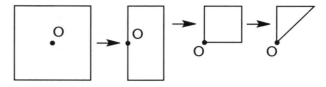

4. Cut a piece of aluminum foil in the form of a circle. Fold it to form a 60° sector, inscribe a design with your ballpoint pen, and unfold it. Identify the symmetry elements in your pattern.

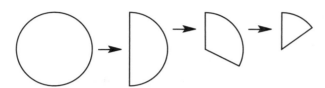

5. In problems 2a and 2b of the preceding section we constructed a cube on face diagonals of a regular dodecahedron, and a regular tetrahedron on face diagonals of a cube. In each case, identify the symmetry elements that are common to both polyhedrons. For example, the three-fold axes of the cube coincide with the three-fold axes of the dodecahedron, and symmetry planes of the cube coincide with symmetry planes of the dodecahedron.

Answers:

3. There are four symmetry planes, spaced at 45°, a four-fold axis of symmetry, and a center of symmetry. (Show that from the existence of the four symmetry planes, the other two symmetry elements must follow.)

4. There are three symmetry planes, spaced at 120°, and a corresponding three-fold axis of symmetry. There is no center of symmetry.

Reflections

Problem:
A person at *A* wishes to go to the edge of the stream to get some water, and then to return to his cabin at *B*. Find the route of least total distance.

Locate the point *B'*, the reflection of *B* in the edge of the stream, and draw a straight line from *A* to *B'*, meeting the bank at *C*. The desired route is then the broken line *ACB*, which has the same total length as *AB'*. Any other path to *B'*, like *ADB'*, would be longer than *ACB'* and, hence, so would the corresponding path *ADB* to *B*.

Problem:
How tall must a mirror be in order for you to see your full length in it?

The sketch shows the path of the light rays from the head and feet to the eyes. The mirror need be only half as tall as you.

Problem:
A cord of length *l* is hung loosely between two poles, attached at points *A* and *B*, respectively, and a weighted wheel is put on the

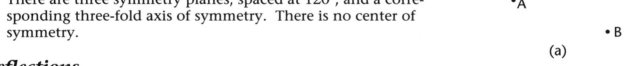
•A

• B

(a)

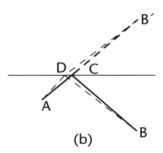

(b)

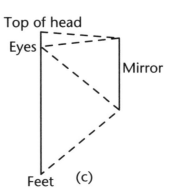

(c)

cord. It stretches the
cord taut and rolls down
it, coming to rest at the
lowest possible point.
How do you locate this
point?

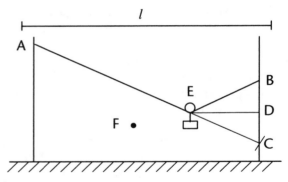

Answer:
From attachment point
A swing an arc of radius
l, intersecting the oppo-
site pole at point *C*, and draw *AC*. Locate the point *D* midway between *B* and *C*. The wheel will come to rest at point *E*, which is at the
same level as *D*. Show that for any lower point, *F*, the sum of the
distances *AF* and *FB* is greater than *l*.

Problem:
Construct the path of a billiard ball that starts at *B* and after striking
the cushion three times enters the pocket at *P*. Assume that the angle
of reflection from the cushion is exactly equal to the angle of
incidence.

Draw the set of imaginary reflected tables as shown, and suppose that
the ball is struck so that it heads toward *C*. This path from *B* to *C*
crosses three lines (at *D*, *K*, and *J*) corresponding to the three bounces
specified in the problem.

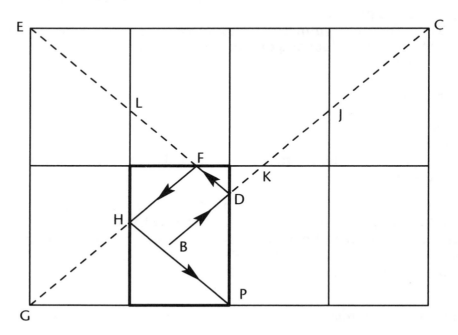

After striking the cushion at *D* the ball heads toward *E*, where the
path *DE* is the reflection of *DC*. Then, after striking the cushion at *F*
the ball heads toward *G*, where *FG* is the reflection of *FE*. Finally, the
ball strikes the cushion at *H* and is reflected toward the pocket *P*,
where *HP* is the reflection of *HG*. Note that along the imaginary path
DC, *DK* represents *DF*, *KJ* represents *FH*, and *JC* represents *HP*. Stated

differently *DK* is the first reflection of *DF, KJ* is the second reflection of *FH* (*FH* → *FL* → *KJ*), and JC is the third reflection of *HP* (*HP* → *HG* → *LE* → *JC*).

Problem:
Find additional three-reflection paths from *B* to *P*.

A billiard ball goes along a path that strikes all four edges and returns to the starting point. Prove that the length of the path is twice the length of the table diagonal.

Problem:
When you look into an ordinary mirror, your right side becomes your image's left side; and your left side becomes your image's right side. But consider the case of two mirrors at right angles. There are now three images: If you are at *A*, your images are at *B*, *C*, and *D*. Show that the image at *C*, in the opposite quadrant, does not have left and right reversed—if you move your right hand, the image also moves its right hand.

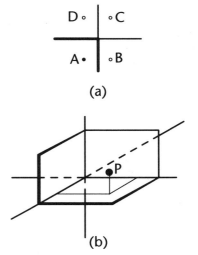

(a)

(b)

Also, show that if you use, say, your right eye to look at this image, you will have to look exactly into the corner in order to see the image's right eye.

Problem:
A set of three mirrors perpendicular to each other is called a corner reflector. Given a point *P* within the corner,

(a) Complete the sketch, showing the seven reflections of *P*.
(b) In our discussion of the billiard-ball reflections, the ball went from *B* to a point *D* near the corner, was reflected twice in the neighborhood of the corner, and then returned from the corner along a path *FH* parallel to the original path *BD*. Show that an incoming ray of light that strikes the corner reflector will, after three reflections, return along a path parallel to its incoming path. (A set of corner reflectors on the Moon was used to reflect a laser beam from the Earth with sufficient intensity and parallelism for it to be detected at the source and for the round-trip time of the beam to be measured.)
(c) Show that an eye must look exactly into the corner in order to see itself in this opposite-octant image.
(d) Show that this image has your right an   eft sides reversed.
(e) Show that right-left reversal occurs when the image corresponds to an odd number of reflections.

Answer to (a):

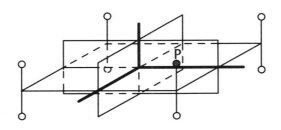

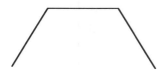

Problems:

In clothing stores you will often find sets of three mirrors put together as shown in the sketch. Where would you stand and how would you orient yourself in order to see your back? Are right and left reversed in this image?

Problem:

You have a kaleidoscope made of three long strips of mirror arranged like an equilateral-triangle prism, and containing a bit of colored glass. Assume that the reflections continue to infinity. Draw a part of this infinite pattern and identify the symmetries.

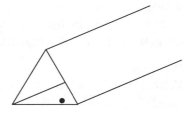

Answer:

A, D, F, G, . . . is one set of three-fold axes

B, J, K, L, . . . is another set of three-fold axes

C, E, M, N, . . . is a third set of three-fold axes

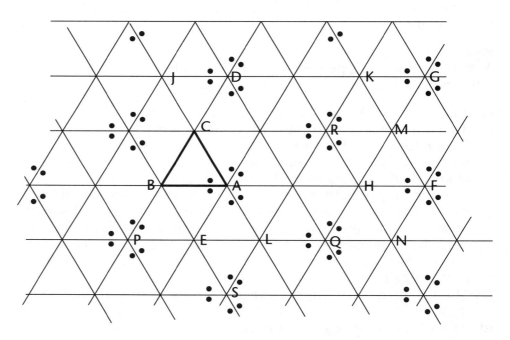

All the lines in this drawing are similar planes of symmetry. Along the directions of the three sets of lines, the pattern repeats every three spaces. Thus, the pattern about point *D* is the same as the pattern about point *G*; it is also the same as the pattern about point *Q*; and it is also the same as the pattern about point *P*.

Along the directions at 30° to these three sets of lines, the pattern repeats every two spaces, as along the directions of *DAS, DRF,* and *PARG.*

Such directions, or lines, in an infinite pattern are called translation axes.

The more usual kaleidoscope contains only two long strips of mirror set at 60° to each other. What are the symmetries of the arrangements that can be seen in it?

How Many Squares? How Many Cubes?

How many squares are in this figure? (The correct answer is not 16.) After you have found the correct answer, apply your method to determine the general formula for the total number of squares in an $n \times n$ arrangement.

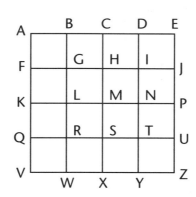

The number of unit squares is 16. The number of 2×2 squares may be found as follows: There are three 2 × 2 squares across the top, namely *ACMK*, *BDNL*, and *CEPM*; just below but overlapping them are three more, namely *FHSQ*, *GITR*, and *HJUS*; just below but overlapping these are three more, namely, *KMXV*, *LNYW*, and *MPZX*. Thus there are 3 × 3 of the 2 × 2 squares. Similarly, there are 2 × 2 of the 3 × 3 squares. Finally, there is only one (or 1 × 1) 4 × 4 square. The total number is thus $1^2 + 2^2 + 3^2 + 4^2 = 30$. In general, for an $n \times n$ arrangement, the total number of squares is

$$1^2 + 2^2 + 3^2 + \ldots + (n-1)^2 + n^2$$

Show that for an $n \times (n + 1)$ arrangement, the total number of squares is $1 \times 2 + 2 \times 3 + 3 \times 4 + \ldots + n(n+1)$, which may also be written as $(1^2 + 2^2 + 3^2 + \ldots + n^2) + (1 + 2 + 3 + \ldots + n)$.

Show that for the corresponding three-dimensional $n \times n \times n$ arrangement, the total number of cubes is $1^3 + 2^3 + 3^3 + \ldots + n^3$; for an $n \times n \times (n + 1)$ arrangement it is $(1^3 + 2^3 + 3^3 + \ldots + n^3) + (1^2 + 2^2 + 3^2 + \ldots + n^2)$; for an $n \times (n + 1) \times (n + 2)$ arrangement it is

$$(1^3 + 2^3 + 3^3 + \ldots + n^3) + 3(1^2 + 2^2 + 3^2 + \ldots + n^2) + 2(1 + 2 + 3 + \ldots + n)$$

Problem:
Derive the general formula for an $n \times (n + a) \times (n + b)$ arrangement.

Formulae for the sums of squares and of cubes. If you have had some algebra, you may be interested in deriving formulae for the sums of successive squares and of successive cubes that are used in the preceding expressions. (You have already derived the formula for the sum of successive integers.)

Assume that the sum $1^2 + 2^2 + 3^2 + \ldots + n^2 = an^3 + bn^2 + cn + d$, where the coefficients a, b, c, and d are to be determined. Then for the next larger value of n,

$$1^2 + 2^2 + 3^2 + \ldots + n^2 + (n+1)^2 = a(n+1)^3 + b(n+1)^2 + c(n+1) + d$$

Subtract the first equation from the second to get

$$(n + 1)^2 = a(3n^2 + 3n + 1) + b(2n + 1) + c$$

Equate the coefficients of n^2 and of n, and equate the constant terms:

n^2: $1 = 3a$

n: $\quad 2 = 3a + 2b$

1: $\quad 1 = a + b + c$

from which

$$a = \frac{1}{3}, \; b = \frac{1}{2}, \; c = \frac{1}{6}$$

The desired formula for $1^2 + 2^2 + 3^2 + \ldots + n^2$ is thus

$$\frac{n^3}{3} + \frac{n^2}{2} + \frac{n}{6} = \frac{n(n + 1)(2n + 1)}{6}$$

By the same method you can show that

$$1^3 + 2^3 + 3^3 + \ldots + n^3 = \left[\frac{n(n + 1)}{2}\right]^2$$

You may recognize this last expression in brackets as the sum of the arithmetic series $1 + 2 + 3 + \ldots + n$. Thus,

$$1^3 + 2^3 + 3^3 + \ldots + n^3 = (1 + 2 + 3 + \ldots + n)^2$$

Note:
In our derivation of the formula for $1^2 + 2^2 + \ldots + n^2$, we assumed that the formula would be of the form $an^3 + bn^2 + cn + d$. We solved for a, b, and c, but no value of d could be obtained by our method. Fortunately, d turns out to be zero, and we find that the formula that we derived holds for all integral values of n, including 0 and 1. Similarly for the sum $1^3 + 2^3 + \ldots + n^3$. In general, however, we would not have been justified in neglecting d simply because we did not find a value for it.

Geometry Bits

The rolling coin. If you roll a coin along a flat surface you must roll it over its entire circumference before it regains its original orientation (sketch (a)). However, if you roll the coin around another coin of the same size, it will regain its original orientation after it has rolled over only half of its circumference. Just wherein is the difference?

(a)   (b)

One way of considering the problem is as follows: Suppose the coin is against a vertical surface (lower position, sketch (c)). Roll it up a distance equal to half its circumference. Its orientation is then reversed (upper position, sketch (c)). Now suppose that the vertical surface is a flexible sheet and can be bent over to form a semicircle of diameter equal to that of the coin (sketch (d)). The orientation of the coin is then the same as its original orientation. In this analysis of the problem, the rotation of the coin has two components: (1) a 180° rotation acquired in rolling up the straight wall, and (2) an additional 180° rotation acquired when the wall is bent over by 180°.

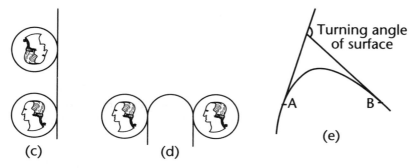

(c)   (d)   (e)

The analysis may be generalized to determine the change in orientation of a wheel rolling along any curved surface (sketch (e)) from one point *A* to another point *B*. It is the sum of (1) the amount of turning acquired by rolling along a straight wall a distance equal to that along the curved surface between *A* and *B*, and (2) the amount of turning between the tangent at *A* and the tangent at *B*.

Painted cube faces. A cube is painted and then cut into 27 small cubes, as in the sketch.

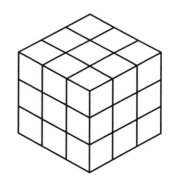

(a) How many small cubes have paint on three faces?

(b) How many small cubes have paint on two faces?

(c) How many small cubes have paint on one face?

(d) How many small cubes have no paint?

The cubes at the eight corners have paint on three faces; the cubes at the middles of the twelve edges have paint on two faces; the cubes at the centers of the six faces have paint on one face; the cube in the center of the large cube has no paint (8 + 12 + 6 + 1 = 27).

Sum of distances to four points. Given a convex quadrilateral *ABCD*. Prove that the sum of the distances from a point to the four corners is least when the point is at the intersection *P* of the diagonals.

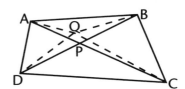

Compare the sum *AP* + *PC* + *DP* + *PB* with the sum of the distances to some other point *Q*, *AQ* + *QC* + *DQ* + *QB*. The broken line *AQC* is longer than the straight line *APC*, and the broken line *DQB* is longer than the straight line *DPB*. Hence

$$AQC + DQB > APC + DPB$$

Twiddling bolts. Two equal bolts, oppositely directed, are meshed together as in the sketch. If they now revolve around each other, neither bolt rotating about its own axis, do they come together, separate from each other, or remain at a fixed distance from each other?

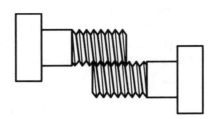

Answer:
If one bolt moves clockwise (looking from its head) around the other, the other moves contraclockwise around the first. From this antisymmetry we conclude that there is no displacement; that is, they neither move together nor separate.

The helical seam. You have a strip of paper (top sketch) with an irregular edge along the bottom, and you roll it up into a tube, starting from the upper left corner. Which of the four lower sketches represents your tube?

If you first imagine that you have rolled the paper as far as the lower left corner, you should be able to see that further rolling will wind the rough edge around the outside as in the first of the four sketches.

The right connections. Given six points connected in pairs by either red lines or blue lines, indicated on the sketch as solid lines and dashed lines, respectively. Prove that this arrangement contains at least one triangle whose three sides are all of the same color.

Of the five lines radiating from each point, either all five have the same color, four have one color and one has the other color, or three have one color and two have the other color. Thus, each point has at least three lines of one color or the other. Suppose, then, that point *A* is connected to points *B*, *C*, and *D* by red lines. Now consider the lines connecting these three points. If any two, say *B* and *C*, are connected by a red line, then the triangle *ABC* is all red. If, however, no two of the three points are connected by a red line, then they must all be connected by blue lines. Then triangle *BCD* is a blue triangle. Thus, in either case, the arrangement contains a triangle of uniform color.

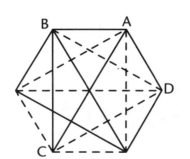

Problems:
(1) I have invited six people to a party. Prove that among these six there is at least one group of the following types:

    (a) A group of at least three who are all acquainted with each other.
    (b) A group of at least three none of whom is acquainted with any of the others in the group.

(2) How many lines are in the diagram?

Answer to (2):
Each of the six points has five lines. However, each line belongs to
two points, one at each end. Hence there are $\frac{6 \times 5}{2}$ = 15 lines.

Grouping the Gothic capital letters. We can organize the twenty-six
capital letters (Gothic style) into several groups such that any letter of
a group can, by bending, stretching, shrinking, or otherwise deform-
ing it or any part of it, be changed into any other letter of the group.
For example, we put E and T into the same group because, by length-
ening the cross piece of the T and then bending down the ends, we
can transform it to the letter E. The letters C and I are similarly
related; but the letters C and O and not related, because converting
one to the other would require either cutting the O or welding together the ends of the C.

Problem:
Organize the twenty-six capital letters into the least number of such
groups. Consider only Gothic style (sans serif) letters.

Answer:
A R
B
C G I J L M N S U V W Z
D O
E F T Y
H
K X
P Q

Problems:
(1) Show that a doughnut and a cup can similarly be stretched and
    distorted into each other.

(2) Suppose you have a hollow rubber ball with a large hole in its
    surface. Assuming that the rubber is very elastic, could you turn
    the ball inside out by pushing it through the hole?
(3) Suppose you have an inner tube (hollow torus) also made of very
    elastic rubber, with a large hole in its surface. Could you turn the
    inner tube inside out through the hole to obtain a similar inner
    tube whose outside surface is the original inside surface, and
    whose inside surface is the original outside surface?

Answers:

2. It is obviously possible; the task is essentially equivalent to turning a sock inside out—a trivial exercise.

3. Some people will quickly respond that it is surely possible. A little thought will show, however, that the possibility is not at all obvious. Following is one approach to determining whether the task is possible:

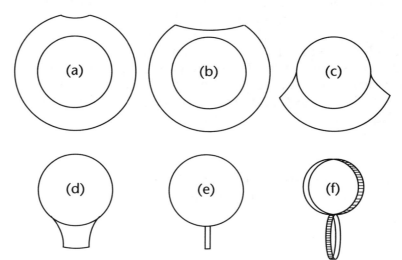

Imagine that we stretch the hole (sketches (b) to (e)) until (sketch (e)) there remains only the larger, upper ring and the smaller lower ring attached to it at right angles. The last sketch shows the final configuration viewed at an angle. Make this 2-ring configuration as follows: Cut two long narrow strips of paper from a sheet in your notebook and mark or color one side of each strip. Paste together the ends of the strips so as to make two rings with the marked surfaces outside. Then paste together the two rings at right angles to each other, as shown in sketch (f). Finally, try to turn this arrangement inside out so that it looks like sketch (f) except that the marked surfaces are inside. You will find that it is not possible. If it were possible, you could then stretch out the small lower ring, proceeding backward through the sketches ((e) to (a)) to attain the original inner-tube configuration, with the marked surface inside. (One might note the large difference between sketches (a) and (e) and wonder whether we have changed the problem; but the only real difference between (a) and (e) is the size of the hole.)

You might try the following experiment: Take an old sock or stocking, cut off the toe, and sew or pin together the two ends along a short length. The result is roughly as shown in this sketch. Try to turn the sock inside out through the opening.

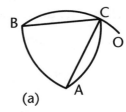

Safety pin

It rolls smoothly but is not round. With point A as center draw an arc BO of somewhat more than 60° (sketch (a)). Then, with B as center, and with the same radius, draw arc AC meeting the arc BO at C. Finally, with C as center, draw arc AB. The three-arc figure ABC has the same width in all directions. If it is fit snugly between a pair of parallel lines and then rotated (sketch (b)), the snug fit will be maintained regardless of its orientation. A log having a cross section like this three-arc figure could serve as a roller for moving heavy loads (sketch (c)).

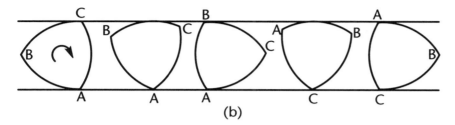

(b)

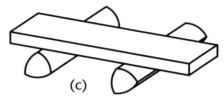

(c)

The chords *AB*, *BC*, and *CA* of sketch (a) form an equilateral triangle. Extend them, as in sketch (d). Then, with *A*, *B*, and *C* as centers, draw the three equal 60° long arcs and the three equal 60° short arcs shown in the sketch. Prove that this figure also has the same width in all directions.

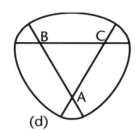

(d)

Instead of basing the figure on an equilateral triangle as in sketches (a) and (d), we might use a star of five, seven, or any larger odd number of points. The roller constructed on the five-pointed star is shown in sketch (e). By extending the sides of the star we get a frame for a roller made of five long 36° arcs and five short 36° arcs (sketch (f)).

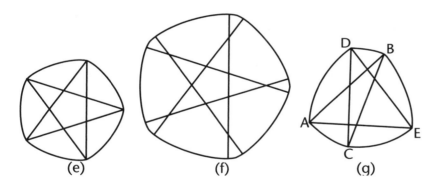

(e)   (f)   (g)

Stars with five or more points need not be symmetrical; we require only that all the sides be of equal length. Sketch (g) shows such a deformed star and the roller that is constructed on it. Drawing a star of this type is straightforward: Draw *AB*, then draw *BC* of the same length, with angle *B* arbitrary but not too large; and then draw *CD* with the same length, again with angle *C* arbitrary but not too large. The final point *E* is not arbitrary; it must be located such that $AE = DE = AB$.

Exercises:

1. Draw an unsymmetrical equilateral five-pointed star. Then draw the arcs between the points in order to make the constant-width roller. Finally extend the sides of the star and make a roller with ten different arcs.
2. Draw a five-arc constant-width roller without first drawing a star.

Problem:
In the preceding directions we mentioned that angles *B* and *C* could be "arbitrary but not too large." Show that a five-pointed equilateral star cannot have an angle greater than 60°.

Problem:
Show that for any orientation of a uniform-width roller between two parallel lines, the line connecting the two contact points (or tangent points) must be perpendicular to the two lines; it cannot be oblique as in the sketch.

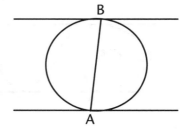

Answer:
The oblique line *AB* is longer than the distance between the two parallel lines. Then, when the roller is turned so that the line *AB* is vertical, the two parallel lines must be moved farther apart in order to accommodate the roller; accordingly, the width of the roller is not uniform. We conclude that for a uniform-width roller, any chord that represents the width is perpendicular to the tangent at each end, like the diameter of a circle. Furthermore, no chord of the roller can be longer than the width.

Problem:
Given a line *AB*, which is to be the width of a roller, and a convex curve connecting the end points *A* and *B*, which is to be part of the boundary of the roller, construct the remainder of the boundary.

Constructions:
1. From the answer to the preceding problem we see that one method is as follows (sketch (j)):

   (1) Construct tangents at several points along the given part of the boundary.
   (2) Construct perpendiculars to the tangents at these points, of length equal to *AB*.

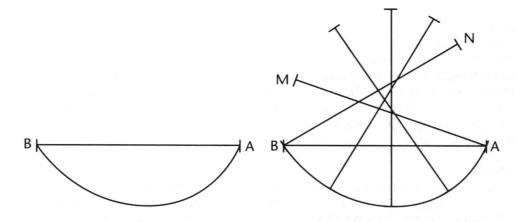

   (3) Draw a curve through all the end points of these perpendiculars. This curve is the desired remainder of the boundary. (The parts of the curve between *B* and *M* and between *A* and *N* are circular arcs. Why?)

2. A method that avoids the construction of tangents and perpendiculars is as follows:

With radius equal to the given width *AB*, and with points along the given curve as centers, draw arcs as shown in sketch (k). The curve that is tangent to all of these arcs is the desired remainder of the boundary. As in the preceding method, we must use an adequate number of points along the given curve in order to get an accurate result.

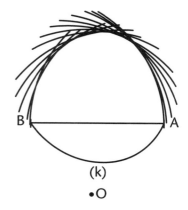

(k)

•O

Problem:

In the preceding problem, the given convex curve is not altogether arbitrary, for it must satisfy one important requirement: Nowhere along the curve may the radius of curvature exceed the desired width *AB*. Why?

Answer:

Sketch (l) illustrates the problem. It shows an arc and its center of curvature *O*, tangents at three points on the arc, and three equal lines perpendicular to these tangents. The lengths of these lines are the desired width, so a curve through the three end points is part of the desired boundary. But the curve through the three points is concave, a consequence of the fact that the desired width is less than the radius of curvature of the given arc, so it cannot be part of a uniform-width roller. (Satisfy yourself that the boundary of a uniform-width roller may nowhere be concave.)

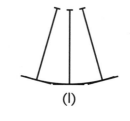

(l)

Sketch (m) shows the result of using the second method when the given curve is a circular arc of radius equal to twice the desired width *AB* of the roller. For the upper part of the boundary we obtain the curve *ACDB*, which is interesting but quite useless for our purpose.

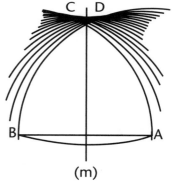

(m)

Most change is gradual. If a plant is 80 cm tall today and was 40 cm tall 3 weeks ago, we may be sure that at some intermediate time it was 60 cm tall, and that at some other intermediate time it was 48.63 cm tall, and so on. We say that the variation of height with time is *continuous.*

Not all change is continuous. One example is the change of date: If yesterday was June 5, then exactly at midnight the date changed *discontinuously* to June 6. At no time was the date June $5\frac{1}{2}$. A physical example is the amount of fissionable material that may be safely assembled into one lump. Small amounts of isolated Uranium-235 decompose very slowly, and the rate of fission per gram increases only very slowly as the amount of U-235 increases; but when the *critical mass* (about 50 kg) is suddenly assembled it explodes within a millionth of a second.

We had another example in our study of the Möbius band, when we made an edge band by cutting along a line parallel to the edge. The edge is twice as long as the circumference of the Möbius band, and so also was the length of the cut. If we increase the width of the edge band, the length of the cut does not change, *until* we finally make the edge band half as wide as the Möbius band, for which case we cut

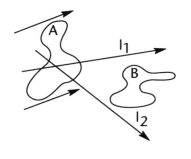

along the centerline of the Möbius band. In this case, the length of the cut is only half of that required for all the other edge bands, for the cut goes only once around the Möbius band.

The freezing of a pure liquid is another example. At temperatures above 0°C (but not above the boiling point), water under atmospheric pressure is a liquid. Below 0°C it is ice. The change is discontinuous—water does not gradually become more and more ice-like (or rigid) as it cools.

In spite of these and other examples of discontinuity, most variation is continuous. In the following we give some simple geometric applications of this idea of continuous variation.

Given two areas A and B in a plane, situated relative to each other as shown, is there a straight line that bisects both? First we show that there is a line in any given direction that bisects A: Given a direction, draw two lines in that direction such that A is between them. (These are the two parallel arrows on the sketch.) The lower line has none of A on its right; the upper line has all of A on its right. If a parallel line moves continuously from one of these lines to the other, at some position it will have exactly half of A on its right; that is, it will bisect A.

There is thus an infinity of lines (all possible directions in the plane) that bisect A. One of these lines, l_1, has all of B on its right; another, l_2, has none of B on its right. In some intermediate direction there is one that has exactly half of B on its right; that line is the line that bisects both A and B.

Is there a pair of perpendicular area bisectors that divide a given area into four equal parts? Suppose that l_1 and l_2 are a pair of perpendicular bisectors of the given area. In general, they do not divide the area into four equal parts; in the sketch it is obvious that areas B and D are much smaller than areas A and C.

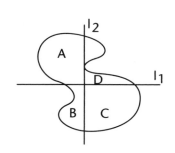

Since l_1 is a bisector, $A + D = B + C$.
Since l_2 is a bisector, $A + B = D + C$.

From these two equations it follows that $A = C$ and $B = D$.

Now rotate the pair of bisectors contraclockwise through 90°; then l_1 will be where l_2 was originally, and l_2 will be where $-l_1$ was originally. During the rotation, the area in the corner between $+l_1$ and $+l_2$ continuously increased from the small area of D to the large area of A, so at some point it was exactly one-fourth of the total area, and then each of the other three areas was also one-fourth of the total area. (Prove this statement.)

Problems:
1. Prove that there is an area bisector that also bisects the perimeter.
2. Prove that there are two perpendicular perimeter bisectors that cut the perimeter into four equal parts.
3. Prove that, given three volumes in space, there is a plane that bisects all three.

A *simple visualization puzzle*. Cut the three pieces shown (the rack, the handbag, and the keeper) out of thin cardboard. Fold the rack and the handbag in the middle. Slip the keeper on the lower arm of the rack and then slip one side of the handbag down into the crease (lower left sketch). Move the handbag and the keeper to the right end of the arm and then put the keeper around the end of the arm and down around the handbag strap. Finally unfold the rack to get the arrangement shown in the final sketch. As a mental exercise, try to imagine the steps in reversing the process and separating the three pieces.

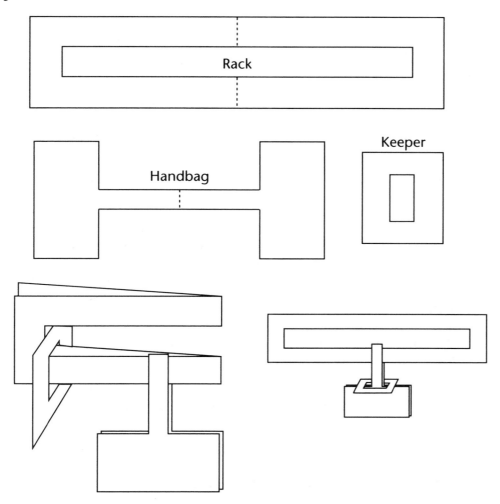

A *string-ring-board puzzle*. The popular puzzles involving strings, rings, and boards are especially valuable for our purpose. Even after the solution procedure has been described, determining just why this procedure works usually remains as a challenging problem demanding clear geometrical visualization. Only one puzzle of this type will be described.

Sketch (a) shows a board about 12–15 cm long, with a central hole about 1 cm in diameter and a flexible string about 75 cm long laced through the board as shown, attached at the ends, and carrying two rings. The rings are too large to pass through the hole, but the puzzle requires that you bring the rings together as shown in sketch (f).

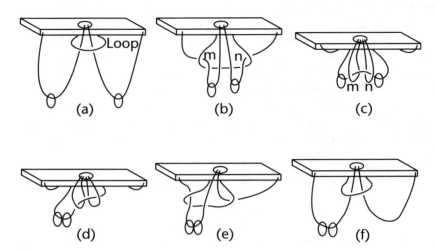

(a)   (b)   (c)

(d)   (e)   (f)

The solution procedure is described in the following five steps. Try to visualize just what happens in each step, especially steps 2 and 4 (that is, (b) → (c) and (d) → (e), respectively). The middle part of the string will be referred to as the loop.

1. Pull down the loop a little and put both rings through it toward you (sketch (b)).
2. Pull up the loop through the hole and then down to the front. In the result (sketch (c)), both rings are on the loop. The puzzle is now essentially solved, for you have only to slide one ring over to the other in order to bring them together.
3. Put both rings on the left side (sketch (d)). The remaining steps merely reverse the preceding steps.
4. Pull the strings back down through the hole in order to get the arrangement shown in sketch (e).
5. Put the two rings through the loop toward the back in order to get the desired configuration (sketch (f)).

In order to return to the original configuration, reverse every step precisely. Why is it necessary to put the rings through the loop in the first step?

Why, after the second step ((b) → (c)), are there four strings coming out of the hole at the top? In order to help you see why, corresponding points in sketches (b) and (c) have been labeled *m* and *n*—when these points are pulled through, each carries a doubled string behind it.

Among the books that describe such puzzles is *Mathematical Puzzles and Other Brain Twisters*, by Anthony S. Filipiak (Bell Publishing Co., a division of Crown Publishers, Inc.). An earlier edition, published by A. S. Barnes & Co., was called *100 Puzzles, How to Make and How to Solve Them*.

Three equal pyramids in a cube. Given the cube shown in the sketch:

1. Saw perpendicular to face *AFBE*, starting at the face diagonal *AB* and going as far as the cube diagonal *AC*.

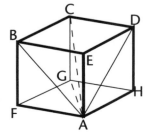

2. Saw perpendicular to face *AEDH*, starting at face diagonal *AD* and going as far as the cube diagonal *AC*.
3. Lift out the top pyramid *A–BCDE*.
4. Split the remainder by sawing down the triangle *AGC*. Show that you now have three equal pyramids, so that the volume of each is one third the volume of the cube.

The friendly pyramids. Sketch (a) shows two pyramids whose sides are all equal equilateral triangles. One pyramid has a triangular base and the other has a square base. The two are in contact along edge *AD*. If the triangular-base pyramid is rotated up about this edge until the two faces are in contact (sketch (b)), how many faces does this combined solid have?

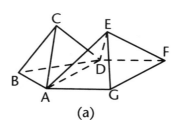

(a)

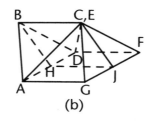

(b)

The correct answer is five, because edges *AB, BC, CG,* and *GA* are all in one plane; and *DB, BC, CF,* and *FD* also lie in one plane. A proof is as follows:
Draw the triangle altitudes *BH* and *CJ*, and the line *HJ* down the middle of the base. We see that *BC = HJ* and *BH = CJ*; also, all four lines lie in the plane of symmetry of the object. Accordingly, *BCJH* is a parallelogram, and *BC* is parallel to *HJ*. The line *HJ* is also parallel to *AG*, so *BC* is parallel to *AG* (because they are both parallel to the same line, *HJ*). Accordingly, the quadrilateral *ABCG* must be a plane figure. (In fact, it is an equilateral parallelogram, or rhombus.) Thus, the two triangles *ABC* and *AEG* have combined to form a single face.

This problem received some publicity in March 1981. It had been given on the Preliminary Student Aptitude Test and the correct answer, 5, had been marked wrong while the incorrect answer, 7, had been marked right.

The nest of triangles. Given a triangle and a point *O* within it. Draw lines from the three vertices to *O*. Now construct more triangles within the given triangles, all with their vertices lying on these three lines and with their sides parallel to those of the given triangle. (Show that it is always possible to draw such triangles.) In such a figure, all points that are similarly situated in all of the triangles lie on a straight line that passes through point *O*. For example, let point *A* be at the midpoint of the right-hand side of the given triangle, point *B* be at 1/3 the length of the bottom side from its right end, and point *C* be at the midpoint of line *AB*. Then if we locate similarly situated points in the other triangles, we shall find that all the midpoints of the right sides lie on the straight line *OA*; and similarly all points like *B* lie on the straight line *OB*, and all points like *C* lie on the straight line *OC*.

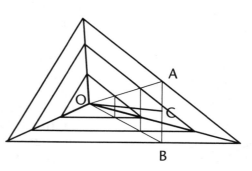

An example of the application of this result is the solution of the following problem: Given three equal circles all passing through a

common point O, and all touching two sides of a triangle that encloses the group. Prove that the center of the inscribed circle of the triangle, the center of the circumscribed circle, and point O all lie on a straight line.

Proof:
Draw lines connecting the centers of the three circles. The lines are parallel to and equidistant from the sides of the triangle. The three angle bisectors of the given triangle meet at P, the center of the inscribed circle, and also pass through the vertices of the little triangle (and bisect its angles). In short, the two triangles form a nest in which P is the principal point.

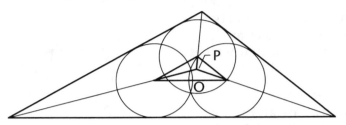

The point O is equally distant from the three vertices of the little triangle and hence is the center of its circumscribed circle. Then, according to the property of nests, the center of the circumscribed circle of the given triangle, the center of the circumscribed circle of the little triangle, O, and the principal point P (which is also the common center of the inscribed circles) all lie on a straight line. (The center of the circumscribed circle is point Q on the sketch.)

This problem was given in the International Mathematics Olympiad of 1981, reported in *Time*, July 27, 1981, p. 67.

Inconsistent drawings. Examine these three drawings (sketches (a), (b), and (c)) and determine the basis of the inconsistency in each.

(a) A group of equidistant parallel lines can represent many different things. In this case, the artist has achieved inconsistency by making the lines represent three cylinders at one end and making them represent two square-cross-section bars at the other end. He might easily have created many other absurdities. For example, he might have made one end represent clotheslines while the other end represents railroad tracks or a set of stairs (sketch (d)).

Question:
Does sketch (a) necessarily represent an impossible object?

Answer:
If all the lines represent wires, the sketch represents a simple wire structure that can be easily constructed.

(b) In sketch (b), if we erase any of the corners, the remainder of the sketch represents a consistent arrangement: three bars at right

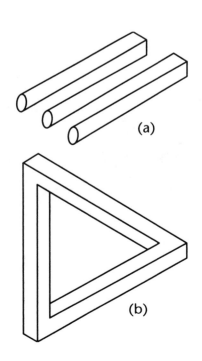

(a)

(b)

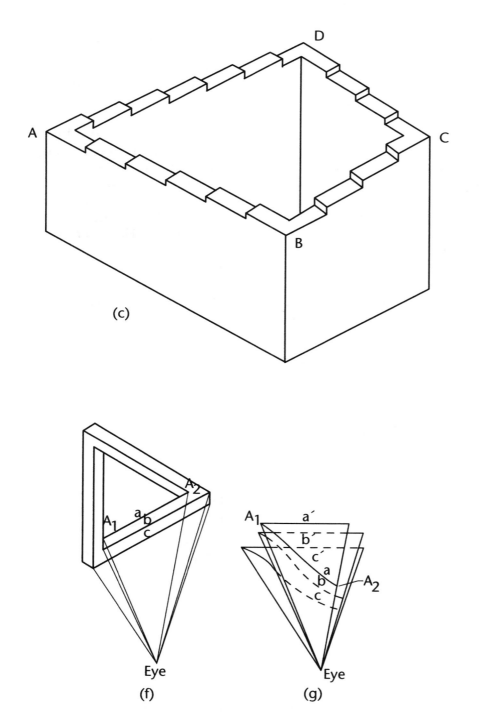

(c)

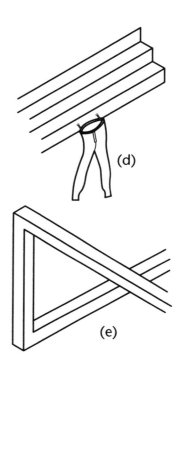

(d)

(e)

(f)

(g)

angles to each other. For such an arrangement, a drawing should show one bar passing behind another, as in sketch (e). Instead, the artist has used the two sets of three lines to construct a corner.

Question:
Does sketch (b) necessarily represent an impossible object?

Answer:
Consider your view of the lower bar, which you see as three parallel

lines, designated *a, b,* and *c* in sketch (f). You assume that the three lines represent three edges of a straight square-cross-section bar extending at right angles to the vertical bar; and so you conclude that the drawing is inconsistent.

The lines lie in three planes that pass through your eye, as shown in sketch (f). Sketch (g) shows the three planes and the three parallel lines *a', b',* and *c'* that you think you see. However, any line across the top plane is indistinguishable by your eye from line *a',* and similarly for lines in the other two planes. In particular, a line *a* (sketch (g)) that starts at point A_1, swings around in the plane, and ends at point A_2 looks like the straight line *a* of sketch (f); similarly for lines *b* and *c*. Thus, the three lines *a, b,* and *c* in sketch (f) can actually represent three edges of some misshapen, contorted bar that connects the two bottom corners of the object shown in sketch (b). However, if your eye were above or below the location shown in the sketches, the distortion of the bar would be apparent. Note also that in this discussion we referred to "your eye." With two eyes, the stereoscopic effect of binocular vision should help avoid the deception unless you are very distant from the object.

Question:
Does sketch (h) necessarily represent an impossible object?

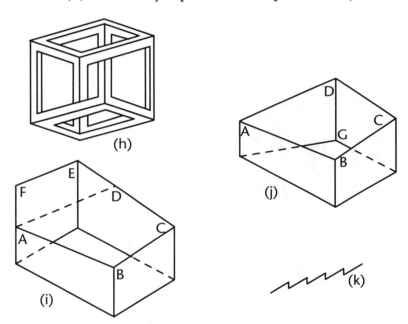

(h)

(i)

(j)

(k)

(c) Suppose the tower had a rectangular cross section and a continuously upward sloping upper edge. A schematic drawing of it might then appear as is shown in sketch (i), where the upper edge is *ABCEF*. On this drawing we locate point *D* on the rear wall such that line *DA* is parallel to line *EF*, and then draw a tower whose upper edge is *ABCDA* (sketch (j)); it slopes upward from *A* to *B*, from *B* to *C*, and from *C* to *D*, but it then slopes sharply downward from *D* to *A*.

The deception in sketch (c) occurs where the artist shows a set of upgoing stairs on edge *DA* similar to a set of stairs that might have been on edge *EF*. The deception is enhanced by making the tower so high that corner *G* (sketch (j)) is hidden, so that it is not obvious that point *D* is higher than point *A*. (Of course, one might claim that there is no deception—that the confusion arises merely because the artist used an unconventional design (sketch (k)) for the down-going stairs from *D* to *A*.)